Sociological
Ambivalence
and
Other Essays

Sociological Ambivalence

and Other Essays

Robert K. Merton

77-2665

THE FREE PRESS
A Division of Macmillan Publishing Co., Inc.
New York

Collier Macmillan Publishers
London

The Free Press
A Division of Macmillan Publishing Co., Inc.
866 Third Avenue, New York, N.Y. 10022

Collier Macmillan Canada, Ltd.

Library of Congress Catalog Card Number: 76–1033

Printed in the United States of America

printing number

1 2 3 4 5 6 7 8 9 10

Library of Congress Cataloging in Publication Data

Merton, Robert King
    Sociological ambivalence and other essays.

    Includes bibliographical references and index.
    CONTENTS: Sociological ambivalence (with E. Barber).--
The ambivalence of scientists.--The ambivalence of
scientists, a postscript.--The ambivalence of physicians.
[etc.]
    1. Sociology. 2. Social structure. 3. Ethnic
attitudes. I. Title.
HM24.M472   301   76-1033
ISBN 0-02-921120-4

Poetic lines from "Under Which Lyre: A Reactionary
Tract for the Times" Copyright 1946 by W. H. Auden.
Reprinted from *Collected Shorter Poems 1927–1957*,
by W. H. Auden, by permission of Random House, Inc.
(*See p. 109.*)

To

André F. Cournand
William T. Golden
Joshua Lederberg

with
boundless admiration
and affection

Contents

Preface

THESE ESSAYS in sociology, a baker's dozen drawn from symposia and journals in various fields of scholarship, were written over a span of forty years, for the most part within the past decade. Owing to the diversity of the sources in which they were first published—journals of medicine, psychiatry, and nursing as well as sociology—they are not readily accessible, and so my publishers proposed that they should be collected in a single volume.

The essays are arranged according to their subject matter rather than the date of original publication. Part I begins with the essay that gives the volume its title and introduces the notion of sociological ambivalence as complementary to the notion of psychological ambivalence. The other papers in this section examine the workings of sociological ambivalence in the form of structurally induced contradictions and of norms and counter-norms in several institutional domains of society: science, medicine and other professions, and complex business organizations.

Part II sets out the theoretical orientation which guides the substantive essays in the volume. The orientation is that variant of functional analysis in sociology which has evolved, over the years, into a distinct mode of structural analysis. This section includes a paper dealing with the structural constraints in society that make for unanticipated consequences of social action and another dealing with structural contexts of the use, nonuse, and abuse of sociological knowledge. One kind of abuse appears in the form of popular misconceptions of how sociologists go about their business, a subject examined in the paper "Canons of the Anti-Sociologist."

The essays in Part III deal with various aspects of ethnic relations. As a group, they were the earliest in this volume to be published. They require extended notice here if only to indicate some implications that were not evident at the time of their first writing.

"Discrimination and the American Creed," originally published in 1948, utilizes the notion of institutionalized evasions of institutional rules to forecast that new laws designed to counter discrimination against blacks would meet for a time with all manner of procedures for evading their full force, procedures such as circumvention, subterfuge, legal fictions, and outright nullification. The paper also modifies a general idea in theoretical sociology, arguing that the familiar gap between creed and practice, as set forth in Gunnar Myrdal's important observations in *An American Dilemma*, fails to delineate the complex sociopsychological dynamics of social control. It proposes instead a threefold interaction between creed, attitude, and behavior. Under specifiable conditions, the behavior of individuals tends to vary independently of their own attitude toward a creed (doctrine or norm). Witness the expedient conformist, the man of ethnic prejudice who does not himself believe in the creed of equal opportunity but conforms to it in practice through fear of sanctions or promise of gain; witness, too, his precise counterpart, the expedient nonconformist, who, in spite of his own freedom from prejudice, engages in discriminatory practices when these provide the easier or more profitable course. The fair-weather liberal and fair-weather bigot emerge as clearly identifiable types in this mode of analysis to join the more familiar types for whom attitude and behavior coincide.

"Intermarriage and the Social Structure," first published in 1941, attempts a structural and functional analysis, greatly limited by the paucity of data then available, of patterns of marriage between black and white Americans. Among other things, the analysis aims to account for the striking pattern of caste hypogamy—i.e., marriage between white women and black men—which was far more common than marriage between white men and black women. From the standpoint of theoretical sociology, this paper follows another—"Social Structure and Anomie"— which attempts to identify and to interpret patterns of social behavior that recur although *they are not normatively prescribed*. It can be argued that it was the discovery of such unprescribed but recurrent patterns of behavior that has given enduring significance to Durkheim's monograph *Suicide*, so that eighty years after its first appearance it remains an early prototype for the formulation of sociological problems as well as a target for sociological criticism. Back in the 1940s, it seemed to Kingsley Davis and myself that the phenomenon of intermarriage might provide another case of identifiable though unprescribed patterns of social behavior. I am indebted to Professor Davis for permission to reproduce part of our correspondence on the subject while we were both engaged in trying to make sense of an imperfectly defined problem.

All apart from providing a curious case of an avowed novice trying to instruct a recognized master in the first principles of his craft, the last paper holds a certain substantive and procedural interest. Published in 1940, "Fact and Factitiousness in Ethnic Opinionnaires" puts into question the early formulation of "attitude scales" by the master psychometrician, L. L. Thurstone. The critique is grounded in an empirical investigation used to illustrate my belief that the Thurstone instruments fail to meet specified basic criteria of linear interval scales. Since these instruments are not therefore "attitude scales," properly so-called, I decided to describe them as "opinionnaires"—that is, sets of opinions—in the thought that this term did not prejudge their metrical nature. The paper goes on to substantive intimations of the analytical problem that was later explored in "Discrimination and the American Creed." At one point, it suggested that the long-debated problem of the relationship between attitudes and behavior extends well beyond the familiar question of their generally being consistent or discrepant. There is the further possibility that when such discrepancies occur, their *directions* are socially patterned; for example, that Northerners avow ethnic attitudes that are apt to be more strongly equitable in substance than their actual practices while it is often the other way with Southerners, whose actual practices are apt to be more nearly equitable than their strongly avowed prejudices. Such patterned discrepancies, to the extent that they occur, would require us to draw different inferences about future behavior from expressions of like opinions among socially differing publics.

As acknowledged in later notes, I am indebted to various editors and publishers for permission to reprint papers appearing in their journals and symposia and to the National Science Foundation for a grant to the Program in the Sociology of Science at Columbia University, which supported the work reported in several of the papers. I must thank Paul F. Lazarsfeld and Louis Schneider for having independently suggested that the essays "Sociological Ambivalence" and "The Unanticipated Consequences of Purposive Social Action" be made more widely accessible; Elinor Barber for agreeing to have our joint paper reprinted in this volume; Raymond Firth for permission to reprint his recent observations on the history and import of the concept "paradigm"; Harriet Zuckerman for advice on the selection and arrangement of the essays; Mary Wilson Miles for again monitoring the preparation of a manuscript; and Thomas F.

Gieryn for again converting the skill of proofreading into the art of copy-editing. Except for a few corrections of obvious errors of fact and syntax, the papers appear as first published. This means, of course, that the remaining errors are indisputably my own.

R.K.M.

Columbia University
April 1976

Part 1

1

Sociological Ambivalence

[with Elinor Barber]

EVER SINCE BLEULER introduced the term early in the century, the ambivalence[1] of human attitudes and behavior has been continually investigated, especially by psychologists. Almost in the Aristotelian vein, Bleuler identified three types of ambivalence: the emotional (or affective) type in which the same object arouses both positive and negative feelings, as in parent-child relations; the voluntary (or conative) type in which conflicting wishes make it difficult or impossible to decide how to act; and the intellectual (or cognitive) type, in which men hold contradictory ideas.

Long before the term was coined, man's experience of ambivalence—of being pulled in psychologically opposed directions—had of course been endlessly noted. Not to move beyond the seventeenth century or outside the borders of France, we have only to look into the writings of Montaigne, La Rochefoucauld, La Bruyère, and Pascal for many pensées and maxims dealing with a wide range of ambivalent experiences. It could scarcely be otherwise. No observer of the human condition could long fail to note the gross facts of mingled feelings, mingled beliefs, and mingled actions. He had only to look inward at his own psyche or outward at the behavior of others. And, of course, Freud himself had noted a few years before Bleuler's coinage the alternation of love and hate for the

Reprinted with permission from *Sociological Theory, Values, and Sociological Change: Essays in Honor of Pitirim A. Sorokin*, Edward A. Tiryakian, ed. (New York: The Free Press, 1963), pp. 91–120.

1. Eugen Bleuler, "Vortrag über Ambivalenz," *Zentralblatt für Psychoanalyse*, 1910, p. 1; *Dementia Praecox, oder Gruppe der Schizophrenien* (Leipzig: Deuticke, 1911.) Later, Freud was to remark that it was only natural for Bleuler to introduce the concept of ambivalence in view of his own alternating hostility and devotion to psychoanalysis. See Ernest Jones, *Sigmund Freud: Life and Work* (London: Hogarth Press, 1955), II, p. 80.

same person, with the early separation of the two sentiments usually leading the hate to be repressed.[2]

Whether examined by the penetrating eye of the early essayists or by the no less penetrating eye of the later psychoanalysts, the facts of ambivalence have been regarded chiefly or wholly in their psychological aspects. The focus has been upon the inner experience and the psychic mechanisms released by efforts to cope with conflicting emotions, thoughts, or actions. To be sure, Freud and those who followed him touched upon some social constellations that make for the experience of ambivalence. After all, in modern psychology as in ancient myth, the Oedipus complex takes account of the double status of the mature male as husband-and-father when it treats the son's mixed feelings of love and hate about his father. Nevertheless, the structure of social relations is taken as a given in these accounts; it does not itself become the focus of systematic investigation.

Another way of putting this is to say that although the social relations between persons have inevitably been drawn into the psychological analysis of ambivalence, they have not been made central to it. Social relations remain peripheral to the analysis. They are taken as facts of historical circumstance rather than examined in terms of the dynamics of social structure to see how and to what extent ambivalence comes to be built into the very structure of social relations.

An example: the pattern of apprentice love, the devotion of a pupil or disciple for his master, brings out the unavoidable yet peripheral place accorded social relations in psychological theories and studies of ambivalence. In the psychological analysis of the pattern, the apprentice esteems the master and takes him as a role-model while aiming to replace the master who, after a time, stands in his way. Without assuming that such ambivalence is typical, we can identify many cases of the pattern in the history of science: Kepler's patent ambivalence toward Tycho Brahe; Sir Ronald Ross's strong ambivalence toward his master Manson in the quest for the malarial parasite, his devotion to his teacher pushing him to extravagant praise, his need for autonomy pushing him to excessive criticism. Or consider, appropriately enough, the checkered history of psychoanalysis itself with the secessionists Jung and Adler displaying their ambivalence toward Freud; in sociology (to come no closer home to our own day) the mixed feelings of the young Comte toward Saint-Simon; in psychiatry, of Bouchard toward Charcot; in medicine, of Sir Everard

2. Jones, *op. cit.*, II, p. 47.

Home toward John Hunter; and so on through an indefinitely long list of apprentice-ambivalence in science.[3]

In all such cases, the structure of social relations between master and disciple must of course be drawn into the interpretation of the pattern of ambivalence. Nevertheless, this structure remains at the periphery of psychological analyses of apprentice love. No effort is ordinarily made to search out the differing probabilities of ambivalence on the part of the apprentice toward the master, depending upon systematic differences in the structure of their relations and in the structure of the field of activity. Were there a double focus on both the psychology and the sociology of ambivalence, the inquiry into apprentice love would consider whether ambivalence, or univalence, is more apt to ensue, according to how these structures differ. For example, the relation between master and apprentice—say, in the world of science—may be one in which, for structural reasons such as a paucity of major chairs in the field, the apprentice "has no place to go" after having completed his basic training, other than the place still occupied by the master. This is one type of structural situation; the one in which ambivalence is apt to develop. But if the structure of the society provides an abundance of other places, some as highly esteemed as that currently occupied by the master, the apprentice may be less motivated for these structural reasons to develop ambivalence toward the master. And, by the same token, the master, in this reciprocity of relations, may be less motivated to develop ambivalence toward the apprentice who, in more confined types of structure, might be regarded as his "premature" successor. Briefly sketched, this example may help us to distinguish a basically psychological from a basically sociological orientation toward the study of ambivalence.

Unlike the psychological orientation, the sociological one focuses on the ways in which ambivalence comes to be built into the structure of social statuses and roles. It directs us to examine the processes in the social structure that affect the probability of ambivalence turning up in particular kinds of role-relations. And finally, it directs us to the social consequences of ambivalence for the workings of social structures.

That the sociological inquiry into ambivalence does not replace the psychological inquiry, but instructively complements it, has been implied by much of what has been said so far. Yet it seems that the great emphasis on the psychological aspects of ambivalence during the past half-

3. Whether further evidence of the apprentice-ambivalence pattern is to be found in the *Festschrift* for Pitirim Sorokin, the reader must decide for himself.

century has, without anyone's intent, somewhat stunted the development
of a sociological theory of ambivalence since it seemed, on the face of it,
to be a distinctively *psychological* subject. As a result, we have had only
scattered and largely uncollated contributions on the sociological side
which have not been systematically drawn into a more nearly psycho-social
theory of ambivalence.

This short discussion cannot, of course, redress the imbalance between
psychological and sociological orientations to the subject of ambivalence.
But it can perhaps send out signals indicating how the two orientations
are related. By centering on the special case of the structural sources of
ambivalence in the relations between professionals and clients, we may be
able to raise some of the principal problems requiring investigation and
still keep our account from becoming so diffuse as to blur these problems.

The Concept of
Sociological Ambivalence

As has been noted, the concept of ambivalence in psychology refers to the
experienced tendency of individuals to be pulled in psychologically opposed directions, as love and hate for the same person, acceptance and
rejection, affirmation and denial. The concept leads directly to distinctive
problems: How is it that these opposed pressures persist? Why doesn't
one or the other prevail? What psychic mechanisms are triggered by
ambivalence, as, for example, the separation of the conflicting components
with one of them—say, hate—being repressed while the overt reaction
to the repressed hate takes the form of a marked expression of loving
care? Such problems are not our concern here. For our purpose, the essential point is that whatever the psychological theory takes as the sources
of ambivalence, it centers on how this or that type of personality develops
a particular ambivalence and copes with it.

The sociological theory of ambivalence is directed to quite other
problems. It refers to the social structure, not to the personality. *In its
most extended sense*, sociological ambivalence refers to incompatible
normative expectations of attitudes, beliefs, and behavior assigned to a
status (i.e., a social position) or to a set of statuses in a society. *In its
most restricted sense*, sociological ambivalence refers to incompatible
normative expectations incorporated in a *single* role of a *single* social
status (for example, the therapist role of the physician as distinct from
other roles of his or her status as researcher, administrator, professional
colleague, participant in the professional association, etc.). In both the

most extended and the most restricted sense, the ambivalence is located in the social definition of roles and statuses, not in the feeling-state of one or another type of personality. To be sure, as we would expect and as we shall find, sociological ambivalence is one major source of psychological ambivalence. Individuals in a status or status-set that has a large measure of incompatibility in its social definition will tend to develop personal tendencies toward contradictory feelings, beliefs, and behavior. Although the sociological and psychological kinds of ambivalence are empirically connected, they are theoretically distinct. They are on different planes of phenomenal reality, on different planes of conceptualization, on different planes of causation and consequences.

The sociological theory deals with the processes through which social structures generate the circumstances in which ambivalence is embedded in particular statuses and status-sets together with their associated social roles. Anticipating our later discussion a bit, we suggest that one source of ambivalence is to be found in the structural context of a particular status. Another source is found in the multiple types of functions assigned to a status—for example, expressive and instrumental functions. These two sources have been identified in a continuing series of sociological analyses of ambivalence during the last twenty years or so: ambivalence in the role of the bureaucrat when individualized and personal attention is wanted by the client while the bureaucracy requires generalized and impersonal treatment[4]; the role of the intellectual expert in bureaucracy, embracing values derived from his profession and values derived from the organization[5]; the ambivalence toward accomplishments by people not warranted by their social status (involving a positive response to the achievement and a negative attitude toward the devalued status)[6]; the ambivalent ex-member of a group[7]; the ambivalence of scientists toward priority which results from their role incorporating potentially incompatible values ("the value of originality, which leads them to want their priority to be recognized, and the value of humility, which leads them to insist on how little they have been able to accomplish")[8]; the ambiv-

4. Robert K. Merton, *Social Theory and Social Structure* (New York: The Free Press, 1968, enlarged ed.) pp. 256–59.
5. *Ibid.*, pp. 266–73, 277.
6. *Ibid.*, pp. 483–86.
7. *Ibid.*, p. 349.
8. Robert K. Merton, "Priorities in Scientific Discovery: a Chapter in the Sociology of Science," *American Sociological Review,* 22 (1957), pp. 647–49. [Reprinted in Merton, *The Sociology of Science: Theoretical and Empirical Investigations,* ed. and with an introduction by Norman W. Storer (Chicago and London: University of Chicago Press, 1973), pp. 284–324.]

alence in the role of the physician which requires him to try "to blend incompatible or potentially incompatible norms into a functionally consistent whole"[9]; and the ambivalence inherent in a wide variety of roles that must deal with both maintenance of the pattern of behavior and with instrumental results, with activity that serves chiefly to maintain social cohesion and activity that serves to get things done.[10]

In all these and kindred instances, people occupying the statuses are exposed to ambivalence. They are exposed to it not because of their idiosyncratic history or their distinctive personality but because the ambivalence is inherent in the social positions they occupy.[11] This is what we mean by saying that sociological ambivalence is a concept focused upon social structure.

In its broadest sense of inconsistent normative expectations embodied in a social status or status-set, sociological ambivalence has been substantially investigated. But very little attention has been accorded ambivalence in its most *restricted, core sense of conflicting normative expectations socially defined for a particular social role associated with a single social status.* It is this special case to which we shall devote the greater part of this discussion. We shall try to analyze the ways in which social function and social structure make for a socially prescribed ambivalence in a particular role, as, for example, in the therapist role of the physician which calls for *both* a degree of affective detachment from the patient and a degree of compassionate concern about him. The core-type of sociological ambivalence puts contradictory demands upon the occupants of a status in a particular social relation. And *since these norms cannot be simultaneously expressed in behavior, they come to be expressed in an oscillation of behaviors: of detachment and compassion, of discipline and permissiveness, of personal and impersonal treatment.*

Before proceeding with the examination of the core-type of sociologi-

9. Robert K. Merton, "Some Preliminaries to a Sociology of Medical Education," in R. K. Merton, G. Reader, M.D., and P. L. Kendall, eds., *The Student-Physician* (Cambridge: Harvard University Press, 1957), pp. 72–76.

10. Robert K. Merton, "Social Problems and Sociological Theory," in R. K. Merton and R. A. Nisbet, eds., *Contemporary Social Problems*, First Edition (New York: Harcourt Brace Jovanovich, 1961), pp. 734–35.

11. For analyses bearing on this conception, see Melvin Seeman, "Role Conflict and Ambivalence in Leadership," *American Sociological Review* 18 (1953), pp. 373–80; Lewis Coser, *The Functions of Social Conflict* (New York: The Free Press, 1956), pp. 61–65; W. C. Mitchell, "The Ambivalent Social Status of the American Politician," *Western Political Quarterly* 12 (1959), pp. 683–89; Werner Cahn, "Social Status and the Ambivalence Hypothesis: Some Critical Notes and a Suggestion," *American Sociological Review* 25 (1960), pp. 508–13.

cal ambivalence, we should sketch out other, related types which have been the object of inquiry. The second type of ambivalence is perhaps the most thoroughly investigated: ambivalence involved in a conflict of statuses within a status-set (i.e., the set of social positions occupied by each individual). There are, for example, the familiar cases of conflict between men's or women's statuses in the occupational sphere and in the family sphere; in their religious status and their secular ones; in their public and private statuses as, say, the judge and friend or the school monitor and his student-colleagues.[12] This type has been studied particularly in the case of voting behavior under the notion of cross-pressures.[13]

This second kind of sociological ambivalence is essentially a pattern of a "conflict of interests or of values" in which the interests and values incorporated in *different* statuses occupied by the same person result in mixed feelings and compromise behavior. More compactly, this involves conflicting interests and values in the individual's status-set.[14] Since the pattern is induced by the social structure, it can be regarded as a form of sociological ambivalence. But this form of ambivalence differs from the first, core type in a basic respect: its frequency and dynamics will differ according to the number of people who happen to have a particular combination of statuses. The more married women at work in the labor market, the more subject to competing obligations. But this is not inherent in their occupying a *single* status and performing a *single* role. That is part of what we intend by describing this type as a derivative rather than core type of sociological ambivalence. It differs from the core type also

12. The literature on this is so voluminous (and still uncollated) that only a few citations must suffice. E. C. Hughes, "Dilemmas and Contradictions of Status," *American Journal of Sociology* 50 (1945), pp. 353–59; Samuel A. Stouffer, *Social Research to Test Ideas* (New York: The Free Press, 1962), pp. 39–67; Mirra Komarovsky, "Cultural Contradictions and Sex Roles," *American Journal of Sociology* 52 (1946), pp. 184–89.
13. As originally set forth in P. F. Lazarsfeld, Bernard Berelson, and Hazel Gaudet, *The People's Choice* (New York: Duell, Sloan and Pearce, 1944), pp. 53–72, and in a great variety of investigations since.
14. On the conflicting demands of several statuses in an individual's status-set, much germane and relatively unexplored data for the sociologist can be found in recurrent situations, subject to legal definition, involving the "conflict of interest." For one excellent account of this pattern from the legal standpoint, see Association of the Bar of the City of New York, *Conflict of Interest and Federal Service* (Cambridge: Harvard University Press, 1960.) The social arrangements expressly devised to reduce the frequency of such patterned conflict of interest provide a rich source for the sociological analysis of this type of ambivalence. On the lack of integration of the status-set, see Merton, *Social Theory and Social Structure*, pp. 422–24, 434–38.

in that the conflicting demands of different statuses ordinarily involve *different* people in the role-sets of the conflicting statuses (the demands of an employer, for example, and of a spouse). But in the core type, the ambivalence is built into the social relation with the *same* people. It involves a structurally induced ambivalence in a single relation—say, of the lawyer with his client—and not a conflict between relations—say, of the lawyer to his family and to his client. Since conflicts in the status-set have been examined repeatedly, it is not our intent to deal with these except as they bear upon the ambivalence that is found in a particular role associated with a particular status.

A third kind, comparable to the preceding one, is found in the conflict between several roles associated with a particular status. This too is a familiar type of sociological ambivalence. The one position of university professor or scientist in a research organization has variously multiple roles associated with it: the roles of teaching or training, of research, administration, and so on. And as some of the readers of this paper have ample reason to know from their own experience, the demands of these several roles in the one status can be at odds. Not only do they make competing demands for time, energy, and interest upon the occupants of the one status, but the kinds of attitudes, values, and activities required by each of these roles may also be incompatible[15] with the others.

A fourth kind of sociological ambivalence is found in the form of contradictory cultural values held by members of a society. These values are not ascribed to particular statuses, but are normatively expected of all in the society (e.g., patriotism and honesty). Thus, Robert Lynd listed twenty paired assumptions by which Americans live, noting that these run at once "into a large measure of contradiction and resulting ambivalence."[16] For examples:

Everyone should try to be successful.
But: The kind of person you are is more important than how successful you are.

The family is our basic institution and the sacred core of our national life.

15. See, for examples, Logan Wilson, *The Academic Man* (New York: Oxford University Press, 1942), Chaps. 4, 5, 10, 11; William Kornhauser, *Scientists in Industry: Conflict and Accommodation* (Berkeley and Los Angeles: University of California Press, 1962), Chap. 7.
16. Robert S. Lynd, *Knowledge for What?* (Princeton: Princeton University Press, 1939), Chapter III.

But: Business is our most important institution, and, since national welfare depends upon it, other institutions must conform to its needs.

Honesty is the best policy.

But: Business is business, and a businessman would be a fool if he didn't cover his hand.

As long as these value premises are widely held and not organized into sets of norms for one or another role in particular, they can be regarded as cases of cultural conflict. When they are so organized, they result in the core type of sociological ambivalence, in which incompatible normative demands are built into a particular role of a particular status. The phenomena of cultural conflict have been investigated at length, and although there are gaps in our understanding of the processes involved in such conflict, we shall not deal with them here.[17]

A fifth type of sociological ambivalence is found in the disjunction between culturally prescribed aspirations and socially structured avenues for realizing these aspirations (what one of us has long described as the "opportunity structure").[18] It is neither cultural conflict nor social conflict, but a contradiction between the cultural structure and the social structure. It turns up when cultural values are internalized by those whose position in the social structure does not give them access to act in accord with the values they have been taught to prize. This type, examined in some detail in studies of "social structure and anomie,"[19] will also be largely ignored in this discussion which focuses on the core type of ambivalence built into a single role of a particular social status.

A sixth type of sociological ambivalence develops among people who have lived in two or more societies and so have become oriented to differing sets of cultural values. Best exemplified by immigrants, this

17. See *ibid.*; Karen Horney, *The Neurotic Personality of Our Time* (New York: W. W. Norton, 1937); and for an emphatic, literary version of this theme, Paul Goodman, *Growing Up Absurd* (New York: Random House, 1960).

18. See R. K. Merton, "Social Conformity, Deviation, and Opportunity Structures," *American Sociological Review* 24 (1959), pp. 177–89.

19. Merton, *Social Theory and Social Structure*, pp. 185–248; Elinor G. Barber, *The Bourgeoisie in 18th Century France* (Princeton: Princeton University Press, 1955), pp. 56 ff., 141 ff.; Leo Srole, "Social Integration and Certain Corollaries," *American Sociological Review* 21 (1956), pp. 709–16; papers by Robert Dubin, Richard A. Cloward, *American Sociological Review* 24 (1959), pp. 147–89; E. H. Mizruchi, "Social Structure and Anomia in a Small City," *American Sociological Review* 25 (1960), pp. 645–54; and in these see citations to other studies of the subject.

special pattern has been intensively investigated at least since the concept of the "marginal man" was introduced by Robert E. Park and effectively developed by Everett V. Stonequist.[20] In a connected but somewhat different vein, reference-group theory has dealt with the ambivalence of people who accept certain values held by groups of which they are *not* members.[21] This type instructively combines elements of the fourth type of ambivalence (cultural conflict) and the second type (conflict within the status-set). Although in this orientation to a nonmembership group the individual does not "belong" to the group whose values he accepts and so does not, in social fact, occupy conflicting statuses, his identification with that group, if only in aspiration or fantasy, subjects him to the conflicting demands of his own groups and of the group to which he aspires. This type of ambivalence is presumably most characteristic of the socially mobile.

Accounts of Social Roles: Depictive, Sociographic, Analytical

Since sociological ambivalence in its core sense refers to *opposing normative tendencies in the social definition of a role*, we need to consider how roles are to be characterized in order to permit the analysis of ambivalence. The fact is that no standardized set of categories has yet been adopted by sociologists and anthropologists for the systematic analysis of social roles. Indeed, we believe it possible to identify three types of accounts of roles that coexist in the social science of today: the depictive, the sociographic, and the analytical.

The *depictive accounts of social roles* are representational portraits. The role of the business executive or the housewife or the labor leader is described in terms so concrete and vivid that the reader would at once recognize people engaged in these roles as soon as he met them. Valuable as these depictive accounts may be as a beginning, they are not the tasks which the sociologist is distinctively or best prepared to discharge. They are, rather, what the novelist or the historian essays to do. The perceptiveness of a Sir Walter Scott or of a Balzac enabled them to paint such representative portraits of major social roles. In doing so, of course, their depictions inescapably caught up some sociologically relevant aspects of these roles. That is part of the reason why their instructive cast of

20. Robert E. Park, "Preface" in Everett V. Stonequist, *The Marginal Man* (New York: Charles Scribner's Sons, 1937), and of course the book itself.
21. Merton, *Social Theory and Social Structure*, pp. 279–440.

characters, playing well-defined social roles, are individually and collectively recognizable, why they provide the reader with that sense of the intuitively familiar which leads him to say: "all this is true; this is how it actually was." That is why, also, *Waverley* or *Ivanhoe* or *Old Mortality* acquaints us with those individualized heroes of mediocrity which Scott takes to typify major social developments in each age of English society he examines. And that is why, even more, the forty volumes of *The Human Comedy* show us, close up, a sociological portrait of characteristic types in every social class and occupation on which Balzac fixed his discerning eye.

Standing between the depictive, graphic art of the sociological novelist and the analytic, abstract formulations of the sociologist are the partly narrative, partly categorized descriptions of the sociographer. The *sociography of social roles* narrates but does not place its principal characters in a more or less complex plot that helps the novelist exhibit a complexity of social relations. Sociography also classifies social roles but in categories drawn from everyday life rather than from the more abstract formulations of sociological theory. The sociographer at work is a little like the man in the street who might describe water as a colorless liquid, transparent and without taste or odor, thus touching upon certain verifiable attributes that happen to have caught his eye (and other sense organs). The sociographer is unlike the poet, even that minor and inadvertent one who saw water as "a thing of beauty, gleaming in the dewdrop; singing in the summer rain; shining in the ice gems . . ." and so on and on.[22] And he is also unlike the chemist who sees pure water as made up of hydrogen (11.188% by weight) and oxygen (88.812%) in the proportion of two atoms of H to one of O, serving as solvent and catalytic agent though poor as a conductor of electric current.

Much of the sociological study of social roles is still on the plane of sociography, though less as time moves on and knowledge accumulates. A typically sociographic account is provided in a study of the roles of men and women in Eskimo society[23] which tabulates more than 300 activities assigned to one or the other sex or shared by them both. The list is characteristically sociographic: house-cleaning, the bringing in of game, types of coiffure, tattooing practices, and so through the long list. In point of vivid imagery, it falls somewhat short of the depictions in

22. It is only fitting that these lines of a prose poem to *A Glass of Water* should have been penned by John Batholomew Gough, that nineteenth-century advocate of total abstinence from more spirited liquids.
23. Naomi M. Giffen, *The Roles of Men and Women in Eskimo Culture* (Chicago: University of Chicago Press, 1930).

such a book as, say, de Poncins' *Kabloona*. Nor is it more than preliminary to a sociological analysis that would try to identify the abstract properties of these activities assigned to sex roles.

That sociographic accounts of social roles are still prevalent can be seen by dipping into textbooks of sociology, those compendia of the current state of the sociological art. Following prevailing practice, these typically describe the components of social roles in the language of everyday speech. Thus, an excellent textbook soundly observes that "the elements of a social role are both obvious and subtle" and then goes on to a sociographic instance: "We know, for example, what a teacher is supposed to do in his professional role: to transmit to his students some kind of information or skill, and to follow more or less acceptable methods of doing so. But in some communities a teacher is also expected to avoid tobacco and liquor. . . ."[24] Or again, the role of a manager in a small business concern is outlined in another text: "The social demands of his role are that he be present at the plant at the appropriate time, dressed in a business suit rather than overalls, that he formulate the work allocation and keep records of production and distribution. . . ."[25]

Such sociographic accounts are of course an indispensable phase in the movement toward the sociological analysis of social roles. Fairly concrete descriptions of the norms embodied in a social role are plainly required before they can be subjected to more abstract analysis. The last part of this paper, for example, is largely sociographic, with only occasional analysis in terms of abstract and systematically arrayed concepts. Nevertheless, this must be recognized as only a transient phase. Sociography is no permanent substitute for sociological analysis.

Beyond depiction and sociography, then, is the third way of examining social roles, the way of the sociological theorist. From the standpoint of theoretical sociology, social roles are combinations of designated properties and compounds of designated components. Particularly at the level of analysis and even at the level of later synthesis, these theoretical accounts do not make for immediate recognizability of the role. They are, to pursue the analogy only a short distance, more like the chemical

24. Ely Chinoy, *Society*, First Edition (New York: Random House, 1961), p. 30. Reflecting the condition of the discipline of sociology, Chinoy implied that such descriptions are only a way-station toward the sociological analysis of roles: "An important task of sociology is to discover not only the obvious and explicit norms which define and regulate man's actions but also those which usually remain hidden below the surface."

25. Arnold M. Rose, *Sociology*, First Edition (New York: A. A. Knopf, 1956), p. 117.

formula of water than like the painting of a waterfall. Just as the formula provides no sensory similitude to what one sees in looking at water, whether in undomesticated nature or in the family kitchen, so these abstract accounts of social roles seem far removed from everyday "reality." And that is why laymen often find sociological analyses absurdly remote from the world of direct and untutored sense experience when they mistakenly assume that sociologists are trying to describe the social world photographically.[26]

Various attempts have been made to devise fruitful classifications of the properties and components of social roles. And, of course, such classifications are necessary for the theoretical analysis of sociological ambivalence. One of these classifications has been set forth by Pitirim Sorokin, who analyzes social roles[27] and relations as combinations of the following properties: direction of the social relation (mutual and twosided or predominantly onesided); its extensity (from a narrow sector of life to almost the entire range); its intensity; its duration and, finally, its type of influence (direct or mediated and indirect).[28] Particular social relations are syntheses of the values of these variables which, on the theory, can be identified in all social relations. The relations between role-partners are not depicted but analyzed in terms of these variables. Sorokin even makes use of the instructive analogy with chemical compounds, saying that "Similarly, in actual social life solidary and antagonistic relationships appear not only in pure forms but also in various combinations of these forms. Of these combined types, three are particularly important . . . these forms are *familistic* (predominantly solidary); *mixed* (partly solidary,

26. In this respect if no other, the conscientiously uninformed criticism of sociological analysis as "unrealistic" because it is not instantly depictive is a little like the early rejection of impressionism and much like the derisive taunts leveled against abstract art.
27. Sorokin explicitly rejects the term "social role," saying that it "adds practically nothing to the more precisely defined term 'the totality of the rights and duties' except some pedagogical value of vividness." But since the term has been widely adopted by sociologists if only because it is a more succinct notation than the phrase preferred by Sorokin and since, in spite of his disclaimer, Sorokin himself goes on to use the term "social role" repeatedly in this same book, and since his objection is largely one of terminological taste, we take the liberty of using the term in conjunction with Sorokin's analysis. For his nominal rejection of the term, see P. A. Sorokin, *Society, Culture and Personality* (New York: Harper and Row, 1947), p. 89n.
28. *Ibid.*, 95 ff. Perhaps a word of further explanation is needed here. It is true that Sorokin is here treating "types of social interaction" rather than "social roles." But these patterned and recurrent social interactions are of course social relations, i.e., relations between the roles established in a social system.

partly antagonistic), of which the *contractual* relationships are especially typical; *compulsory* (pre-eminently antagonistic)."[29]

For the purposes of our own analysis of sociological ambivalence, we should take note of Sorokin's repeated statement that actual social relations are *predominantly* of one type or another, rather than comprising pure types. Later, we shall see that it is precisely the matter of not confining our attention to the dominant attributes of a role or social relation that directs us to the functions and structure of sociological ambivalence. But, for the moment, we need only notice that Sorokin's classification is neither depictive nor sociographic; instead, it is analytical and synthesizing.

Overlapping Sorokin's classification in part is Talcott Parsons's classification of "pattern-variables" which designate aspects of normative patterns embodied in social roles. On this view, every social role is compounded of either affectivity (norms calling for the ready expression of feeling) or neutrality (non-expression of affect); diffuseness (wide-ranging obligations) or specificity (expressly limited obligations); universalism (obligations irrespective of the social status of the other) or particularism (obligations only toward those holding designated statuses); concern with qualities or attributes of the role-partner or with performance; and finally, either self-oriented (the role calling for satisfaction of self-interests) or collectivity-oriented (calling for self-interest to be subordinated to the collective interest).[30]

Whether the Sorokinian or the Parsonsian or some other classification of role-attributes will turn out in the end to be most productive is not at issue here. (It is encouraging that in part the two classifications overlap.) Nor need we pause for more than a moment to note that other abstract aspects of social roles, not expressly included in these classifications, affect the relations between role-partners. The normatively prescribed extent of observability of role-performance, for example, is a crucially significant variable that affects the character of social relations. Other structural attributes of roles include the size and complexity of role-sets, normatively patterned variability in the leeway allowed status-occupants to depart from the strict letter of the norms, patterned restric-

29. *Ibid.*, p. 99.
30. For one among several expositions of the pattern-variables, see Talcott Parsons, *The Social System* (New York: The Free Press, 1951), pp. 51–67. For present purposes, we need not examine Parsons's suggestion that these five pairs exhaust the logical possibilities of variability of role-patterns on this particular plane of generality (p. 66). As Harry M. Johnson notes in his summary, these are not "the only distinctions that one might make in classifying role patterns." *Sociology* (New York: Harcourt Brace Jovanovich, 1960), p. 136n.

tions on the number of role-partners (as in monogamy and other social games), the degree of clarity or vagueness of role-prescriptions, and so on.[31]

Norms and Counter-Norms

At issue is how we conceive the structure of social roles. *From the perspective of sociological ambivalence, we see a social role as a dynamic organization of norms and counter-norms*, not as a combination of dominant attributes (such as affective neutrality or functional specificity). We propose that *the major norms and the minor counter-norms alternatively govern role-behavior to produce ambivalence.*

This line of inquiry differs from that indicated by the caveats of both Sorokin and Parsons to the effect that social relations cannot be exhaustively analyzed in terms of their dominant attributes. Sorokin, as we have seen, warns that role-relations are only predominantly of one kind or another; they are seldom purely familistic or compulsory. And Parsons, writing of the pattern-variables, refers to the primacy of one or another, so that they do not necessarily apply "to every specific act within the role."[32] The role of a public official, for example, which is primarily defined as collectivity-oriented, nevertheless allows the official to be self-oriented in choosing among jobs, although he is expected to be collectivity-oriented in taking a stand on public policies.

Important as such caveats are in their own right, they do not direct us to the structure of social roles caught up in the notion of sociological ambivalence. It is true that the practice of characterizing social roles only in terms of their dominant attributes does not exhaust the normative complexity of these roles. This is plainly the case, for example, when in the Parsonsian scheme the role of the physician in relation to the patient is represented in the formula of affective neutrality, functional specificity, universalism, performance-orientation and collectivity-orientation. Or when, in the Sorokinian scheme, it is characterized as having narrow extensivity (confined to matters pertinent to the health-problem), variously intensive (depending on the acuteness of the problem), predominantly direct, of contingent duration and largely asymmetrical (with

31. As will be glimpsed from these examples, role-attributes are in some respects similar to properties of groups which are, after all, organized in the form of interrelated statuses and associated roles. See Merton, *Social Theory and Social Structure*, pp. 364–86 for a list of group-properties that can be so adapted.
32. Parsons, *The Social System*, p. 61.

the physician largely governing the character of the interaction). Such formulae in terms of dominant attributes alone give no reason to suppose that sociological ambivalence is built into the relation of physician and patient. Since the attributes are not at odds, the connected social roles would appear integrated and stable.

From the standpoint of sociological ambivalence, however, the structure of the physician's role differs from these characterizations, consisting of *a dynamic alternation of norms and counter-norms.* These norms call for potentially contradictory attitudes and behaviors. For the social definitions of this role, as of social roles generally, in terms of dominant attributes alone would not be flexible enough to provide for the endlessly varying contingencies of social relations. Behavior oriented wholly to the dominant norms would defeat the functional objectives of the role. Instead, role-behavior is alternatively oriented to dominant norms and to subsidiary counter-norms in the role. This alternation of subroles *evolves* as a social device for helping people in designated statuses to cope with the contingencies they face in trying to fulfill their functions.[33] This is lost to view when social roles are analyzed only in terms of their major attributes.

To continue with the example of physicians, it is only partly true that their role requires them to be affectively neutral in their professional relations with patients. Rather, this aspect of the role (and, we repeat, not merely the concrete behavior of this or that physician) is more complex than that. As the Columbia studies of the medical student have found, the physician is taught to be oriented toward *both* the dominant norm of affective neutrality (detachment) and the subsidiary norm of affectivity (the expression of compassion and concern for the patient). That is why, in these studies, we have treated this part of the physician's role not as one of affective neutrality (with only idiosyncratic departures from this norm) but as one involving "detached concern," calling for alternation between the instrumental impersonality of detachment and the functional expression of compassionate concern.[34] As physician and patient inter-

33. Henry L. Lennard and Arnold Bernstein, *The Anatomy of Psychotherapy* (New York: Columbia University Press, 1960), Chaps. VII–VIII, *et passim.*
34. The concept of detached concern calls attention to the major point that each of these abstractly opposed norms may be functionally necessary for the task in hand at differing times in the interaction between physician and patient. On the concept, see Merton, Reader, and Kendall, eds., *The Student-Physician, op. cit.,* p. 74; Seminar on the Sociological Study of the Medical School, Bureau of Applied Social Research, Columbia University, March 25, 1954, 1–2; April 22, 1954, 1–7; April 29, 1954, 1–5; November 4, 1954, 1–2. As indicated in these

act, different and abstractly contradictory norms are activated to meet the dynamically changing needs of the relation. *Only through such structures of norms and counter-norms*, we suggest, *can the various functions of a role be effectively discharged.* This is not merely a matter of social psychology but of role-structure. Potentially conflicting norms are built into the social definition of roles that provide for normatively acceptable alternations of behavior as the state of a social relation changes. This is a major basis for that oscillation between differing role-requirements that makes for sociological ambivalence.

Sources of Ambivalence toward the Professions

As we have repeatedly noted, the opposed feelings, beliefs and actions embraced in the concept of psychological ambivalence can in part be understood as responses to conflict in patterned situations and social structure as caught up in the concept of sociological ambivalence.[35] This final section of our paper sets out observations on the socially patterned bases of ambivalent attitudes and feelings toward the professions and, to some extent, of professionals toward clients. As we have also noted, sociographic accounts are a necessary but only temporary phase in the development of analytical accounts, and since this particular subject is still in its early stages of development, we shall find ourselves dealing with it in largely sociographic rather than analytical terms.

Sociological studies of the comparative prestige of occupations in industrial society have uniformly found that the professions outrank all

---

memoranda, the concept of detached concern can be linked up with the structure of role-sets, but we do not treat this matter here. See Renée C. Fox, "Training for Detached Concern in the Anatomy Laboratory," Bureau of Applied Social Research, Publication A–253, 1957 and Gene N. Levine, "The Good Physician: Some Observations on Physician-Patient Interaction," Bureau of Applied Social Research, Working Paper No. 3, Evaluation Studies of the Cornell Comprehensive Care and Teaching Program, 1957. [See H. I. Lief and Renée C. Fox, "The Medical Student's Training for 'Detached Concern,' " pp. 12–35, in H. I. Lief, V. Lief, and N. R. Lief, eds., *The Psychological Basis of Medical Practice* (New York: Harper & Row, 1963); Renée C. Fox, *Experiment Perilous* (New York: The Free Press, 1959); R. H. Coombs and L. J. Goldman, "Maintenance and Discontinuity of Coping Mechanisms in an Intensive Care Unit," *Social Problems* 20 (1973), pp. 342–43].

35. This section draws upon our paper presented to the American Sociological Association at its annual meeting in August, 1958.

other broad classes of occupations.[36] It may well be that these findings which consistently attest the high standing of the professions have deflected the attention of sociologists from the sources and consequences of the hostility that, over the years, has also been directed against the professions.[37] (Remember only G. B. Shaw's quip that a profession is a conspiracy against the laity.) Yet it is well known, understandably by the sensitive professionals themselves, that the professions have been and often still are the targets of hostility as well as the objects of esteem. The professions are, in varying extent, the objects of ambivalence: of praise, sometimes extravagant praise, and of sharp, sometimes immoderate, censure. In short, they are the object of all manner of positive feelings and all manner of negative ones.

The sources and extent of ambivalence toward different types of professions probably differ. But the fact is that a demonstrably useful classification of the professions has yet to be developed, and so it would be premature for us even to speculate about the nature of ambivalence directed toward each type. That is why we involuntarily restrict our discussion to sources of ambivalence that seem more or less common to the professions as a whole. Nevertheless, we record our impression that ambivalence toward a profession will differ according to the degree to which it is *prophylactic or preventive*, scotching the troubles of people before they become marked; the degree to which it is *preparatory*, designed to help people anticipate special kinds of contingencies; and according to the degree to which it is *remedial or therapeutic*, helping people to cope with troubles after they have arisen.

Throughout our discussion, also, we center attention on the sources of negative components in ambivalence toward the professions. We do so, not because they necessarily predominate over the positive components, but only because, as we have noted, most inquiries into the standing of the professions have tended to emphasize the high regard in which they are held.

In accord with our discussion of sociological ambivalence, we shall

36. For a detailed overview of this subject, see Albert J. Reiss, Jr. *et al.*, *Occupations and Social Status* (New York: The Free Press, 1961), and the cross-cultural comparisons of the standings of occupations in six industrialized countries by Alex Inkeles and Peter H. Rossi, "National Comparisons of Occupational Prestige," *American Journal of Sociology* 61 (1956), pp. 329–39.

37. In part, this may be an artifact of the research tools used in the social ratings of occupations. Since these inquiries typically call for net ratings, and often do not expressly include statements of the negative as well as the positive bases of evaluation, they reinforce the tendency to attend to the net position of the professions being located toward the top of the hierarchy of prestige.

examine only those sources of hostility toward the professions that are built into the normative structure of professional work and into the patterned conditions under which that work is ordinarily done. In other words, we do not examine such obvious sources of hostility as the conspicuously deviant practices of certain professionals: charging fees judged excessive by established standards, violating professional confidences, evident incompetence, and so on. Such deviant practices do, of course, arouse hostility; indeed, they may be its principal source, although no one yet knows. But since the violating of professional norms, malpractice of every sort, is an unproblematic and almost self-evident source of hostility toward the malpractitioner (and the guild of which he is a part), it does not require much analysis. In such cases, the sociological problem would be one of trying to track down the sources of deviant behavior by the professional, and that is not our interest here. Instead, we confine ourselves to *sources of hostility between professionals and clients that stem from the institutionally patterned relations between them and from the patterned situations in which they usually deal with one another.* In particular, we center on the paradox that the very effort of the professional to live up to the norms of professional conduct can make for hostility, distrust, and resentment on the part of clients and the public.

Situational Contexts of Professional Care and Ambivalence

Before turning to the sources of ambivalence built into the role of the professional, we must consider the patterned conditions under which people obtain professional care. Troubled by sickness, by legal difficulties, by moral dilemmas, by marital or economic problems, some people will seek professional help, for it is the task of the professions to try to solve other people's problems. The professions are not alone among the occupations in being assigned the role of handling the troubles of others. But they tend to deal with troubles of profound rather than minor significance to clients and to have their work held to exacting technical and moral standards.

Often, people facing such troubles will not get professional help simply because they cannot pay for it. This is a basic and conspicuous source of the inadequate provision of needed professional care and an immense library of investigation has been devoted to it. But beyond these economic obstacles to the use of professional help are the less conspicuous social and psychological obstacles which help explain the ambivalence toward professions. Each culture prescribes the occasions on which it is appropriate to seek professional help, but this cultural prescription is not uniformly distributed throughout the society. Some social strata and groups have the patterned value that people "should be able to handle" particular kinds of problems by themselves. Such a conception held for a long time, and in some groups still holds today, in the case of childbirth; it is still the case for many who will not turn to the psychiatrist; just as it is for some who will not make use of social workers, marriage counselors, architects, lawyers, and other professionals. Studies of people in trouble consistently report these attitudinal and value hindrances to the use of professional help, apart from the obstacle of not being able to afford the price of such help.[38] Groups having this do-it-yourself sentiment that self-respecting people should be able to look after certain problems for themselves burden those members of the group who do make use of professional help with self-blame and guilt that can be transformed into hostility toward the profession.

Furthermore, clients are normally in a state of anxiety when they do seek out a professional. Concerned with troubles important to them, clients cannot easily remain emotionally detached, for involvement in a contingent situation where the outcome matters is an excellent generator of anxiety. This condition has important consequences for the emergence of ambivalence toward a profession.

In the anxious eyes of the client, virtually every remark and every act of the professional is imbued with disproportionate significance. What the professional does or fails to do *matters* to the anxious client even when, in fact, it does not matter by affecting the objective situation. All this tends to produce an excess of emotional response: exaggerated praise for every satisfying episode and exaggerated blame for every disturbing one. Emotions of love and hate become focused on the professional and, by generalization, on the profession at large. Affective involvement with the problem and uncertainty about its outcome thus help to account both for the disproportionate esteem sometimes accorded the professions and for the sometimes disproportionate distrust and hostility directed toward them.

38. Earl L. Koos, *Families in Trouble* (New York: King's Crown Press, 1946); Gerald Gurin, Joseph Veroff and Sheila Feld, *Americans View Their Mental Health* (New York: Basic Books, 1960); Harry Stack Sullivan, *The Psychiatric Interview* (New York: W. W. Norton, 1954), who notes: "... [as] psychiatric experts, we are very much afflicted by the fact that all people are taught that they *ought not* to need help, so that they are ashamed of needing it or feel that they are foolish to seek it or expect it. And along with this, they come for psychiatric assistance with curious expectations as to what they are going to get, perhaps partly because this is so necessary to prop up self-esteem" (p. 37).

Motivated by anxiety, the client thus develops exaggerated hopes and exaggerated fears. Above all, he has a profound desire to know "how things really stand." He is peculiarly unable to tolerate that ambiguity that comes from uncertainty of outcome. He develops an insatiable desire for information, of the kind that would be supplied by a definite diagnosis of his situation and by a firm prognosis. A classic historical instance of such status- or condition-anxiety, it will be remembered, was analyzed by Max Weber in his account of religious anxiety among the Calvinists "in an age in which the after-life was . . . more important . . . than all the interests of life in this world."[39] Even though they regarded the outcome as predestined, believers focused their anxiety on the need to know whether they were in a state of grace or not. This is reminiscent of clients confronting professionals of every kind with the anxiety-inspired insistence on knowing how things stand and how they are going to turn out.

This anxiety, we suggest, lies back of the pattern, familiar to all the professions, of clients complaining that they are not being sufficiently informed. In particular cases, this complaint requires no special interpretation: the professional has simply failed to appreciate the anxious concern of the client and has not told him as much as he could easily have done. But in other cases, the troubles that led clients to consult a professional create a profound need for reassurance that cannot be readily satisfied so that clients' feelings are typically skewed toward the belief that they have not been told what they should be told.

"Adequate communication" is of course a functional requirement for the effective working of social relations generally; it is by no means peculiar to client-professional relations. But since this relation is typically acted out when at least one of the two parties to it is in a state of anxiety, the extent of this requirement is stepped up until, at the extreme, it approaches insatiability. For this reason, clients tend to feel uninformed and consequently uneasy and hostile even in cases when the professional is doing all that he is in a position to do. (We repeat: our discussion excludes the obvious instances of hostility generated by professionals' malpractice; these are socially important but analytically trivial.)

Structural Sources of Ambivalence

From these few observations on the situational context in which professional and client have contact, we turn now to structural sources of

39. Max Weber, *The Protestant Ethic and the Spirit of Capitalism* (New York: Charles Scribner's Sons, 1958), pp. 109–15.

ambivalence. These are sources located in the normative structure of the relations between client and professional that affect the role-behavior of both. We want to see how the institutionalized relationship itself comes to generate ambivalence toward the professions.

The Attribute of Continuity.   Once again, we begin with a familiar fact. The relation between a professional and a client is *normatively* presumed to be of indefinite duration, to involve enduring though intermittent interaction between the same people. This contrasts with the norm governing transactions in other parts of the marketplace, which holds that the buyer should shift his custom whenever he believes that he can do better elsewhere. Of course, business transactions often involve continuing relations between buyer and seller; the *fact* is not in question. All we want to emphasize is that the professions are skewed in the direction of having a *normative* presumption of continuity in the client-professional relation. When the client changes his professional, this is apt to be construed as a deviation from the norm, whereas in other economic transactions such changes in personnel are typically in accord with the norm. All this is expressed in the sentiment, found among all the professions, that "clients should not shop around."

The functional basis for this sentiment is well known. Continuity of relationship helps the professional to learn enough about the client to give him the individualized help he often needs and typically craves. Such continuity is functionally significant not only in medicine, where it has become a virtual slogan expressing the technical advantage of knowing more and more about the particular patient and the interpersonal advantage of making for mutual understanding, but also, and for much the same reasons, in the other professions as well.

The norm prescribing a continued relationship, however, also provides a basis for *the accumulation of ambivalence.* For in some unknown proportion of cases, it constrains the client to continue with the relationship long after he has come to be dissatisfied with it. We suggest, in short, that a heavier load of client dissatisfaction is required to break down a professional relationship than other relationships involving the exchange of services or goods. To the extent that the norm of continuity has this effect, ambivalence becomes more characteristic of client-professional relations than of those in which the customer feels free to take his trade elsewhere. Less turnover in the parties to the client-professional relationship may thus not signify greater satisfaction, but only a greater commitment to maintain the relationship, in spite of accumulating dissatisfaction.

This conception that the normatively prescribed duration of social relations affects the accumulation of ambivalence generated in the relation and the related conception that different types of social relations can tolerate varying degrees of personal dissatisfaction before being terminated have much greater generality, of course, than their application to the special case of the professions. The first conception implies, for example, that ambivalence would be more frequent as well as more intense in marriages than, say, in acquaintanceships. For since marriage is normatively defined as a presumptively continuing relation, it will be less readily terminated under the "same load of dissatisfaction" than the acquaintanceship. In generalized form, the hypothesis holds that social relations which are normatively defined as presumptively "permanent or as having an indefinitely extended duration"[40] will tolerate heavier loads of hostile attitudes than those defined as temporary, with the result that a backlog of ambivalence can the more readily accumulate.

The second part of this general conception holds that institutional norms affect the rate at which personal satisfaction or dissatisfaction with a social relation becomes expressed in the form of continuing or discontinuing the relation. This is a theoretical issue of some importance. The conception developed here helps us to disentangle the interpersonal from the social-structural elements in the history of social relations. It serves to correct the widely held but sociologically naive notion that the persistence of a particular social relation depends largely or wholly on the extent of personal satisfaction with it. The degree of satisfaction is only the interpersonal element; the norms—in this case, the norm of indefinitely extended duration—provide the element of social structure. And the actual outcome of a relation involving a given degree of interpersonal conflict will be affected by its normative structure.[41] As a result, the client–professional relation tends to accumulate ambivalence (on the part of both client and professional, although we center here only on the client).

The Attribute of Professional Authority. The authority assigned the professional by virtue of special competence also helps accumulate ambivalence among clients. As with continuity, so with authority: the func-

40. For the view that the normatively expected (as distinct from the actual) duration of a social relation (or of a group) is a significant variable in social structure, see Merton, *Social Theory and Social Structure*, p. 366.
41. For a related analysis of friendship as a social relation, see P. F. Lazarsfeld and R. K. Merton, "Friendship as Social Process," in Morroe Berger, Theodore Abel, and C. H. Page, eds., *Freedom and Control in Modern Society* (New York: D. Van Nostrand, 1954), esp. pp. 28–37; and for ambivalence in other types of close relations, see R. K. Merton, M. Fiske, and A. Curtis, *Mass Persuasion* (New York: Harper, 1946), pp. 62–63.

tional basis for the institutionalized right of the professional to prescribe action for the client is manifest. But however great its legitimacy, authority is known to have a high potential for creating ambivalence among those subject to it. Authority generates a mixture of respect, love and admiration and of fear, hatred, and, sometimes, contempt.

In its own way, professional authority can reinforce the anxieties that prompted the client to seek help in the first place. As he develops dependence on the authoritative professional for solving (or helping him to solve) his problems, the client develops a coordinate fear of being rejected by the authority-figure and not infrequently condemns himself for not living up to the expectations of the professional.

Furthermore, the authority is an agent of frustration. However benevolent his intent, the professional must often impose various kinds of frustration upon the client.[42] The client may be required to abandon favored practices or values. He may be required to live a more limited version of his former life, as with medically, legally or religiously prescribed regimens. He may be asked to change his eating habits or his work habits, to give up claims to property or to turn his attention from interests that have long had meaning for him to new activities which he finds thoroughly uninteresting although they are said to be "good" for him.

There is, then, a distinct potential in the authoritative relation of the professional to the client for generating considerable ambivalence. We should emphasize again that we are examining sources of the frustration of clients which are patterned in the role of the professional; we are not referring to idiosyncratic sources of frustration which can be assigned to the particular personality of this or that professional or of this or that client. We focus on *frustrations induced by the professional living up to his role*. These are not the more conspicuous, important but different frustrations resulting from the apparent failure to solve his client's pressing problem, a matter effectively analyzed by Everett Hughes.[43] Although no systematic evidence is yet available, we assume from the foregoing hypotheses that professions differ in the coefficients of frustration they typically induce in clients.

One particular norm embedded in the professional's authority requires the client to make known to his doctor, his lawyer, his social worker or

42. For this observation in the case of the physician, see Talcott Parsons, *The Social System*, op. cit., p. 442.
43. Everett C. Hughes, "Mistakes at Work," *The Canadian Journal of Economics and Political Science* 17 (1951), pp. 320–27, and Hughes, *The Sociological Eye: Selected Papers* (Chicago: Aldine–Atherton, 1971), pp. 316–25.

his clergyman information about himself that he has regarded as private. That is why the doctrine of privileged communications was designed to legitimatize access to such private but functionally important information.[44] There is evidence that such reports can serve the psychological function of providing the client with "the luxury of an intimate disclosure to a stranger," a stranger committed to sympathetic listening rather than harsh judgments. But even legitimatized disclosures of the private self can disturb the client and leave a residue of hostility toward the professional. The disclosures of feelings and actions that are, by his own standards and those of his reference groups, shameful, can damage his self-image and make it difficult for him to maintain his self-esteem. However technical or benevolent the purpose of the professional, his probing is often experienced by the client as an invasion of privacy, violating the sentiment that certain matters should be kept wholly to oneself.[45] In short, functionally appropriate and role-prescribed behavior by the professional can nevertheless make for ambivalence. This can be construed as one of the costs incurred by professionals at work.

"Living Off" the Profession. As the role of the professional is socially defined, he is to subordinate his own interests to the interests of the client he has accepted. More strictly, he cannot legitimately advance his own interests at the expense of his clients'. Yet the interests built into the professional role have a dual character: they require him to give the best possible service to his clients, to remove or ameliorate their troubles so far as he can, and at the same time the continuing problems of clients provide him with his livelihood. It is in this objective sense that professionals have an institutionalized stake in trouble, that they "live off" the troubles of their clients.[46]

This sets the stage for clients to suspect the motivations of the professionals who minister to their needs. Various elements in the client-professional relationship converge to produce the suspicion that the professional may be using his authority principally in his own interest rather than in that of the client. First, the client typically lacks the specialized knowl-

44. For one among many observations on this, see Parsons, *op. cit.*, p. 452.
45. On resistances to full observability and on ambivalence toward those who insistently probe into matters socially defined as private, see Merton, *Social Theory and Social Structure*, pp. 397–98. For perceptively analyzed cases of such resistance to invasion of "privacy," see Aaron Lusk, *Night Calls: A Study in General Practice* (London: Tavistock Publications, 1961), pp. 115, 117, *passim*.
46. For the notion of "living off" an occupation as contrasted with "living for" it, see Max Weber, *Essays in Sociology*, trans. and edited by H. H. Gerth and C. W. Mills (New York: Oxford University Press, 1946), p. 84.

edge to judge the aptness of the professional's decisions. Second, his anxiety about his fate tends to distort his appraisal of what is being done. Third, since it is often (not always) the case that a professional stands to gain from the continuation of his clients' troubles, this complicates the task of gauging his motivations, a task that is at best difficult in all human relations and particularly so in this type of situation. Fourth, the frustrations imposed upon the client by the professional tend to skew the client's interpretation of even the most disinterested activities of the professional toward their being seen as self-interested. Beset by uncertainty, attendant anxiety and thorough awareness that they must pay for the continued relationship, clients come to feel that professionals unnecessarily prolong their ministrations: the patient feels that he is asked to come back time and again long after the necessity is really past; the client believes that the law case is drawn out long after it could have been satisfactorily settled or that it is being settled too soon and for too little. The definition of the professional's role as collectivity-oriented rather than self-interested may mitigate these sources of ambivalence but scarcely eliminate them. And once again, we emphasize that we are not dealing here with cases in which professionals do, by the standards of the time, exploit the troubles of their clients. We are concerned with legitimate practices and patterned situations, not with deviant practices, that produce ambivalence.

Discrepant Appraisals of Role-Performance. We have singled out the composite of self-interest-and-client-interest incorporated into the professional's role because this seems to provide a pervasive potential for ambivalent interpretations of the professional's behavior. But this is, of course, only a special case of a more general pattern deriving from a basic fact of social structure. Social structures are variously differentiated into social statuses, roles and strata, with these having their distinctive (and sometimes opposed) as well as their shared values and interests. This leads us to expect that people occupying different positions in a social structure will tend to differ in their appraisals of the same social situations.[47] Applying this general conception to the particular case in point, we should anticipate that different criteria of the effectiveness of professional work would be employed by professionals and their clients, if only as a result of their different statuses, with attendant differences in values, knowledge, and interests. Hughes has noted that it is difficult to define

47. On this conception, see Merton, *Social Theory and Social Structure*, pp. 424 ff.; R. K. Merton and R. A. Nisbet, eds., *Contemporary Social Problems* (New York: Harcourt Brace Jovanovich, 1961), pp. ix–xi, 733.

"a failure or mistake" in any line of work and that "even where the standards may be a little clearer than in medicine and education, the people who work and those who receive the product as goods or services will have quite different degrees and kinds of knowledge of the probabilities and contingencies involved."[48]

Having few other points of reference, laymen tend to appraise professional performance in terms of outcome: whether it succeeds or fails to solve the problem. Professionals tend to judge performance in terms of what is accomplished in relation to what, under the circumstances, could be accomplished. The fact that certified medical specialists are more apt than general practitioners to be sued for negligence does not lead physicians to assume that specialists are less competent but only that they are more likely to undertake difficult cases that involve far more contingencies.[49]

Unlike the bitter relatives of the deceased, physicians will maintain that "the operation was a success but the patient died" just as they will maintain (among themselves) that "the operation was botched but the patient survived." The possible discrepancy between quality of performance and actual outcome is recognized in every field of specialized activity. Laymen may be impressed by the box score of district attorneys who have "won" 98 per cent of all the cases they have prosecuted but fellow-lawyers will want to know how often the district attorney converted uncertain prosecutions into sure things by permitting the defendant to plead guilty to a lesser charge. On the average, the quality of performance and actual outcome may be closely connected, as witness the confession by the barrister, quoted by Bryce, who said that "when I was young I lost a good many causes which I ought to have won, and now, that I have grown old and experienced, I win a good many causes which I ought to lose."[50] But clients have a way of being primarily interested in their own cases, not in an averaging out of performance. Neither the clients in the first brace of our barrister's cases nor his opponent's clients in the second can be expected to appreciate the statistical jest with which he concludes: "So, on the whole, justice has been done."

Apart from actually inept professional work, the status-patterned discrepancy in the criteria used by laymen and professionals to appraise performance is another source of hostility toward the professional who failed to solve the problem (even though he may have done all that was

48. Hughes, "Mistakes at Work," *op. cit.*, pp. 323 ff.
49. *Medical News*, April 7, 1958.
50. James Bryce, *The American Commonwealth* (New York: The Macmillan Co., 1914), Vol. II, p. 275.

possible). The client and his associates are concerned with the outcome; unable to appraise the objective possibilities, they will devaluate some proportion of sound but unsuccessful performance by professionals.

The Social Diffusion of Ambivalence

Until now, we have dealt with some patterned sources of the negative component in ambivalence as these turn up in the relation between one client and one professional. Hostilities generated in such particular cases can be aggregated to account for part of the total volume of hostility directed against a profession in the society. We believe that this would account for only a part, because processes of communication in larger social systems so operate that the experiences of frustrated and hostile clients become more widely known and help to shape the attitudes and feelings of others who have not themselves had these experiences.

Since clients are involved in other social relations, their experiences with professionals affect not only themselves but, in some measure, others in their role-sets. In noting this, we only apply to this particular subject the general conception that the structure of status-sets and role-sets provides a basic form of interdependence in society. In some parts of the social structure, the degree of this interdependence is reduced by segregating and insulating the various statuses and roles of individuals. What happens in one status is not made known to role-partners in other statuses. In the case of experiences with professionals, however, we believe that there is a motivated tendency for clients to break through such insulation from the role-sets of their other statuses. The deep involvement with their troubles and the widespread interest in the institutionalized treatment of such troubles motivates people to talk about these experiences. The *fact* that people like to talk about their experiences with professionals has been noticed time without number. Everyone knows that much small talk is devoted to detailed accounts of an operation or a law suit or the building of a house. But there is still need to trace the consequences of this conspicuous pattern for the diffusion of attitudes toward the professions.

For the reasons set out in earlier parts of this paper, we assume once again that, in these conversations, clients will attend selectively to certain parts of their range of experience with professionals. They will center on dramatic experiences rather than on routine ones. They will be motivated to tell of extraordinary successes and dismal failures, and tend to magnify both in the telling. The polarized reports would serve to spread ambivalent attitudes and to provide a context for hearers when next they have dealings with professionals. Furthermore, it is probably the case that the more a relation between a client and his professional has deteriorated, the more will the client be motivated to tell intimates and strangers about his miserable experiences (since these, almost as much as the weather, provide common ground for phatic communion).[51] Much of the tendentious wit directed against the professions finds expression in these circumstances. In this way, systems of social interaction can reinforce and diffuse the components of ambivalence toward the professions.

Summary

The first part of this essay distinguishes psychological from sociological ambivalence and indicates the connections between them. The restricted sense of sociological ambivalence, as incorporated in a single role of a single status, is related to five other kinds of ambivalence caught up in the extended sense of the concept.

The second part deals with principal modes of characterizing social roles: depiction in representational detail, as by the novelist; description in categorical but fairly concrete terms, as by the sociographer; and analysis in terms of abstract attributes and components, as by the theorist. The analysis of sociological ambivalence proceeds from the premise that the structure of social roles consists of arrangements of norms and counter-norms which have evolved to provide the flexibility of normatively acceptable behavior required to deal with changing states of a social relation. As an example of this in the role of the physician, we identify "detached concern" rather than affective neutrality.

The third part examines patterned sources of ambivalence toward the professions. The principal conception developed here is that such ambivalence is generated, under specifiable conditions, by professionals living up to the requirements of their role as well as by the obvious situations in which they fail to meet these requirements.

51. It was the perceptive and conceptive anthropologist Bronislaw Malinowski who coined the useful term "phatic communion." It refers to the use of conversation to reveal or share feelings or to establish an atmosphere of sociability rather than to communicate ideas or facts. This concept was, of course, congenial to the literary critic and functional analyst of language, I. A. Richards, who made good use of it for literate cultures.

2

The Ambivalence
of Scientists

SCIENCE, AND THE MEN AND WOMEN who create science, can be examined
from different though connected points of view. There is the standpoint
of the body of scientific knowledge itself. This requires little interest in
scientists, centering only on the fruits of their work. What has been found
out? how sound is the evidence? what are the implications for new knowledge? Beyond this is the perspective of the philosophers and logicians of
science who concern themselves with the assumptions underlying scientific
ideas and the logic of inquiry. Still another angle of vision is that of the
psychology of the scientist, focused on the processes of learning and of
that special kind of learning that is creative investigation. These and other
perspectives on science each contribute to our understanding of the life
and work of scientists, but I shall say nothing about them here.

Ambivalence in the
Social Institution of Science

Instead, I shall stick to my last and examine a restricted set of questions
in the sociology of science. From this perspective, science appears as one
of the great social institutions, coordinate with the other major institutions of society: the economy, education and religion, the family and the
polity. Like other institutions, science has its corpus of shared and transmitted ideas, values and standards designed to govern the behavior of
those connected with the institution. The standards define the technically

Reprinted with permission from *Bulletin of The Johns Hopkins Hospital*, 112
(February 1963), pp. 77–79. The third Daniel Coit Gilman Lecture delivered at The
John Hopkins University School of Medicine on September 25, 1962. The investigation providing the basis for this lecture has been greatly aided by a fellowship
awarded by the John Simon Guggenheim Memorial Foundation.

and morally allowable patterns of behavior, indicating what is prescribed, preferred, permitted or proscribed. The culture of science refers, then, to more than habitual behavior; its norms codify the values judged appropriate for the people engaged in doing science.

A major characteristic of social institutions is that they tend to be patterned in terms of potentially conflicting pairs of norms. This sets a task for those governed by the institution to blend these imposed inconsistencies into reasonably consistent action. This is what I mean by saying that sociological ambivalence is imbedded in social institutions generally and, in its distinctive fashion, in the institution of science as well. Consider only, in swift review, some institutionally defined pairs of norms and note the tension that can be generated by potential inconsistency within each pair. (I adopt the Lyndian pattern established in Chapter 1.)

The scientist must be ready to make his newfound knowledge available to his peers as soon as possible.

But: He must avoid an undue tendency to rush into print. (Compare Faraday's motto: "Work, Finish, Publish" with Ehrlich's motto: "Viel arbeiten, wenig publizieren.")

The scientist should not allow himself to be victimized by intellectual fads, those modish ideas that rise for a time and are doomed to disappear.

But: He must remain flexible, receptive to the promising new idea and avoid becoming ossified under the guise of responsibly maintaining intellectual traditions.

New scientific knowledge should be greatly esteemed by knowledgeable peers.

But: The scientist should work without regard for the esteem of others.

The scientist must not advance claims to new knowledge until they are beyond reasonable dispute.

But: He should defend his new ideas and findings, no matter how great the opposition. (Compare C. N. Yang on the scientific credo: "it will not do to jump to hasty conclusions" and Pasteur: "do not fear to defend new ideas, even the most revolutionary.")

The scientist should make every effort to know the work of predecessors and contemporaries in his field.

But: Too much reading and erudition will only stultify creative work. (Compare Cayley's omnivorous reading of other mathematicians— that same Cayley who, with Euler and Cauchy, is among the three most prolific mathematicians of all time—with the irritation of his collaborator, Sylvester, at being expected to master what others had done. And, of course, there is always Schopenhauer's sin against the Holy Ghost: "to put away one's original thoughts in order to take up a book.")

The scientist should pay scrupulous attention to detail.

But: He must avoid the excessive accuracy of the pedant, fastidious only when it comes to inconsequentials.

Scientific knowledge is universal, belonging to no nation.

But: Each scientific discovery does honor to the nation that fostered it.

The scientist should recognize the prime obligation to train up new generations of scientists.

But: He must not allow teaching to preempt his energies at the expense of advancing knowledge. Of course, this reads just as persuasively in reverse. (Remember the complaints about Faraday that he had never trained a successor as Davy had trained him and consider the frequent criticism of scientists who give up research for teaching.)

Young scientists can have no happier condition than being apprenticed to a master of the scientific art.

But: They must become their own men, questing for autonomy and not content to remain in the shadow of great men. (I reiterate a brace of cases in point: Kepler's ambivalence toward Tycho Brahe; Sir Ronald Ross's ambivalence toward Manson, his devotion to the master pushing him to extravagant praise, his need for autonomy pushing •him to excessive criticism; in psychiatry, Bouchard's ambivalence toward Charcot and the secessionists Jung and Adler displaying theirs toward Freud; Sir Everard Home's mixed feelings about John Hunter, and the rest in the list of ambivalent apprentices in science.)

And so, on and on, with norms garnered from the literature of science which can be paired into actual contradictions, potential contradictions or near-contradictions. Before turning to one conspicuous kind of ambivalence experienced by scientists, I should first say a word about the spirit in which this inquiry is conducted. Embodying as they do some of the prime values of world civilization, scientists have been placed on pedestals where they have no wish to be perched—not, at least, the greatest among them. This is not the result of a conspiracy, not even a conspiracy of good will. It is only that men and occasionally, women of science have been pictured, through collective acts of piety, as though they were more than human, being like gods in their creativity, and also as less than human, being deprived of the passions, attitudes and social ties given to ordinary mortals. As a result, scientists have been dehumanized by being idealized and, on occasion, idolized. Contributing greatly to this centuries-long process of distortion are the pious biographers who convert indubitably great scientists into what Augustus de Morgan once described as "monsters of perfection." Yet an honest appreciation would see them as men and women, not gods, and so subject to the pressures, passions and social relations in which people inevitably find themselves. Rather than deny their human qualities, we must examine them. As the historian of science, A. C. Crombie, observed for one of the most notable cases in point:

> We must completely misunderstand Newton the man and we run the risk of missing the essential processes of a mind so profoundly original and individual as his, if we exclude from our field of historical investigation all those influences and interests that may be distasteful to us, or seem to us odd in a scientist.

A comprehensive monograph on the subject would consider, first, how potentially contradictory norms develop in every social institution; next, how in the institution of science, conflicting norms generate marked ambivalence in the lives of scientists; and finally, how this ambivalence affects the actual, as distinct from the supposed, relations between scientists. In this chapter, I shall consider only the socially patterned sources of one kind of ambivalence—toward the claiming of priorities in cases of multiple scientific discovery. This one type is not necessarily typical of the rest. But by examining it in the needed detail, we can perhaps catch a glimpse of the ways in which ambivalence is socially generated by each of the other potentially opposed pairs of norms in the institution of science: erudition *vs.* originality, apprentice-emulation *vs.* personal autonomy, and so on.

Ambivalence toward
Priorities in Scientific Discovery

As is well known, scientists typically experience multiple independent discoveries as one of their occupational hazards. These create occasions for acute stress. Few scientists indeed react with equanimity when they learn that one of their own best contributions to science—what they *know* to be the result of long hard work—is "only" (as the telling phrase has it) a rediscovery of what was found some time before or "just" another discovery of what others have found at about the same time. No one who systematically examines the disputes over priority can ever again accept as veridical the picture of the scientist as one who is exempt from affective involvement with *his* ideas and *his* discoveries of once unknown fact. The value of observing the behavior of people under stress in order to understand them better in all manner of other situations need not be emphasized here. By observing the behavior of scientists under what they experience as the stress of being forestalled in a discovery, we gain clues to ways in which the social institution of science shapes the motives, social relations and affect of working scientists. I have tried to show elsewhere[1] how the values and reward-system of science, with their pathogenic emphasis upon originality, help account for certain deviant behaviors of scientists: secretiveness during the early stages of inquiry lest they be forestalled, violent conflicts over priority, a flow of premature publications designed to establish later claims to having been first. These, I suggest, are normal responses to a badly integrated institution of science, such that we can better understand the report of a sample of American "starred men of science" that, next to "personal curiosity," "rivalry" is most often the spur to their work.

In saying that the social institution of science is malintegrated, I mean that it incorporates potentially incompatible values: among them, the value set upon originality, which leads scientists to want their priority to be recognized, and the value set upon humility, which leads them to insist on how little they have in fact been able to accomplish. These values are not real contradictories, of course—'tis a poor thing, but my own—but they do call for opposed kinds of behavior. To blend these potential incompatibles into a single orientation and to reconcile them in practice is no easy matter. Rather, the tension between these kindred values creates an inner conflict among scientists who have internalized both of them. Among other things, the tension generates a distinct resistance to the systematic study of multiple discoveries and associated conflicts over priority.

This resistance is expressed in various ways: by seeking to trivialize the subject, by regarding the conflicts over priority as rare or aberrant, by motivated misperceptions of the facts of the case or by a hiatus in recall and reporting. Such resistance often leads to those wish-fulfilling beliefs

1. See R. K. Merton, *The Sociology of Science: Theoretical and Empirical Investigations*, ed. and with an Introduction by Norman W. Storer (Chicago and London: University of Chicago Press, 1973), Parts 3, 4, and 5.

and false memories that we describe as illusions. And of such behavior the annals that treat of multiple discoveries and priorities are uncommonly full. So much so, that I have arrived at a rule-of-thumb that seems to work fairly well. The rule is this: whenever the biography or autobiography of a scientist announces that he had little or no concern with priority, there is a reasonably good chance that, not many pages later in the book, we shall find him deeply embroiled in one or another battle over priority. A few cases here must stand for many.

The authoritative biography of that great psychiatrist of the Salpêtriè̄e, Charcot, states that, despite his many discoveries, he "never thought for a moment to claim priority or reward." Our rule of thumb leads us to expect what we find: some 30 pages later, there is a detailed account of Charcot insisting on having been first in recognizing exophthalmic goiter and a little later, emphatically affirming that he "would like to claim priority" [the language is his] for the idea of isolating patients who are suffering from hysteria.[2]

Or again, Harvey Cushing writes of the brilliant Halsted that he was "overmodest about his work, indifferent to matters of priority . . ."[3] Alerted by our rule-of-thumb we find some 20 pages later in the book where this is cited, a letter by Halsted about his work on cocaine: "I anticipated all of Schleich's work by about six years (or five) . . . [In Vienna], I showed Wölfler how to use cocaine. He had declared that it was useless in surgery. But before I left Vienna he published an enthusiastic article in one of the daily papers on the subject. It did not, however, occur to him to mention my name."[4]

But perhaps the most apt case of such denial of an accessible reality is provided by Ernest Jones, writing in his comprehensive biography[5] that "Although Freud was never interested in questions of priority, which he found merely boring, he was fond of exploring the source of what appeared to be original ideas, particularly his own . . ." This is an extraordinarily illuminating statement. For, of course, no one could have known better than Jones—"known" in the narrowly cognitive sense—

2. Georges Gullain, *J.–M. Charcot: His Life, His Work* (New York: Hoeber, 1959), pp. 61, 95–96, 142–43.
3. In his magisterial biography, *Harvey Cushing* (Springfield: Charles C. Thomas, 1946), pp. 119–20, John F. Fulton describes Cushing's biographical sketch of Halsted, from which this excerpt is quoted, as "an excellent description."
4. *Ibid.*, p. 142.
5. Ernest Jones, *Sigmund Freud: Life and Work* (London: Hogarth Press, 1957) III, p. 105. Contrast David Riesman, who takes ample note of Freud's concern with priority, in *Individualism Reconsidered* (New York: The Free Press, 1954), pp. 314–15, 378.

how very often Freud turned to matters of priority: in his own work, in the work of his colleagues (both friends and enemies) and in the history of psychology altogether. In point of fact, Dr. Elinor Barber and I have found that Freud expressed an interest in priority on more than 150 occasions. With characteristic self-awareness, he reports that he even dreamt about priority and the due allocation of credit for accomplishments in science. He oscillates between the poles of his ambivalence toward priority: occasionally taking multiple discoveries to be practically inescapable, as when he reports a fantasy in which "science would ignore me entirely during my lifetime; some decades later, someone else would infallibly come upon the same things—for which the time was not now ripe—, and would achieve recognition for them and bring me honour as a forerunner whose failure had been inevitable." At other times, he reluctantly or insistently acknowledges anticipations of his own ideas or reports his own anticipations of others; he "implores" his disciple Lou Andreas-Salomé to finish an essay in order "not to give me precedence in time"; he admonishes Adler for what he describes as his "uncontrolled craving for priority" just as he admonishes Georg Groddeck for being unable to conquer "that banal ambition which hankers after originality and priority"; over a span of 40 years, he repeatedly reassesses the distinctive roles of Breuer and himself in establishing psychoanalysis; he returns time and again to his priority-conflict with Janet, reporting that he had brought the recalcitrant Breuer to publish their joint monograph early because "in the meantime, Janet's work had anticipated some of his [Breuer's] results"; he writes nostalgically about the days of "my splendid isolation" when "there was nothing to hustle me . . . My publications, which I was able to place with a little trouble, could always lag far behind my knowledge and could be postponed as long as I pleased, since there was no doubtful 'priority' to be defended"; again and again, he allocates priorities among others (Le Bon, Ferenczi, Bleuler, Stekel being only a few among the many); he even credits Adler with priority for an error; and, to prolong the occasions no further, he repeatedly intervenes in priority-battles among his disciples and colleagues (for example, between Abraham and Jung), saying that he could not "stifle the disputes about priority for which there were so many opportunities under these conditions of work in common."[6]

In view of even this small sampling of cases in point, it may not be

6. For a more detailed account and the bibliographic references to Freud, see Merton, *The Sociology of Science*, pp. 385–91.

audacious to interpret as a sign of resistance, Jones's remarkable statement that "Freud was never interested in questions of priority, which he found merely boring. . . ." That Freud was ambivalent toward priority, true; that he was pained by conflicts over priority, indisputable; that he was concerned to establish the priority of others as of himself, beyond doubt; but to describe him as "never interested" in the question and as "bored" by it requires the extraordinary feat of denying, as though they had never occurred, scores of occasions on which Freud exhibited profound interest in the question, many of these being occasions which Jones himself has detailed with the loving care of a genuine scholar. It is true that Freud appears to have been no more concerned with this matter than were Newton or Galileo, Laplace or Darwin, or any of the other giants of science about whom biographers have announced an entire lack of interest in priority just before, as careful scholars, they inundate us with a flood of evidence to the contrary. This denial of the realities they report and segregate seems to be an instance of that keeping of intellect and perception in abeyance which so typically reflects deep-seated resistance.

Such resistance has obvious parallels with other occasions in the history of thought, not least with psycho-analysis itself, when amply available facts with far-reaching theoretical implications were regarded as unedifying or unsavory, ignoble or trivial and so were conscientiously ignored. It is a little like the psychologists who once ignored sexuality because it was a subject not fit for polite society or regarded dreams, incomplete actions and slips of the tongue as manifestly trivial and so undeserving of thorough inquiry.

Complicating the problem in the case of multiple discoveries and priority-conflicts is the fact that investigation requires the detached examination of the behavior of scientists by other scientists. Even to assemble the facts of the case is to be charged with blemishing the record of undeniably great men and women of science, as though one were a raker of muck that a gentleman would pass by in silence. Even more, to investigate the subject systematically is to be regarded not merely as a muck-raker, but as a muck-maker.

The behavior of fellow-scientists involved in priority-disputes tends to be condemned or applauded, rather than analyzed. It is morally judged, not systematically investigated. The disputes are described as "unfortunate" with the moral judgment being substituted for the effort to understand what the disputes imply for the psychology of scientists and the sociology of science as an institution. At least since Goethe, we find references to "all those foolish quarrels about earlier and later discovery, plagiary, and quasi-purloinings."[7] We are free, of course, to find this behavior unfortunate or foolish or comic or sad. But these affective responses to the behavior of our ancestors- or brothers-and-sisters-in-science seem to have usurped the place that might be given to analysis of this behavior and its implications for the ways in which science develops. It is as though the physician were to respond only evaluatively to illness, describe it as unfortunate or painful, and consider his task done or as though the psychiatrist were to describe the behavior of schizophrenics as absurd and to substitute this sentiment for the effort to discover what brings that behavior about. The history of the sciences shows that the provisional emancipation from sentiment in order to investigate phenomena methodically has been a difficult task, that it has been achieved at different times in the various sciences and at different times for selected problems in each of the sciences. I suggest that only now are we beginning to emancipate the study of the actual behavior of scientists from the human tendency to respond to that behavior in terms of the sentiments and values which we have made our own rather than to examine it in reasonably detached fashion.

Norms and Behavior in Science

Contributing to the substitution of sentiment for analysis is the often painful contrast between the actual behavior of scientists and the behavior ideally prescribed for them. When confronted with the fact that their discovery is a rediscovery or, much worse, when confronted with the suggestion that it is a plagiary, their behavior scarcely matches the image of the dispassionate man of science, exclusively absorbed by his scientific work. It is often seen as ugly, harsh and greedy for fame. And in the bitter social conflict that ensues, the standards governing behavior deteriorate. One or another of the discoverers caught up in a multiple—or often a colleague or fellow-national—suggests that he rather than his rival was really first and that the independence of the rival is at least unproved. Grouping their forces, the other side counters with the opinion that plagiary had indeed occurred, that let him whom the shoe fits wear it and furthermore, to make matters quite clear, the shoe is on the other foot. Reinforced by group loyalties and sometimes by ethnocentrism, the controversy gains

7. Goethe's *Briefe*, in his *Werke* (Weimar: H. Boehlaus, 1903), Vol. 27, pp. 219–23. I am indebted to Aaron Noland, of the *Journal of the History of Ideas*, for calling my attention to this passage.

force, mutual charges of plagiary abound, and there develops an atmosphere of thoroughgoing hostility and mutual distrust.

This is not exactly in accord with the ideal image of scientists and particularly, of the greatest among them. When we identify ourselves with the role-models provided by great scientists of the past and by lesser as well as outstanding ones of the present, we find it painful to observe their behavior in these situations of conflict. Regarded in terms of sentiment rather than of understanding, it may seem a bit sordid for a Galileo to engage in seemingly egotistic attacks on one Grassi who tried "to diminish whatever praise there may be in this [invention of the telescope] which belongs to me"; or to go on to assail another who "attempted to rob me of that glory which was mine, pretending not to have seen my writings and trying to represent themselves as the original discoverer of these marvels"; or finally, to say of a third that he "had the gall to claim that he had observed the Medicean planets . . . before I had [and used] a sly way of attempting to establish his priority."[8]

For all of us who harbor the ideal image of the scientist it can be only disconcerting to have Edmond Halley forthrightly described by the first Astronomer Royal, John Flamsteed, as a "lazy and malicious thief" who manages to be just as "lazy and slothful as he is corrupt."[9] Or to have Flamsteed assert that he found Newton "always insidious, ambitious, and excessively covetous of praise."[10]

Almost all those firmly placed in the pantheon of science—a Newton, Descartes, Pascal, Leibniz or Huyghens; a Lister, Faraday, Laplace or Davy—have at one time or another been caught up in these fierce disputes. As we approach our own day, we hear an echo of these angry and agitated words reverberating through the corridors of the peaceful temple of science. Since these episodes involve our contemporaries and often our associates, they become, we must suppose, even more painful to observe and more difficult to analyze with detachment. Even the social scientists who may not be directly involved, at least for the moment, feel acutely uncomfortable. Uneasy and distressed, they can hardly bring themselves to study this behavior. For when sociological analysis is stripped bare of

8. Galileo, "The Assayer," 1623, trans. by Stillman Drake in *Discoveries and Opinions of Galileo* (New York: Doubleday, 1957), pp. 232–33, 245.
9. Francis Baily, *An Account of the Rev. John Flamsteed, the First Astronomer-Royal, Compiled from his own Manuscripts, and other Authentic Documents, never before published* (London: Printed by Order of the Lords Commissioners of the Admiralty, 1835), pp. 323–24.
10. *Ibid.*, pp. 73–74.

sentiment, it often leaves the sociologist shivering in the cold. And to respond with detachment to these hot conflicts of their associates becomes all the more difficult. The study of multiple discoveries and priorities accordingly remains undeveloped.

The disputants themselves manifest ambivalence toward their own behavior. Even while he is assembling documents to prove his priority, for example, Darwin registers his mixed feelings, writing Lyell: "My good dear friend, forgive me. This is a trumpery letter, influenced by trumpery feelings." In a postscript he assures Lyell that "I will never trouble you or Hooker on the subject again." The next day, he writes: "It seems hard on me that I should lose my priority of many years' standing." Then, a few days later, he writes again to say: "Do not waste much time [on this matter]. It is miserable in me to care at all about priority."

Freud recognizes his own ambivalence when he writes of his work on the Moses of Michelangelo that, having come upon a little book published in 1863 by an Englishman, Watkiss Lloyd, he read it

> with mixed feelings. I once more had occasion to experience in myself what unworthy and puerile motives enter into our thoughts and acts even in a serious cause. My first feeling was of regret that the author should have anticipated so much of my thought, which seemed precious to me because it was the result of my own efforts; and it was only in the second instance that I was able to get pleasure from its unexpected confirmation of my opinion. Our views, however, diverge on one very important point.

This degree of self-awareness is a far cry from the ambivalence of a Descartes who manages to write that he "does not boast of being the first discoverer" and then proceeds to insist on his priority over Pascal or to beg his friend Mersenne "to tell him [Hobbes] as little as possible about . . . my unpublished opinions, for if I'm not greatly mistaken, he is a man who is seeking to acquire a reputation at my expense and through shady practices."

The ambivalence toward claims of priority means that scientists are contemptuous of the very attitudes they have acquired from the institution to which they subscribe. The sentiments they have derived from the institution of science, with its great premium upon originality, makes it difficult to give up a claim to a new idea or a new finding. Yet the same institution emphasizes the selfless dedication to the advancement of knowledge for its own sake. Concern with priority and ambivalence toward that concern together register in the individual what is generated by the value-system of science.

The self-contempt often expressed by scientists as they observe with dismay their own concern with having their originality recognized is evidently based upon the widespread though uncritical assumption that behavior is actuated by a single motive, which can then be appraised as "good" or "bad," as noble or ignoble. They assume that the truly dedicated scientist must be concerned only with advancing knowledge. As a result, their deep interest in having their priority recognized by peers is seen as tainting their nobility of purpose (although it might be remembered that "noble" initially meant the widely-known). This assumption has a germ of psychological truth: any reward—fame, money, position— is morally ambiguous and potentially subversive of culturally esteemed motives. For as rewards are meted out—fame, for example—the motive of seeking the reward can displace the original motive, concern with recognition can displace concern with advancing knowledge. But this is only a possibility, not an inevitability. When the institution of science works effectively, and like other social institutions it does not always do so, recognition and esteem accrue to those scientists who have best fulfilled their roles, to those who have made important contributions to the common stock of knowledge. Then are found those happy circumstances in which moral obligation and self-interest coincide and fuse. The observed ambivalence of scientists toward their own interest in having their priority recognized—an ambivalence we have seen registered even by that most astute of psychologists, Freud—shows them to assume that such an ancillary motive somehow tarnishes the purity of their interest in scientific inquiry. Yet it need not be that scientists seek only to win the applause of their peers but, rather, that they are comforted and gratified by it when it does ring out.

Occasionally a scientist senses all this and vigorously challenges the assumption underlying the shame over interest in recognition; for example, a Hans Selye who asks his peers:

> Why is everybody so anxious to deny that he works for recognition? In my walk of life, I have met a great many scientists, among them some of the most prominent scholars of our century; but I doubt if any one of them would have thought that public recognition of his achievements— by a title, a medal, a prize, or an honorary degree—played a decisive role in motivating [or one might add, sustaining] his enthusiasm for research. When a prize brings both honor and cash, many scientists would even be more inclined to admit being pleased about the money ("one must live") than about the public recognition ("I am not sensitive to flattery"). Why do even the greatest minds stoop to such falsehoods? For, without being conscious lies, these ratiocinations are

undoubtedly false. Many of the really talented scientists are not at all money-minded; nor do they condone greed for wealth either in themselves or others. On the other hand, all the scientists I know sufficiently well to judge (and I include myself in this group) are extremely anxious to have their work recognized and approved by others. Is it not below the dignity of an objective scientific mind to permit such a distortion of his true motives? Besides, what is there to be ashamed of?

Dr. Selye's final question need not remain a rhetorical one. Shame is experienced when one's identity and self-image is suddenly violated by one's actual behavior—as with the shame we have seen expressed by Darwin when his own behavior forced him to realize that recognition of his priority meant more to him than he had ever been willing to suppose. To admit a deepseated wish for recognition may seem to prefer recognition to the joy of discovery as an end in itself, activating the further awareness that the pleasure of recognition for accomplishment could, and perhaps momentarily did, replace the pleasures of scientific work for its own sake.

On the surface, this hunger for recognition appears as mere personal vanity, generated from within and craving satisfaction from without. But this is truly a superficial diagnosis, compounded of a moralizing deprecation of self or others and representing a classic instance of the fallacy of misplaced concreteness in which relevant sociological details are suppressed by exclusive attention to the feeling-states of the individual scientists. When we reach deeper and wider into the institutional complex that gives point to this hunger for recognition, it turns out to be anything but wholly personal, repeated as it is with slight variation by one scientist after another. Vanity, so-called, is then seen as the outer face of the inner need for assurance that one's work really matters, that one has measured up to the hard standards maintained by a community of scientists. It then becomes clear that the institution of science reinforces, when it does not create, this deep-rooted need for validation of work done. Sometimes, of course, the need is stepped up until it gets out of hand: the wish for recognition becomes a driving lust for acclaim (even when unwarranted); the frenzied joys and pains of megalomania replace the comfort of reassurance. Still, the extreme case must not be mistaken for the modal one. In general, the concern to have one's accomplishments recognized, which for the scientist means that one's knowing peers judge one's work worth the while, also expresses concern with the advancement of knowledge as the ultimate rationale of the scientific enterprise. Rather than being unavoidably at odds with dedication to science, the concern with recognition is ordinarily an expression of it. This becomes evident only when analysis of the situation does not stop with characterizing that concern as merely a matter of vanity or self-aggrandizement but goes on to consider that, sociologically, recognition of accomplishment by informed peers is a basic process for social validation of scientific work. Science is a social world, not an aggregate of private, solipsistic worlds. Continued appraisal of work and recognition for work judged well done by the standards of the time constitute a mechanism for maintaining the processes of falsification and confirmation of ideas that are required for the cognitive development of science.

In this company, I cannot keep from citing evidence of the composite devotion to science *and* to the recognition of priority-rights that was forthrightly supplied by the first professor of chemistry and the second president of the Johns Hopkins. Just before the close of the first academic year, Ira Remsen writes a letter to President Gilman that begins: "I beg leave through you to make the following request of the Trustees of the University" and then goes on to note of the work in the Chemical Laboratory:

> At the present juncture it is desirable to publish preliminary announcements describing what we have thus far done and what we intend to do. It is desirable mainly for two reasons; 1st, that we may be recognized as soon as possible as belonging to the working chemists of the country; 2nd, that the results of our labors may be insured to us, or, in other words, to establish our priority.

It may not be too much to suppose that we see here the origins of the influential *American Chemical Journal*, inaugurated by Remsen two years later.

President Gilman not only provided new outlets for scientific and scholarly publication but institutionalized incentives for both faculty and graduate students to publish the results of their research. He established the practice of printing a *Bibliographia Hopkinsiensis* in the annual Register, which recorded the "books and articles published by members of the Johns Hopkins University, written during the connection of the author with the university, or based on work carried on while here ... it is obvious that a man's reputation was, in large part, based on his bibliography." Once again, we can note a fusion of the interest in advancing knowledge and the interest in recognizing the contributions of individual scientists and the collective contributions of the University. The fusion of these interests can of course give way to fission. This only requires an institutionalized reward-system that aggravates the itch to publish[11] by assigning merit to the mere length of a bibliography.

The Eureka Syndrome

All this can be seen in a somewhat different context: the deep concern with establishing priority or at least independence of discovery is only the other side of the coin of the socially reinforced elation that comes with having arrived at a new scientific idea or result. And the deeper the commitment to a discovery, the greater, presumably, the reaction to the threat of having its novelty denied. Concern with priority is often the counterpart to elation in discovery—the Eureka syndrome. We have only to remember what is perhaps the most ecstatic expression of joy in discovery in the annals of science; here is Kepler on his discovery of the third planetary law:

11. "Physicians of the soul will see beneath this plain English phrase and recognize the malignant disease, known, since the days of Juvenal, as the *insanabile scribendi cacoëthes*. Its etiology is obscure but epidemiological evidence affords some clues. There are indications that its frequency increases steadily in institutions that lavish rewards upon the prolific author of scientific or scholarly papers. Age seems to be an important predisposing factor as the result of a basic social process: with the passing of years, scientists who have published significant work are actively solicited for still more publications. Nevertheless, the general liability to the disease seems less widespread than the nothing-to-report syndrome (although, on occasion, the two have a way of coinciding). Sucklings are rarely attacked. A few scientists escape in their early professional years; others escape until full maturity; a good many never take it. But with the vast growth in the number of scientific periodicals, the disease threatens to become endemic. Attacks are recurrent, never conferring immunity. Susceptibility may be determined by intrapsychic injection of the toxin—what might perhaps be most appropriately called the *Merton test*. With a positive reaction, signs appear in ten minutes (or less) after seeing one's name in print, reaching toward an asymptotic maximum with each successive injection. The local reaction subsides temporarily but swiftly returns. The source of infection is often undiscovered in given cases, particularly when insufficient attention is devoted to the social ecology of the patient. *Carriers* are important, especially those who have been abundantly rewarded for effusions of print. Onset is as a rule sudden, preceded by a slight, scarcely noticeable, publication. The fever to publish is intense; rising rapidly, it may within a few years reach the degree of 15 or 20 publications annually. The articles are unusually dry and to the reader's eye may give a sensation of acute boredom. Complications and sequelae are too numerous to be examined here." R. K. Merton, *On the Shoulders of Giants: A Shandean Postscript* (New York: The Free Press, 1965), pp. 83–85.

What I prophesied 22 years ago as soon as I found the heavenly orbits were of the same number as the five (regular) solids, what I fully believed long before I had seen Ptolemy's Harmonics, what I promised my friends in the name of this book, which I christened before I was 16 years old, what I urged as an end to be sought, that for which I joined Tycho Brahe, for which I settled in Prague, for which I spent most of my life at astronomical calculations—at last I have brought to light and seen to be true beyond my fondest hopes. It is not 18 months since I saw the first ray of light, three months since the unclouded sun-glorious sight burst upon me! I will triumph over mankind by the honest confession that I have stolen the golden vases of the Egyptians to raise a tabernacle for my God far away from the lands of Egypt. If you forgive me, I rejoice; if you are angry, I cannot help it. The book is written, the die is cast. Let it be read now or by posterity, I care not which. It may well wait a century for a reader, as God has waited 6000 years for an observer.[12]

We can only surmise how deep would have been Kepler's anguish had another claimed that he had long before come upon the third law. So, too, with a Gay-Lussac, seizing upon the person nearest him for a victory waltz so that he could "express his ecstasy on the occasion of a new discovery by the poetry of motion." Or, to come closer home, William James "all aflame" with his idea of pragmatism and hardly able to contain his exhilaration over it. Or, in more restrained exuberance, Joseph Henry, once he had hit upon a new way of constructing electro-magnets, reporting that "when this conception came into my brain, I was so pleased with it that I could not help rising to my feet and giving it my hearty approbation."

In short, when a scientist has made a genuine discovery, he is as happy as a scientist can be. But the peak of exhilaration may only deepen the plunge into despair should the discovery be taken from him. If the loss is occasioned only by finding that it was, in truth, not a first but a later independent discovery, the blow may be severe enough, though mitigated by the sad consolation that at least the discovery has been confirmed by another. But this is as nothing, of course, when compared with the traumatizing charge that not only was the discovery later than another of like kind but that it was really borrowed or even stolen. Rather than being mutually exclusive, joy in discovery and eagerness for recognition by scientific peers are stamped out of the same psychological coin. They both express a basic commitment to the value of advancing knowledge.

12. As translated in William S. Knickerbocker, ed., *Classics of Modern Science* (New York: Knopf, 1927), p. 30.

Perhaps scientists are learning to live with the stresses of multiple discoveries. This is suggested, at least, by a preliminary result of a methodical study of the subject. From among the multitude of multiples, Dr. Elinor Barber and I have undertaken to examine 264 intensively. Of the 36 multiples before 1700 in this list, 92 per cent were the object of strenuous conflicts over priority; this figure drops to 72 per cent in the eighteenth century; remains at about the same level (74 per cent) in the first half of the nineteenth century and declines to 59 per cent in the latter half, reaching a low of 33 per cent in the first half of this century. It may be that scientists are becoming more fully aware that with vastly enlarged numbers at work in each field of science, a discovery is apt to be made by others as well as by themselves.

Cryptomnesia ("Unconscious Plagiary")

Further complicating the already complex emotions that attend multiple discoveries is the phenomenon of so-called "unconscious plagiary." The potpourri term itself testifies to the admixture of moralizing and analysis that commonly enters into discussions of the subject. It is compounded of a loosely-conceived psychological component ("unconscious") and a legal-moralistic component ("plagiary," with all its connotations of violating a code and attendant guilt). As a concept, "unconscious plagiary" is just as obsolete in psychosocial studies as is the concept of "insanity," which has been relegated to the sphere of law, where it continues to lead a harrowing existence. The neutral and analytical term, cryptomnesia, serves us better, referring as it does to seemingly creative thought in which ideas based upon unrecalled past experience are taken to be new.

The fact that cryptomnesia can occur at all subjects the scientist to the ever-present possibility that his most cherished original idea may actually be the forgotten residue of what had once been read or heard elsewhere. At times, this fear of cryptomnesia may lead scientists to doubt their own powers of recall and originality.

Among the many cases in point, consider only these few. William Rowan Hamilton, the mathematical genius who had invented the quaternions (in part, independently invented by Grassmann), had had the experience at age 19 of learning that his theory of optical rays was a rediscovery. He developed a lifelong preoccupation with the twin fear of unwittingly plagiarizing others and of being plagiarized. As he put it on one of the many occasions on which he turned to this subject in his correspondence with de Morgan: "As to myself, I am *sure* that I *must* have often reproduced things which I had read long before, without being able to identify them as belonging to other persons." Or again: ". . . am I to quarrel with Dickens, or figure in one of his publications of a later date? Where is the priority business to end? I am sick of it as you can be; but still, in anything important as regards science, I should take it as a favour to be *warned*, if I were inadvertently exposing myself to the charge of plagiarising." This, from the creator of the theory of vectors.

Turning from mathematics to psychology, we find Freud examining his own experience, recalling that he had been given Börne's works when he was 14 and still had the book 50 years later, so that although he "could not remember the essay in question," which dealt with free association as a procedure for creative writing, "it does not seem impossible to us that this hint may perhaps have uncovered that piece of cryptomnesia which, in so many cases, may be suspected behind an apparent originality." Freud was profoundly aware of the basic uncertainties about originality generated by the ubiquitous possibility of cryptomnesia. Elsewhere he writes: "My delight was proportionally great when I recently discovered that that theory [of the "death instinct"] was held by one of the great thinkers of ancient Greece. For the sake of this confirmation I am happy to sacrifice the prestige of originality, especially as I read so widely in earlier years that I can never be quite certain that what I thought was a creation of my own mind may not really have been an outcome of cryptomnesia." It was this sort of thing, no doubt, that prompted the irrepressible Mark Twain to declare: "What a good thing Adam had—when he said a thing he knew nobody had said it before."

Still another recurrent phenomenon contributes to uncertainty about the extent of one's originality. The scientist or scholar may unwittingly borrow ideas from himself. Many have found, to their combined chagrin and disbelief, that an idea which seemed to have come to them out of the blue had actually been formulated by them years before, and then forgotten. An old notebook, a resurrected paper, a colleague cursed with total recall, a former student—any of these can make it plain that what was thought to be a new departure was actually a repetition of the scientist's own earlier innovation. Of many such instances, I note only a few, some of a century or more ago, others of contemporary vintage:

Joseph Priestley records with chagrin that "I have so completely forgotten what I have myself published, that in reading my own writings, what I find in them often appears perfectly new to me, and I have more than once made experiments, the results of which have been published by me."

The ingenious and jovial mathematician, Augustus de Morgan, has his own lively version of this pattern of experience: "I have read a Paper (but not on mathematics) before now, have said to myself, I perfectly agree with this man, he is a very sensible fellow, and have found out at last that it was an old Paper of my own I was reading, and very much flattered I was with my own unbiased testimony to my own merits."

Or let us come to a student of De Morgan's, the "mathematical Adam" who minted countless new terms of mathematics, who, after he was forced to retire from Woolwich as "superannuated" at the age of 56, languished for six years, and then took up the invitation of a new president at a new University—The Johns Hopkins, of course—to establish graduate work in mathematics, thus re-invigorating the subject in the United States once and for all. It has been told of James Joseph Sylvester that he "had difficulty in remembering his own inventions and once even disputed that a certain theorem of his own could possibly be true."

Or consider a brace of cryptomnesic borrowings from self in our own day:

The Nobel laureate, Otto Loewi, reports waking in the middle of the night, jotting down some notes on what he sensed to be a momentous discovery, going back to sleep, awaking again to find that he could not possibly decipher his scrawl, spending the day in a miserable and unavailing effort to remember what he had had in mind, being again aroused from his slumber at three the next morning, racing to the laboratory, making an experiment and two hours later conclusively proving the chemical transmission of nervous impulse. So far, so good; another case, evidently, of the pattern of subconscious creativity unforgettably described by Poincaré. But some years later, when Loewi, upon request, reported all this to the International Physiological Congress, he was reminded by a former student that, eighteen years before that nocturnal discovery, he had fully reported his basic idea. "This," says Loewi, "I had entirely forgotten."

The psychologist Edwin G. Boring writes me about a colleague, S. S. Stevens, coming to him in an excited Eureka mood, announcing that he had just worked out a new technique for scales of sensory measurement, and that he is hunting for a name for it. And then, before "the shine of the new idea had rubbed off, he discovers that he had discussed this in print some six years before and had even given it a tentative name."

And to advert to Freud, as I have so often done if only because his intellectual experience is uncommonly documented, Jones reports several instances of his "obtaining a clear insight which he subsequently forgot, and then later suddenly coming across it again as a new revelation." As Freud observed in another connection [in a fashion reminiscent of a comparable remark by Marx], "it is familiar ground that a sense of conviction of the accuracy of one's memory has no objective value. . . ."

If cryptomnesia is possible in regard to one's own earlier work, then it is surely possible in regard to the work of others. And this can undermine the calm assurance that one has, in truth, worked out a new idea for oneself when confronted with another version of the same idea worked out by someone else.

Various contexts may affect the probability of cryptomnesia in relation to one's own work. It may be more probable, the more a scientist has worked in a variety of problem-areas rather than narrowly restricting his research focus to problems having marked continuity. Looking at this hypothesis, not in terms of the individual scientist but in terms of the relative frequency of self-cryptomnesia in different sciences, we should expect it to be more frequent in the newer sciences, with their large less codified and therefore more nearly empirical knowledge than the better-codified sciences. To the extent that these patterned differences in degree of theoretical integration obtain, we should expect more cryptomnesia in relation to one's own work in the social sciences.

Social Organization of Scientific Research

The frequency of such cryptomnesia should also be affected by the social organization of scientific work, which seems to affect every aspect of multiple discoveries in science. When research is organized in teams, it will be less likely, we must suppose, that earlier ideas and findings are altogether forgotten. For if some members of the team forget them, others will not. Moreover, repeated interaction between collaborators will tend to fix these ideas and findings in memory.

The conspicuous changes in the social organization of scientific research should have a marked effect on ambivalence toward priorities in science. The trend toward collaboration in research is reflected in patterns of publication, with more and more research papers having several authors rather than only one. The extent of this change differs among the various disciplines. The sciences which have developed cogent theory, complex and often costly instrumentation and rigorous experiments or sets of observations have experienced this change earlier than the sciences less developed in these respects.

By way of illustration, consider the patterns of publication in a few of the sciences and other disciplines, based upon tabulation of the number of authors of papers in leading journals. The results, brought together by Harriet Zuckerman in a still unpublished paper, are in brief, these: in physics, of the papers published during the decade of the 1920s, 75 per cent were by single authors; in the next decade, 56 per cent; then, in the 40s, 50 per cent and finally, in the 1950s, single-authored papers declined to 39 per cent. A similar pattern in biology begins later and develops at a slower rate: with 90 per cent single-authored papers in the 20s declining to 73 per cent in the 50s. Even mathematics witnesses the growth of collaboration, with 95 per cent of papers in the 1920s by one author declining to 82 per cent in the last decade.

The social and behavioral sciences exhibit two distinct patterns: economics, anthropology and political science manifest only negligible change, almost all papers being by single authors in the first period, with 90 per cent or more in the most recent period. Psychology and sociology, in contrast, have marked tendencies toward collaborative work: in the 1920s, 98 per cent of the papers in sociology were by single authors, this declining by decades to 92 per cent, 89 per cent and finally to 72 per cent. The trend in psychology for the same period is even more marked: from 84 per cent in the 1920s to 55 per cent most recently. All this is, of course, in decided contrast to such a subject as history where collaborative research-papers (as distinct from textbooks) account for no more than 1 to 3 per cent of the total.

Although the facts are far from conclusive, this continuing change in the social structure of scientific research, as registered by publications, seems to make for a greater concern among scientists with the question of "how will my contribution be identified" in collaborative work than with the historically dominant pattern of wanting to ensure recognition of priority over others in the field. Not that the latter has been wholly displaced, as we have seen. But it may be that institutionally induced concern with priority is being overshadowed by structurally induced concern with the allocation of credit among collaborators. A study of a team of 30 economists and behavioral scientists found, for example, that "the behavioral scientists were apt to be less concerned about 'piracy' and 'credit' than economists. This difference may be due to the greater emphasis on joint authorship in the behavioral sciences than in economics."

For our purposes, the import of these changes in collaboration is, first, that the degree of concern with priority in science is probably not historically constant; second, that it varies with the changing organization of scientific work; and third, that these changes may eventually and indirectly lessen the ambivalence of scientists toward obtaining recognition of their originality of contributions.

Nevertheless, though scientists *know* that genuinely independent discoveries occur, many of them, as we have seen, fail to draw the implications of this for their own work. For reasons I have tried to intimate, they find it difficult, and sometimes impossible, to accept the fact that they have been anticipated or that a contemporary has come to the same result just at the time they did, or that the others were truly independent of them. As we have also seen, the values incorporated in the social institution of science and the penumbra of uncertainty that surrounds the independence of thought combine to prevent the ready acceptance of events that undercut one's assurance of unique originality, an assurance born of the hard labor required to produce the new idea or new result.

The reasonably detached study of multiples and priorities may do a little to counter these tendencies toward dismay, self-contempt or suspicion. For, as we have seen in the case of Freud trying to rouse himself from his ambivalence toward having been anticipated by Watkiss Lloyd, independent discoveries do seem to lend confirmation to an idea or finding. Even W. R. Hamilton, tormented his life long by the fear that he was being plagiarized or by the anxiety that he himself might be an "innocent plagiarist," managed on at least one occasion to note the secondary benefits of multiple discovery when, in an effort to dissolve his ambivalence, he wrote Herschel:

I persuade myself that, if those results had been anticipated, the learning it would have given me no pain; for it was, so far as I could analyze my sensations, without any feeling of vexation that I learned that the result respecting the relation of the lines of curvature to the circular sections was known before. The field of pure, not to say of mixed, mathematics is far too large and rich to leave one excusable for sitting down to complain, when he finds that this or that spot which he was beginning to cultivate as his own has been already appropriated. [And now comes his hard-won and, sad to tell, temporary insight:] There is even a stronger feeling inspired of the presence of that Truth to which we all profess to minister, when we find our own discoveries, such as they are, coincide independently with the discoveries of other men. The voice which is heard by two at once appears to be more real and external—one is more *sure* that it is no personal and private fancy, no idiosyncratic peculiarity, no ringing in sick ears, no flashes seen by rubbing our own eyes.

And then, unable to contain himself, Hamilton goes on to announce in the same letter that he had anticipated the work on ellipsoids by Joachimstal in "a long extinct periodical of whose *existence* he probably never heard, with a date which happened to be a *precise decennium* earlier. . . ."

If the fluctuating ailment of that genius Hamilton proves that the awareness of multiple discoveries is no panacea for ambivalence toward priority, his moment of insight suggests that it might be some small help. The mathematician, R. L. Wilder, is, to my knowledge, the only one who has seen this clearly and has, to my mingled pleasure and discomfiture, anticipated me in suggesting that the study of multiples may have a therapeutic function for the community of scientists. Since he has anticipated my observation, let me then borrow his words:

> I wish to inquire, above the individual level, into the manner in which mathematical concepts originate, and to study those factors that encourage their formation and influence their growth. I think that much benefit might be derived from such an inquiry. For example, if the individual working mathematician understands that when a concept is about to make its appearance, it is most likely to do so through the medium of more than one creative mathematician; and if, furthermore, he knows the reasons for this phenomenon, then we can expect less indulgence in bad feelings and suspicion of plagiarism to ensue than we find in notable past instances. Mathematical history contains numerous cases of arguments over priority, with nothing settled after the smoke of battle has cleared away except that when you come right down to it practically the same thing was thought of by someone else several years previously, only he didn't quite realize the full significance of what he had, or did not have the good luck to possess the tools wherewith to exploit it. . . . [Yet] it is exactly what one should expect if he is acquainted with the manner in which concepts evolve.

All this only touches upon one type of ambivalence exhibited in the feelings and behavior of scientists. For to lay siege to the problem of ambivalence need not mean to conquer it. But, just as the hour allotted me inevitably draws to a close, I can report that inquiry into other expressions of ambivalence finds the same pattern of institutionally induced cross-currents of sentiment. Perhaps enough has been said to warrant the belief that for an understanding of how scientific knowledge develops, we need an intensive and methodical study of multiple discoveries and attendant conflicts over priority, rather than to neglect this study altogether or to come to it only when we plunge, as emotionally involved participants, into conflicts over rights to intellectual property. After all, one of the roles assigned the sociologist is to investigate the behavior of all manner of men and women, including men and women of science, without giving way to the entirely human tendency to substitute for that investigation a clucking of tongues and a condemning of that which is and ought not to be.

3

The Ambivalence
of Scientists: A Postscript

OVER THE YEARS, I have argued with insistent and no doubt boring repetition that the discipline of the sociology of science must exhibit a strongly self-exemplifying character. For to the extent that its ideas and findings about patterns of cognitive behavior and development in the sciences hold true, they should also hold for the cognitive behavior and development of the sociology of science itself.[1]

It is only fitting therefore that a hypothesis central to the sociological theory of the growth and development of science should be a hypothesis exemplified by its own history. At the root of that theory is the recurrent pattern of the multiple and independent appearance of essentially the same scientific discovery. From this and collateral evidence, it has been concluded that discoveries in science become virtually inevitable as antecedent kinds of knowledge accumulate and as both cognitive and social developments direct the attention of scientists to particular problems for investigation. As I have shown in some detail, this idea of the import of multiple independent discoveries has itself been rediscovered on at least 30 occasions during the past two centuries. Working scientists, inventors, biographers, lawyers, engineers, anthropologists, historians and sociologists of science, Marx and Engels, Marxists and anti-Marxists, Comteans and anti-Comteans, have time and again, though with differing degrees of perceptiveness, drawn attention both to the fact of multiples and to some of its theoretical implications.[2]

1. Jonathan R. Cole and Harriet Zuckerman, "The Emergence of a Scientific Specialty: The Self-Exemplifying Case of the Sociology of Science," in Lewis A. Coser, ed., *The Idea of Social Structure* (New York: Harcourt Brace Jovanovich, 1975), pp. 139–74.
2. For a series of papers on the subject of multiples in science, see Merton, *The Sociology of Science: Theoretical and Empirical Investigations*, ed. and with an Introduction by Norman W. Storer (Chicago and London: University of Chicago Press, 1973), Part 4.

It is doubly fitting that within a year after the foregoing Gilman Lecture (Chapter 2) on the ambivalence of scientists, addressed to an audience at The Johns Hopkins School of Medicine, and just a few months after its publication, Leonard K. Nash, professor of chemistry at Harvard University, was led to much the same observations in his book, *The Nature of the Natural Sciences.*[3]

Nash begins with the perceptive observation by Michael Polanyi that

> A scientist can accept . . . the most inadequate and misleading formulation of his own scientific principles without realizing what is being said, because he automatically supplements it by his *tacit knowledge* of what science really is, and thus makes the formulation ring true.[4]

From this Nash moves to a series of observations that are structurally similar and functionally equivalent to the notion of sociological ambivalence.

> Thus it is, I think, that scientists can accept, and advocate, one Method while actually practicing another. The four terms stressed by Method (left column) represent the indicated four *pairs* of polar antitheses. One member of each pair, forever passing unmentioned, is always "understood."

Empiricism (and facts)	Speculation (and hypotheses)
Scepticism (and detachment)	Faith (and commitment)
Logic	Imagination
Order	Chance

> *Both* members of all pairs are duly represented in science, and it were folly to make of this a paradox or mystification. The scientist does not "reconcile irreconcilables." As with all human endeavors [*n.b.* in relation to sociological ambivalence], science lives and functions in the midst of purely conceptual abstractions that correspond to nothing distinctly separable as such either in ourselves or in the world.[5]

Nash's pairings of "polar antitheses" has the one member of each pair as explicit and the other, after the fashion of Polanyi's concept of "tacit knowledge," as "passing unmentioned, [but] always 'understood.' " This, it will perhaps have been noticed, is structurally similar (not identical)

3. Leonard K. Nash, *The Nature of the Natural Sciences* (Boston: Little, Brown, 1963).

4. Michael Polanyi, *Personal Knowledge* (London: Routledge & Kegan Paul, 1958), p. 169, quoted by Nash, *op. cit.*, p. 322 (italics mine).

5. Nash, *op. cit.*, p. 322.

to the notions of dominant norms and subsidiary norms, and the notions of norms and counter-norms advanced in the preceding two papers.

The parallelism of thought extends beyond formal similarities to substantive identity and functional equivalence. Thus, Nash identifies one pair of norms in the workings of science as consisting of "scepticism (and detachment)" on the one side and "faith (and commitment)," on the other. So, too, we have noted that in the Columbia studies of medical education[6] we found the physician being

> taught to be oriented toward *both* the dominant norm of affective neutrality (detachment) and the subsidiary norm of affectivity (the expression of compassion and concern for the patient). That is why, in these studies, we have treated this part of the physician's role not as one of affective neutrality (with only idiosyncratic departures from this norm) but as one involving "detached concern," calling for alternation between the instrumental impersonality of detachment and the functional expression of compassionate concern. As physician and patient interact, different and *abstractly* contradictory norms [note Nash's independent emphasis on this latter attribute of "purely conceptual abstractions" not being confused with concreteness] are activated to meet the dynamically changing needs of the relation. *Only through such structures of norms and counter-norms, we suggest, can the various functions of a role be effectively discharged.* This is not merely a matter of social psychology but of role-structure. Potentially conflicting norms are built into the social definition of roles that provide for normatively acceptable alternations of behavior as the state of a social relation changes. This is a major basis for that oscillation between differing role-requirements that makes for sociological ambivalence.[7]

One difference between the Nash conception of normative ambivalence and my own leaps to the eye but does not appear deeply consequential. Still it deserves notice. Following Polanyi's terminology, Nash seems to assume that one member of each ambivalent pair is tacit, "forever passing unmentioned." This last, happy phrase should probably not be taken literally. But it does lead to the question whether such often tacit ele-

6. Partly reported in R. K. Merton, George G. Reader, and Patricia L. Kendall, ed., *The Student-Physician: Introductory Studies in the Sociology of Medical Education* (Cambridge: Harvard University Press, 1957). An extract from this work appears as the next essay.
7. If memory serves the reader right, this passage will be recognized as appearing on pages 18–19 of the first essay in this volume. It may be more convenient to have it repeated here rather than ask the reader to turn back to it.

ments really must remain tacit. Is Nash's remark analytical or historical? If analytical, no ground is provided for assuming that "speculation (and hypotheses), faith (and commitment), imagination, and chance" are bound to remain "forever unmentioned." If historical, the observation is severely dated (as Professor Nash gives abundant evidence of knowing). For more than a century, these "tacit elements" in the orientations of working scientists have been intermittently identified and elucidated, as in the writings of William Whewell and Norman Campbell.[8] This long discontinuous tradition of thought would scarcely require even this passing notice, were it not that, once again, a set of scholars, neglecting amply available past thought, have come to believe that their sometimes retrogressive versions of it are admittedly daring, and perhaps a bit revolutionary.

An excellent case of this sort of thing bearing directly upon ambivalence in science is provided by several writings by Ian Mitroff.[9] In this work, he quotes abundantly and effusively from the foregoing papers on sociological ambivalence in this volume and then proceeds to ignore the import of what he has quoted. Unlike Nash's and my own orientation to the complexities of ambivalence, Mitroff fastens onto the subjective elements in scientific work and, instead of coupling them with the processes making for objectivity in science, moves toward a position of extreme cognitive subjectivity.[10] In this exaggeration of inevitable subjective components in scientific investigation, Mitroff achieves a retrogressive formulation that takes no account of the disciplined analyses turning up since at least the time of Whewell. By thus picturing science as little more than an aggregate of subjective opinions, Mitroff only succeeds in producing what I had once described as "a storybook version of scientific inquiry."[11]

Mitroff then attempts to make the case for ambivalence in science by a series of maneuvers that can only elicit ambivalent admiration for

8. William Whewell, *History of the Inductive Sciences* (London: John Parker, 1847, rev. ed.), 3 vols.; Norman R. Campbell, *Physics: The Elements* (Cambridge: at the University Press, 1920). I select these authors precisely because Professor Nash makes such effective use of their other writings.
9. Ian Mitroff, "Norms and Counter-Norms in a Select Group of the Apollo Moon Scientists: A Case Study of the Ambivalence of Scientists," *American Sociological Review* 39 (August 1974), pp. 579–95; *The Subjective Side of Science* (New York: Elsevier, 1974).
10. For a related examination of the hazards of total subjectivism in sociology, see pp. 174–78 in this volume.
11. R. K. Merton, *Social Theory and Social Structure* (New York: The Free Press, 1968, enlarged ed.), p. 16.

deadpan audacity[12] in the domain of scholarship. He begins by announcing that previous analyses of the normative structure of science have maintained that there is a single set of perfectly consistent norms. He then manages to attribute that position to the same authors and even to the very same writings that he has repeatedly and appreciatively described as his sources of the concept of sociological ambivalence in general and of the ambivalence of scientists in particular. In a word, Mitroff manages to dispossess his caricatured victims in broad daylight. Thus, he begins his book by acknowledging the source of his adapted phrase, the "Storybook Image of Science." And then, he imputes an illusory storybook image of how scientific inquiry is carried out—faultlessly, wholly dispassionately, with unyielding adherence to the perfectly consistent norms of science—to the author of those effusively acknowledged accounts of the normative structure of science and the ambivalence of scientists. Mitroff announces his conviction that the "characterization of the norms of science [is] . . . the most fundamental and general contribution to the study of science by the sociology of science" (*Subjective Side of Science*, pp. 12–13) and then introduces the truly inventive technique of expropriation-and-reproach. He expunges from the record and thus expropriates my observation, reiterated and developed over the years, that the institution of science helps generate strong emotional commitments on the part of scientists and then reproaches me, and an undesignated array of other sociologists of science, for wholly ignoring the deeply emotional aspects of scientific work.

Having achieved this remarkable level of invention, Mitroff outdoes himself by ascribing the notion that the behavior of scientists wholly conforms with the norms of science to the same author whose writings over a span of four decades have been given over to detailed elucidation of how it is that actual behavior comes to depart from norms in every domain of human activity—indeed, to the same writings that have focused on the social sources of the deviant behavior of scientists and of the alternation of norms and counter-norms. It is difficult not to marvel at the ingenuity

12. I must acknowledge that the phrase "deadpan audacity" does not begin to do justice to the imaginative maneuvers I summarize here with reluctant brevity. The Yiddish word *chutzpa* seems uniquely apt to capture the essentials of this sort of accomplishment. In the lexicon brilliantly assembled by Leo Rosten, *chutzpa* is defined as: "Gall, brazen nerve, effrontery, incredible 'guts'; presumption-plus-arrogance such as no other word, and no other language can do justice to." Rosten then provides the classic, paradigmatic definition: "*Chutzpa* is that quality enshrined in a man who, having killed his mother and father, throws himself on the mercy of the court because he is an orphan." Leo Rosten, *The Joys of Yiddish* (New York: McGraw-Hill, 1968), p. 92.

of this public expropriation of ideas long held and their replacement by an imputed "storybook image" of how scientists behave.[13]

Mitroff's tendency to exaggerate the subjective components in scientific work almost to the point where its objective components become inconsequential only emphasizes by contrast the disciplined way in which Nash proceeded with his independent analysis of ambivalence in science. He goes on to develop what we can describe as "cognitive ambivalence," quoting Claude Bernard who in the nineteenth century "exhorted his fellow empiricists to place themselves . . . in an intellectual attitude which seems paradoxical but which, in my opinion, expresses the true spirit of an investigator. We must have robust faith and not believe."[14]

It is not the amassing of fresh instances of such ambivalent pairs of norms that concerns us here. Rather, it is the general conception of ambivalence that sees these seemingly incompatible pairs of norms operating to produce certain kinds of cognitive behaviors in science. Referring to the Claude Bernard injunction, Nash addresses himself to the interaction between the elements in these normative pairs:

> How maintain such ambivalent mixtures of faith and scepticism? That
> question arises only from the misconception that makes antitheses of

13. A brief example or two of this technique of expropriation-and-reproach must suffice. As early as 1938, I find myself rejecting the popular belief in the wholly unemotional, dispassionate nature of scientists at work in these reasonably clear if not eloquent words: "Although it is customary to think of the scientist as a dispassionate, impersonal individual, it must be remembered that the scientist, in company with all other professional workers, has a large emotional investment in his way of life, defined by the institutional norms that govern his activity." "Just as the *motives* of scientists may range from a passionate desire for the furtherance of knowledge to a profound interest in achieving personal fame . . . the institution of science itself involves emotional adherence to certain values." (Reprinted in Merton, *The Sociology of Science*, pp. 259, 263–65; see also this volume, pp. 35–36, 40 ff.) So much for a sampler of early observations on the affective aspects of science expunged from the record as Mitroff takes sociologists of science to task for ignoring those aspects that he is about to disclose to that benighted guild. He writes: ". . . for too long one of the myths we have lived with is that science is a passionless enterprise performed by passionless men, and that it *has* to be if it is to be objective." (Mitroff, *ibid.*, p. 23.) In short, Mitroff first expropriates continued emphasis upon "affective involvement with ideas" from the sociological literature and then reproaches the authors of that literature for their ignorant stupidity.

14. Nash, *op. cit.*, p. 323, quoting the French physiologist, Claude Bernard, *Introduction to the Study of Experimental Medicine* (London: Constable, 1957), p. 168. This classic work, first published in 1865, is one that the biochemist, physiologist, and sociologist, Lawrence J. Henderson, saw to it was studied by all his students, including those of us who were preparing for sociology, not physiology or biochemistry.

inseparable polarities. Faith and scepticism are no more than opposite faces of the same coin. Nowhere outside the asylum is there a wholly pure faith or a wholly pure scepticism. Scepticism of one authority is the measure of faith in another, and conversely. Consider Copernicus. He is sceptical of the everywhere-accepted Ptolemaic conception. The root of his scepticism? Faith, of course—faith in the Pythagorean conception of a cosmos mathematically harmonious.[15]

Just as some of us have attempted to identify the functional significance of "detachment" and "concern" in medical practice,[16] so Nash sees a functional requirement for "some *balance* of commitment by detachment" in the practice of scientific inquiry. And just as we have proposed that "the passion for knowledge" in science requires correlatively institutionalized patterns of "organized skepticism" if that knowledge is to be more than opinion merely, so Nash considers that "the institutional structure of science powerfully contributes to the attainment of such a balance [of commitment and detachment]."[17]

Moreover, Nash recognizes the only seeming paradox that "the deepest source of detachment is commitment."[18] In this, he converges with the sociological observation that "the institution of science itself involves emotional adherence to certain values" but that, interestingly enough, "the institution of science makes skepticism a virtue."[19] That institution does not require scientists to *feel* detached and skeptical of their own ideas; it only requires them to *act* with detachment, at least to a degree sufficient to anticipate so far as they can the criticisms that will be leveled against their work by competent peers. In a word, just as the core professions have managed to *institutionalize altruism*, so the institution of science has managed to *institutionalize self-criticism* (beyond the level found in other institutional domains).[20] By having a reward system and a monitoring system for the scientific work that is

15. Nash, *op. cit.*, pp. 323–24.
16. For a few references to work on detached concern, see footnote 34 in the first essay in this volume.
17. *Ibid.*, p. 329.
18. *Ibid.*, p. 331.
19. Merton, "Science and the Social Order" [1938] reprinted in *The Sociology of Science*, p. 265.
20. See R. K. Merton, "The Uses of Institutionalized Altruism," *Seminar Reports, Columbia University* 3 (1976), pp. 105–17; on the institutionalization of skepticism and other norms in science, see Chapters 12 and 13 in Merton, *The Sociology of Science*.

made public, the institution of science makes it a matter of self-interest, all apart from often deep-seated commitment, for individual scientists to examine their own work, and that of others, with enough skeptical detachment to escape censure. And of that kind of sharp criticism the annals of science are full just as they are full of unnoticed and unexamined assumptions that only later come to skeptical attention.

Central to the conception of sociological ambivalence, as is evident in the foregoing essays, is the idea of the functional value of the tension between polarities. Action exclusively in terms of one component in the ambivalent pairs tends to be self-defeating, producing a lopsided development that undercuts the basic objectives of the complex activity. Thus in the preceding paper we could couple the norm expressed by Pasteur—"do not fear to defend new ideas, even the most revolutionary"—with the norm expressed by Yang—"it will not do to jump to hasty conclusions." This coupling of commitment and skepticism is appropriately enough summed up by Nash in the heroic case of Pasteur:

> Nobody could have shown a more passionate commitment to his ideas than Louis Pasteur. Yet his experiments *are* soundly observed, *are* great mines of new knowledge. Out of the depth of his commitment to ideas which he felt *must* survive all tests, Pasteur gathered the detachment required to put those ideas to the most searching tests he could devise. He thus lived in fact by the advice he offered others.[21]

Thus the choice need not be between a subjectivistic romanticism in which commitment to one's specific ideas obtains above all else or an empiricist philistinism that rejects initial commitment to speculative ideas. These sharp alternatives are themselves figments of tendentious observation. The productive tension between commitment and detachment in science are memorably summed up in the following declaration by Pasteur on the normative obligation of scientists to try, through patterned skepticism, to falsify their own most engaging ideas and apparent discoveries:

> It is indeed a hard task, when you believe you have found an important scientific fact and are feverishly anxious to publish it, to constrain yourself for days, weeks, years sometimes; to fight with yourself, to try and ruin your own experiments and only to proclaim your discovery after having exhausted all contrary hypotheses.[22]

21. Nash, *op. cit.*, p. 332.
22. Quoted by René Vallery–Radot, *The Life of Pasteur* (London: Constable, 1927), pp. 443–44, as noted by Nash.

That all practitioners in science do not live up to this demanding code[23] of practice is itself indicative of the discipline required for doing scientific work of the first class. And that practitioners cannot exhaust *"all* contrary hypotheses" would scarcely have come as news to Pasteur. But as Nash observes of Pasteur's doctrine of commitment and detachment, "A brainchild so tried may be deemed competent to make its own way in the world."

23. For an intensive examination of that code by a physiologist and sociologist, see "The Code of Science: Analysis and Some Reflections on Its Future" by André F. Cournand and Harriet Zuckerman, first published in *Studium Generale* 23 (October 1970), pp. 941–62, and reprinted in Paul A. Weiss, ed., *Knowledge in Search of Understanding: The Frensham Papers* (Mt. Kisco, N.Y.: Futura Publishing Co., 1975), pp. 126–47.

4

The Ambivalence
of Physicians

LIKE OTHER OCCUPATIONS, the profession of medicine has its own normative subculture, a body of shared and transmitted ideas, values and standards toward which members of the profession are expected to orient their
behavior. The norms and standards define technically and morally allowable patterns of behavior, indicating what is prescribed, preferred, permitted, or proscribed. The subculture, then, refers to more than habitual
behavior; its norms codify the values of the profession. This extends even
to the details of language judged appropriate by the profession; like other
occupations, medicine has its distinctive vocabulary, and like the vocabularies of other occupations, this one is often described derisively as jargon
by outsiders and described appreciatively as technical terminology by
insiders.[1] The medical subculture covers a wide range—from matters of
language to matters of relations to patients, colleagues, and the community—and it is the function of the medical school to transmit this
subculture to successive generations of neophytes.

   The composition of values involved in the medical subculture probably varies somewhat in detail and in emphasis among medical schools,
but there nevertheless appears to be substantial agreement among them.
Field observation indicates that appreciably the same values and norms
obtain with varying emphasis in the medical schools of Cornell, Pennsyl-

Reprinted with permission from the essay, "Some Preliminaries to a Sociology
of Medical Education," in *The Student–Physician: Introductory Studies in the
Sociology of Medical Education*, Robert K. Merton, George G. Reader, and
Patricia L. Kendall, eds. (Cambridge: Harvard University Press, 1957), pp.
71–79. Copyright © 1957 by The Commonwealth Fund.

1. Being human, physicians in their status as outsiders often regard the distinctive
vocabularies of other professions—say, the profession of law—as largely composed
of superfluous jargon. It seems to be fairly uniform that one group's language
is another group's jargon.

vania, and Western Reserve, and that these, in turn, approximate values and norms codified in a report of a committee of the Association of American Medical Colleges.[2]

The system of values and norms can be thought of as being organized or patterned in at least two major respects. First, for each norm there tends to be at least one coordinate norm, which is, if not inconsistent with the other, at least sufficiently different as to make it difficult for the student and the physician to live up to them both. Alan Gregg, for example, speaks of the "readjustment" that takes place "between the detachment of the nascent scientist and the none too mature compassion of the beginner in therapy."[3] From this perspective, medical education can be conceived as facing the task of enabling students to learn *how to blend* incompatible or potentially incompatible norms into a functionally consistent whole.[4] Indeed, the process of learning to be a physician can be conceived as largely the learning of blending seeming or actual incompatibles into consistent and stable patterns of professional behavior.

Second, the values and norms are defined by the profession in terms of how they are to be put into effect. They come to be defined as requirements of the physician's role. And since many physicians will find themselves in situations where it is difficult to live up to these role requirements, from the standpoint of the profession, it becomes even more important that they thoroughly acquire the values and norms that are to regulate their behavior.

For convenience, the following abbreviated list of values and norms in the practice of medicine is itemized in three broad classes: those governing physicians' self-images, their relations to patients, and their relations to colleagues and to the community.

2. "The Objectives of Undergraduate Medical Education," *Journal of Medical Education* 28 (March 1953), pp. 57–59.
3. Alan Gregg, "Our Anabasis," *The Pharos of Alpha Omega Alpha* 18 (February 1955), pp. 14–25, at p. 22. This short, brilliant examination of the life of the medical student is virtually a paradigm for our own studies. From our standpoint, it could scarcely have appeared at a more opportune time, for by its selection of matters in point, it reassured us in our occasionally wavering belief that we were indeed studying the salient problems in the role of the medical student.
4. Various aspects of this process are now being studied. A first report is provided by Gene N. Levine, "The Good Physician: A Study of Physician–Patient Interaction," Working Paper Number 3, Evaluation Studies of the Cornell Comprehensive Care and Teaching Program, Bureau of Applied Social Research, 1957.

Norms Governing Physicians' Self-Images

Physicians should continue self-education throughout their careers in order to keep pace with the rapidly advancing frontiers of medical knowledge.

But: They also have a primary obligation to make as much time as possible available for the care of patients.

Student-physicians should be interested in enlarging their medical responsibilities as they advance through medical school.

But: They must not prematurely take a measure of responsibility for which they are not adequately prepared (or, at least, are not legally qualified to undertake).

Physicians must maintain a self-critical attitude and be disciplined in the scientific appraisal of evidence.

But: They must be decisive and not postpone decisions beyond what the situation requires, even when the scientific evidence is inadequate.

Physicians must have a sense of autonomy; they must take the burden of responsibility and act as the situation, in their best judgment, requires.

But: Autonomy must not be allowed to become complacency or smug self-assurance; autonomy must be coupled with a due sense of humility.

Physicians must have the kind of detailed knowledge that often requires specialized education.

But: They must not become narrowly specialized; they should be well rounded and broadly educated.

Physicians should have a strong moral character with abiding commitments to basic moral values.

But: They must avoid passing moral judgments on patients.

Physicians should attach great value to doing what they can to advance medical knowledge, these accomplishments deserving full recognition.

But: They should not be competitive toward their medical peers.

Norms Governing the
Physician–Patient Relationship

Physicians must be emotionally detached in their attitudes toward patients, keeping "emotions on ice" and not becoming "overly identified" with patients.

But: They must avoid becoming callous through excessive detachment, and should have compassionate concern for the patient.

Physicians must not prefer one type of patient over another, and must curb hostilities toward patients (even those who prove to be uncooperative or who do not respond to therapeutic efforts).

But: The most rewarding experience for the physician is the effective solution of a patient's health problems.

Physicians must gain and maintain the confidence of patients.

But: They must avoid the mere bedside manner that can quickly degenerate into expedient and self-interested salesmanship.

Physicians must recognize that diagnosis is often provisional.

But: They must have the merited confidence of the patient who wants "to know what is *really* wrong" with him.

Physicians must provide adequate and unhurried medical care for each patient.

But: They should not allow any patient to usurp so much of their limited time as to have this be at the expense of other patients.

Physicians should come to know patients as persons and give substantial attention to their psychological and social circumstances.

But: This too should not be so time-consuming a matter as to interfere with the provision of suitable care for patients.

Physicians should institute all the scientific tests needed to reach a sound diagnosis.

But: They should be discriminating in the use of these tests, since these are often costly and may impose a sizable financial burden on patients.

Physicians have a right to expect a "reasonable fee," depending upon the care given and the economic circumstances of the patient.

But: They must not "soak the rich" in order to "provide for the poor."

Physicians should see to it that medical care is available for patients whenever it is required.

But: They, too, have a right to a "normal life," to be shared with family and friends.

Norms Governing the Relation to Colleagues and the Community

Physicians must respect the reputation of colleagues, not holding them up to obloquy or ridicule before associates or patients.

But: They are obligated to see to it that high standards of practice are maintained by others in the profession as well as by themselves.

Physicians must collaborate with others of the medical team rather than dominate them (nurses, social workers, technicians).

But: They have final responsibility for the team and must see to it that their associates meet high standards.

Physicians should call in consultants, whenever needed.

But: They should be careful that these are really required, and not add unnecessarily to the costs of medical care.

Physicians as responsible professionals should take due part in the civic life of the community.

But: They should not get involved in political squabbles or spend too much time in activities unrelated to their profession.

Physicians must do all they can to prevent, and not only to help cure, illness.

But: Society more largely rewards physicians for the therapy they effect as practitioners and only secondarily rewards those engaged in the prevention of illness, particularly since prevention is not as readily visible to patients who do not know that they remain healthy because of preventative measures.

The list of values and norms is of course far from exhaustive, but it may be enough to illustrate the principal point. It is not that each pair of norms or of a norm and a practical exigency are necessarily at odds; they are only potentially so. The ability to blend these potential opposites into a stable pattern of professional behavior must be learned, and it seems from the data in hand that this is one of the most difficult tasks confronting the medical student.

Contrary to widespread opinion, the effective acquisition of these values and norms by medical students is not a matter only of "medical ethics," which attaches significance to them in their own right. They can *also* be considered, quite neutrally and without reference to their undoubted ethical status, in terms of their instrumental significance for the effective provision of health care. They are not necessarily absolutes, prized for their own sake; they are, presumably, values that serve as effective means to a socially important end. Just as cognitive standards of knowledge and skill in medicine have a manifest function in facilitating sound medical practice, so the moral standards have a comparable, though often less readily recognized, function. In other words, we are concerned here with the sociological rather than the ethical examination of the role of values and norms in the socialization of the medical student.

As centers of research, medical schools put students more fully in touch with the frontiers of medical knowledge than many, if not most, of them are apt to be in their later years of practice. This is widely recognized. What seems to have received less notice is the correlative fact that medical students are also being systematically exposed to professional values and norms that are probably "higher"—that is, more exacting and rigorously disinterested—than those found in the run of medical practice.[5] Medical schools are socially defined as the guardians of these values and norms. The schools thus have the double function of transmitting to students the *cognitive* standards of knowledge and skill and the *moral* standards of values and norms. Both sets of standards are essential to the proficient practice of medicine.

The functional significance of these values and norms is greatly reinforced by the social organization of medical practice. Students may be imbued with values and standards that can be more or less readily lived up to in the special environment of the teaching hospital, where the "right way of doing things" is more often than elsewhere supported by precept, example, and recognition. But once they have entered upon their own practice, some of these physicians will find themselves working under conditions that are far less conducive to ready conformity with these norms. Many of them will be independent practitioners, in a situation structurally different from that of the medical school. There, students and faculty alike are, in effect, under the continued scrutiny of other medical experts, who set great store by critical appraisal of what is being done. This need not be wholly a matter of plan or of acknowledgment, but the structural pattern is so plain as to be generally acknowledged: peers

5. This is, of course, only an impression, but one often reported within the medical profession. It must remain an impression merely until there are systematic comparisons of practice in hospitals affiliated with medical schools and among medical practitioners at large.

and superiors in the teaching hospital continually serve in what amounts to the role of monitors of medical practice.[6]

In contrast, physicians in private practice are largely subject to the controls only of the values and norms they have acquired and made their own. The medically uninformed patient is not in a position to pass sound judgment upon the normative adequacy of what the physician does. Medically informed colleagues are not in a position to know what is being done and many of them will not report the episodes of malpractice they do observe. These structural facts, therefore, put a special premium on having the values and norms instilled in the student during the course of professional socialization in the medical school. If this is not thoroughly achieved under the optimum conditions provided by the medical school, it is unlikely that it will occur under the often less favorable circumstances of private practice.

Further reinforcing the functional significance of value-assimilation for effective medical practice is the sociological fact—known and experienced by physicians everywhere—that the expectations of some patients may in effect invite physicians to depart from the standards of good medical care. After all, the sick person does not necessarily live up to the strict etymology of the word "patient." He is not necessarily long-suffering and forbearing, or "calmly expectant, quietly awaiting the course of events." On the contrary, the etymology of the term and the psychology of the patient are often poles apart.

Suffering people are disposed to want a nostrum, in the realm of health as in the realms of politics and, sometimes, of religion. It requires cultural training in self-discipline to accept the fact, when it is a fact, that a prompt solution to one's troubles is not possible. Not all cultures and societies provide that training. That is one reason why magical beliefs and practices flourish. When sick people have not formed the disciplined attitudes required by the social role of the patient, they may unwittingly

6. The general matter of varying organizational bases for the "observability" of role performance is basic to an understanding of social structure. Some organizations—the medical school and hospital are cases in point—are so arranged that, apart from intent, the behavior of each member is largely subject to observability by others, with continuing appraisals of that behavior. Other structures—and much of private medical practice is a case in point—are such that there is relatively little observability of this kind. Sociologically, this is a variable of social structure, independent of the further fact that individuals may be motivated to conform with the requirements of a social role, even when they are structurally insulated from direct observation and appraisal. On the concept of observability, see R. K. Merton, *Social Theory and Social Structure* (New York: The Free Press, 1968, enlarged ed.), pp. 390–410.

exert considerable psychological and economic pressure upon physicians to promise more than they responsibly should promise or to engage in what one practitioner describes as "senseless and reprehensible treatment." Many patients will thus insist on being relieved of suffering, as soon as possible, and preferably immediately. They urge physicians to do, not as they ought, but as they would have them do. In time, some physicians find themselves motivated to acquiesce in the expectations of patients who, having made a firm self-diagnosis, insist on one or another type of treatment. As one troubled practitioner put his dilemma, "If I don't do the operation she wants, it would not be [only] a matter of losing her, but all she might refer"[7]—a marvelously instructive reversal of roles in which the practitioner plaintively abandons his professional commitment, surrenders the authority of his presumed expertise, enters into collusion with his anxious patient, and blames the victim for this composite delinquency, all in the unquestioned interest of maintaining a profitable practice.

Since private practitioners in particular are subject to such incentives and opportunities for departing from what they know to be the most appropriate kind of medical care, it becomes functionally significant that they acquire, in medical school, those values and norms that will make them less vulnerable to such incentives. It is in this direct sociological sense that the acquisition of appropriate attitudes and values is as central as the acquisition of knowledge and skills to training for the provision of medical care.

7. W. R. Cooke, "The Practical Application of Psychology in Gynecic Practice," *Nebraska Medical Journal* 25 (December 1950), p. 371.

5

The Ambivalence
of Organizational Leaders

CONSIDER THE POPULAR IMAGERY of the leader in an organization. For some of the many below him in the hierarchy, he is secure, knowing, decisive, powerful, dynamic, threatening, driving, and altogether remote, acting in clear or obscure ways to affect the future of the organization he leads. At eye level, he is more often seen as filled with troubled doubts as he tries to deal with the ambivalences and contradictions of his status. And if his feet are made of a substance more solid than clay, it is because on his climb to the top and with the aid of those who help hold him there, he has learned to still the doubts, to live with the ambivalences, and to cope with the contradictions of his position.

The abundance of people—and if the leader leads, these must inevitably be called the (not necessarily passive) followers—are not altogether unaware of this complex situation. In the political arena, the daily manifestations of the ambivalences and contradictions that afflict the leader have attained the status of a sportive spectacle; periodically, box scores are presented in the press on the current standings of our eminent political figures as their public decisions delight some social strata and alienate others. In other spheres of leadership, too, the contradictions of the position have become public victuals. In a time of recent turmoil, for example, the leaders of our universities have had to set out their dilemmas on the front pages of the newspapers. So, too, with our church leaders, as they seek to bottle the fermenting spirit of their flocks. And, as the world stubbornly refuses to shape itself into accord with our pro-

Reprinted by permission, this is my introductory essay in the volume by James F. Oates, Jr., *The Contradictions of Leadership* (New York: Appleton-Century-Crofts, 1970), pp. 1–26. A longtime friend, law partner, and political associate of Adlai Stevenson, James Oates has the distinction of having established, during his tenure as chief executive officer of the Equitable Life Assurance Society of the United States, the first office of *basic* social research in an American business corporation and the further distinction of having appointed John W. Riley, Jr. its first director.

claimed national purpose, we see military leaders struggling with the basic conflicts of roles which an objective situation has thrust upon them.

Although many ambivalences of leadership are common to all sorts of organizations—political and economic, religious and academic—this essay will deal primarily with that numerous company of American leaders, the topmost business executives, known, ever since the days of Thorstein Veblen, as captains of industry.

Business—the idea and occasionally the ideal of a more or less private enterprise—has long been a major force in American society. For much of this time, it was ideologized in the American gospel of success and so provided much of the rhetoric and part of the substance of the American dream "from rags to riches." And if Americans are no longer as convinced as they were a half-century ago of the self-evident truth of Cal Coolidge's epigram—"The business of America is business"—recent soundings of public opinion show that they are ever more widely convinced of Ted Sorensen's inverted epigram—"The business of business is America."

Routes of Upward Mobility

Whether it is an organization for business or another purpose, there are only two routes to the top: one from within, the other from without. Each has its particular advantages and handicaps; each produces its own syndrome of ambivalence.

The leader coming from within the organization is the more likely to know it well: its signal strengths and weaknesses, its style of management and the quality of its managers, its living history and its aspirations, its markets, products and prospects. But perhaps he will know it too well. Friendships and personality clashes have much the same tendency to induce myopia in a leader. And corporate associations of long standing, except in the case of the most detached and widely experienced of managers, have a way of limiting the leader's horizons, of impairing his vision, of restricting his view of possibilities for the future. What has stood the organization in relatively good stead in the past—in terms of organizational goals and of the methods deployed to move toward them—may continue to be carried on. This may be good enough for the immediate if not the longer-run future. But the very value of his intimate knowledge of the past successes of the organization may induce what Veblen unforgettably described as a "trained incapacity": a state of affairs in which one's abilities come to function as inadequacies. Recurrent actions based upon training, skills, and experiences that have been successfully applied in the past result in inappropriate responses *under changed conditions.* Thus, to adopt a barnyard illustration used in this connection by Kenneth Burke, chickens can be readily conditioned to interpret the sound of a bell as a signal for food. The same bell may now be used to summon the trained chickens to their doom as they are assembled to suffer decapitation. As the leader from within adopts organizational measures in keeping with his past experience and employs them under new conditions that are not recognized as *significantly* different, *the very soundness of training for the past leads to maladaptation in the present.* In Burke's almost echolalic phrase: "People may be fit by being fit in an unfit fitness." Their past successes incapacitate them for future ones. To move from the barnyard to the railroad yard, on such sand, for one, has the history of the American railroads been written.

The assumed advantages and handicaps of the internal route to the top are typically reversed with the leader coming from outside the organization. He does not know the company in depth. Practically all of his first months, if not years, will be spent in its study—its past performance gauged against its past potentials, the capabilities of its people, material resources, aggregate aspirations. The organization must endure a period of contemplative inaction. But if his lack of firsthand acquaintance with the organization is a defect, it also has its qualities. He brings few built-in biases toward the particular organization and its parts (although he will, of course, inevitably have his own collection of biases grown outside). But having no emotional involvement with the past of the organization, he is—or the more easily can be—capable of opening himself to all kinds of innovative possibilities. He can more readily perceive ideas that may have been floating around the organization for years. He brings, surely, a fresh—not necessarily a correct—approach to the problems and opportunities of the organization he now leads, and an expertise gained outside the intellectual confinement inherent in every organization. Still, he brings with him from outside no guarantee of success, as is attested by the path of corporate leadership, liberally strewn with the bones of "boy wonders," "financial wizards," and "management geniuses" of all shapes and sizes.

The ambivalences of organizational leadership begin, then, at the beginning. They are found in the route the leader followed to get there, whether from within or from without. They begin with the sum total of his previous organizational experience and with the interaction of his own capability for adaptive growth and all the foibles and creative impulses of the organization he leads.

Varieties of Organizational Ambivalence

Regardless of his origin, the newly made leader of the organization soon confronts another ambivalent situation. As leader, it is his obligation to bring to his position a vision of the future, a sense of direction as to where he wants the organization to go. He must obey the further organizational imperative, on pain of failure, of sharing his private vision with the total organization. For vision that is remote from the values and wants of the many around him becomes transformed into self-defeating fantasy. Within these obligations are planted the seeds of several conflicts and ambivalences.

The more sharply the leader defines his vision, the more confident he is of his own role (and vice versa). But in sharpening his vision he has narrowed his options. And in narrowing his options he has limited the number and kind of his subordinates who will, with enthusiasm, perceive and work toward the goals encompassed in that vision. For people who are to release their energies toward the attainment of goals must have a voice and a hand in shaping those goals. They must have a sense of some mastery over their own destinies. Yet with each slice of power released by the leader—and it is power, i.e., the ability to make something happen, that, in the final analysis and however broadly defined, is the core of leadership—the greater becomes his own condition of uncertainty.

A second kind of conflict is in the offing between the leader who projects his own vision and the organization itself. The more "different" and the more radical that vision happens to be, the greater will be the conflict. For just as the leader comes to his position as the synergistic sum of his experiences, so too he leads an organization which is the synergistic sum of *its* experiences. Indeed, the experiences of the organization will be more deeply ingrained—through its history, traditions, culture, and the sheer inertial structure of all organizational life—than those of any of its individual members. Under such conditions, flexibility in the executive grip may, with only seeming paradox, produce a steadier hand.

Whether his vision is large or small, the leader will want—indeed, will have an emotional need—to shape the organization, to change it, to mold it into a creation that, at least in part, he can claim as his own. Yet, inexorably, he in turn will be shaped, probably without his recognition, by the organization, by its needs, its capabilities, its standards. At some distant time, should he look back, he will be unable to distinguish between the changes he has wrought and the ones that have been wrought in him. "It is a time," wrote Emerson, "when things are in the saddle." Or, to paraphrase a typically Churchillian aphorism: "We shape our organizations and afterwards our organizations shape us." Even the most self-confident of leaders will on occasion find it impossible to disagree.

Another ambivalence confronting the leader is built into the circumstance that although nothing succeeds like success, in organizations increments of success become self-limiting. This means for the leader that the organization will be at one and the same time a continuing source of great pleasure and acute pain. The leader will demand that the organization improve its performance, raise its standards, increase its efficiency. And when, through the objective measurement of the budget or some other device, improvement is discovered and entered into the corporate record, the leader will take great pleasure in it. But to obtain even a tittle of improvement, the leader will find that he must pass through a prolonged period of anguish, during which he feels (and sometimes is) personally responsible for the outcome and, in any case, is held accountable for it. And he will find, too, that unlike an individual who is able to assimilate and use new information for sometimes spectacular improvements in performance, a complex organization functions, for the most part, on precisely the reverse principle: that, after a certain point, as organizational efficiency improves, further improvement becomes increasingly difficult.

Still another ambivalent requirement exacted of the leader calls for him to have pride in his organization, to induce or reinforce the pride of other members of the organization, and still to keep the extent of that collective pride in check. The leader must somehow arrange for that composite of pride that is justified by accomplishment and commitment but, at the same time, he must recognize that pride can become overweening, no longer sustained by continuing accomplishment. This is often expressed in what Theodore Caplow has designated as the "aggrandizement effect": "the upward distortion of an organization's prestige by its own members." Having studied 33 different types of organizations —among them, banks and Skid Row missions, department stores and university departments—he found that members overestimated the prestige of their own organization (as seen by outsiders) eight times as often as they underestimated it. (In judging the prestige of other organizations than their own, people tend to agree.) Now, as Proverbs in the Good Book reminds us in its own brand of organizational sociology: Pride goeth before destruction, and a haughty spirit before a fall. In other words, organizations and their leaders who become happily absorbed in reflecting upon past glories at the expense of providing for new accomplishments are in deep trouble. They come increasingly to live and work in an unreal world of self-induced fantasy. And sooner or later, contact with the world of reality forces the prideful leader and his followers alike to discover that both utilitarian and moral assets waste away if they are not energetically renewed and extended. For the rest of the social system will not stand still. And so organizations which would move with it must continue to engage in both innovative and adaptive change.

While the leader is concerned, perhaps above all else, with pulling the entire organization to higher levels of performance, he will often be put in the contradictory position of being unable to meet the demands for facilities to provide superior performance by the organization's individual parts. He is presented with a classical dilemma of organizational decision. Deeply committed to the goals of the organization, two or more separate departments are each doing their utmost to serve the best interests of the total organization by maximizing their distinctive kinds of contribution to it. But, often, even typically, maximizing the contribution of one part means limiting the contributions of other parts. One thinks of the bright young men and women attracted to the field of electronic data processing who, were the decision in their domain, would systematize the entire universe overnight. There is, in the striving for organizational excellence—although many hesitate to concede it—a balance to be struck that means curbing the single-minded drive for maximum performance by the component parts. The dilemma of decision can be transcended only by having the distinct parts rise to a concern for the whole. Commitment to the goals of the organization then takes precedence over commitment to the goals of the department. All this presents leadership with the geeing-and-hawing that leaves the corporate mule in danger of succumbing to the dead-center obstinacy of noncooperation.

Leadership as Social Exchange

From his relations to his subordinates emerge a variety of other dilemmas, ambivalences, and contradictions for the organizational leader. It is the manager's responsibility, perhaps his very first responsibility, to sustain the people who report to him. He is, in fact as well as in word, "the first assistant of his subordinates." Yet who is to sustain the leader? Granting that topmost leadership is "the loneliest position on earth"—a bit of familiar hyperbole—it is not necessarily so for most organizational leadership; not, that is, under the proper circumstances. Those circumstances have to do, of course, with the kind of support that the subordinates give to their superior in his position of leadership. Turned half-circle and viewed from the position of leadership, this means the degree of confidence that the leader reposes in each of his subordinates.

There is, in every superior–subordinate relationship, a complex of interactions. At the root of them all, when they are effective interactions, is the confidence or trust that each has in the other. For the ultra-rationalists among us, it comes hard to recognize that in organizational life, the prime ingredient of reciprocal confidence is not competence alone, although the importance of competent performance of roles should not be underrated. It is the first stone on which confidence is built. After all, no one is better situated than subordinates to distinguish between a superior's authentic competence and its mere appearance.

This reminds us that leadership is not so much an attribute of individuals as it is a social transaction between leader and led, a kind of social exchange. And again, though some leaders sense this intuitively, the rest of us must learn it more laboriously. Leaders assist their associates in achieving personal goals by contributing to organizational goals. In exchange, they receive the basic coin of effective leadership: trust, confidence, and respect. You need not be loved to be an effective leader, but you must be respected.

Identifiable social processes produce the respect required for effective leadership. First, respect expressed *by* the leader breeds respect *for* the leader. As he exhibits a concern for the dignity of others in the organizational system and for their shared values and norms, he finds it reciprocated. Second, as has been said, he demonstrates technical competence in performing his own roles. He does not merely talk about competence, he exhibits it. Third, the effective leader is in continuing touch with the germane particulars of what is going on in the human organization. For this, it helps, of course, to be located at strategic nodes in the network of communication that comprises much of every organization. But structural location is not enough. Once situated there, he provides with calculated awareness for two-way communication. He not only lets the other fellow get an occasional word in edgewise; he lets him get a good number of words in straightaway. And the effective leader listens: both to what is said and to what is not said in so many words but is only implied. He allows for both negative and positive feedback. Negative feedback, as a cue to the possibility that, in his plans and actions, he has moved beyond the zone of acceptability for his colleagues and subordinates; positive feedback, as a cue that he has support for his initiating actions.

Fourth—and on this accounting, finally—although the leader in a position of authority has access to the power that coerces, he makes use of that power only sparingly. He gives up little and gains much in employing self-restraint in the exercise of his power. For once he has gained the respect of associates, it is they, rather than the leader directly, who work to ensure compliance among the rest of their peers. Leaders only deplete their authority by an excess of use, and that excess is not long coming when leaders, having lost the respect of their subordinates, anxiously try to impose their will. Group experiments in sociology have found that the more often group leaders use the coercive power granted them, the more apt are they to be displaced. The experiments confirm what has long been thought; at its most effective, leadership is sustained by *noblesse oblige*, the obligation for generosity of behavior by those enjoying rank and power. Force is an ultimate resource that maintains itself by being sparingly employed.

In a word, what instills confidence between superior and subordinate is joint commitment: commitment to one another and to agreed-upon organizational goals. It is this mutual commitment that encourages even the leader who is temperamentally inclined to retain the reins of power in his own hands to delegate authority as well as responsibility to his subordinates, that allows him to rely more on corporate consensus than on authoritarianism in the making of decisions, and that, in turn, motivates the subordinate to request (or through muted symbolism, to demand) the exercise of responsibility and power commensurate with his position rather than to suffer in silence the close-handed intransigence of the oligarchic leader.

Styles of Organizational Leadership

This train of thought need not be pursued very far in order to identify what has been emerging as one of the major contradictions facing modern organizations, including, as a prime special case, business organizations. This contradiction is found in the tendencies working simultaneously toward democratic rule and the more traditional authoritarian rule. This is something far deeper and more fundamental than a matter of the relationship between two or more individuals or even groups of individuals. It not only affects the style of management, the relationship between organizational units, and the definition and operation of management, but touches upon the very purposes of the organization itself.

In recent years, behavioral scientists—notably such organizational investigators and theorists as McGregor, Herzberg, Argyris, Likert, Lawrence, and, in his own way, Peter Drucker—have shown to a growing number of corporate executives that efficiency and productivity lie in the direction of a more democratic or participative management. This proposition can be overstated and it often has been. Nevertheless, there is now a growing abundance of evidence testifying that *under certain conditions* democratic leadership is the more efficient in making for productivity of products *and* of valued human by-products.

All the same, styles of leadership continue to vary. The repertoire of styles is extensive; and, it would seem, only few leaders have or acquire the versatility to shift from one to another style as changing circumstances require. There is the authoritarian style in which the leader is insistent, dominating, and apparently self-assured. With or without intent, he creates fear and then meets the regressive needs of his subordinates generated by that fear. He keeps himself firmly at the center of attention and manages to keep communication among the others in the system to a minimum. Ready to use coercion at the slightest intimation of divergence from his definitions of the situation, the authoritarian may be effective for a while in times of crisis when the organizational system is in a state of disarray. But, particularly for organizations in a democratically toned society, extreme and enforced dependence upon the leader means that the organizational system is especially liable to instability.

The democratic style of leadership, in contrast, is more responsive. It provides for extended participation of others, with policies more often emerging out of interaction between leader and led. It provides for the care and feeding of the self-esteem of members of the system, but not in that counterfeit style of spreading lavish flattery on all and sundry egos in the vicinity, after the fashion once advocated by the merchants of interpersonal relations who would have us make pseudo-friends by inauthentic expressions of sentimentality. (Remember G. K. Chesterton's finely wrought distinction: "Sentiment is jam on your bread; sentimentality, jam all over your face.") The democratic style of leadership does not call for indiscriminate and unyielding faith in your fellow man; some people are *not* to be trusted or respected or supported in their incompetence and willful malevolence. What the democratic style does call for is the introduction and maintenance of systems of relations that make for a grounded trust in others and for the human by-product of enabling people in the system to actualize their capacities for effective and responsible action and so to experience both authentic social relations and personal growth, each giving support to the other.

Precisely because one is committed to the ideal of democracy, one must be mindful of countertendencies in organizational systems. To begin with, there is a tendency toward what the German sociologist, Robert Michels, as long ago as 1915, excessively described as "the iron law of oligarchy." He was led to this "law" through which newly organized minorities acquire dominion within organizations by examining the case of democratic organization. He found there the seeming paradox that leaders initially committed to democratic values abandoned those values as their attention turned increasingly to maintaining the organization and especially their own place within it. The danger is plain. Leaders long established are often the last to perceive their own transition toward oligarchy, toward a form of control in which power is increasingly confined to the successively few. And leaders long established are apt to confuse the legitimacy of their rule with the indispensability of themselves. We all remember that royal proclamation by Louis XIV: "L'état, c'est moi!" And we can recall the more recent story of de Gaulle periodically intoning to himself: "Quand je veux savior ce que pense la France, je m'interroge" ("When I want to know what France thinks, I ask myself"). In this specific sense, many a long-established business leader is incorrigibly Gaullist.

The Michels brand of organizational pessimism poses grave problems for the business leader who would be both competitive and compassionate. The temper of the age suggests, however, the necessity of developing a response that utilizes a countervailing force to Michels's iron law. Such a force finds expression in the rule of thumb which says that the solution to the deficiencies of democracy is more democracy.

A particular ailment of organizational leadership was long since diagnosed by Chester Barnard as "the dilemma of the time lag." In this phrase he referred to the problem of discrepancy between organizational requirements for immediate adaptive action and the slow process of obtaining democratic approval of it. This is an authentic dilemma, not easily resolved. Democratically organized groups can cope with it only by having their members come to recognize *in advance* that, remote as they are from the firing line of daily decision, there will be occasions in which decisive action must be taken before it can be fully explored and validated by the membership. This comes hard for democratic organizations whose members often prefer to pay the price of recurrent maladaptations in order to avoid having their leadership converted into Caesarism or Bonapartism. But to earn the right for leases of independent decision, democratic leaders must provide for continuing accountability. They must be accountable not only in terms of the criteria they themselves propose but in terms of the often more extensive criteria adopted by other members of their organization and by the wider society.

Conflicting Interests

This brings us directly to another kind of ambivalence and dilemma confronting the organizational leader. One of the traditional responsibilities of the corporate leader, no less than the political one, and the cause of many contradictions in which the corporate executive is involved, is the need to balance the interests of groups which have a legitimate (and sometimes not so apparently legitimate) call on the resources of the organization.

The most obvious interest in the business corporation is economic and the most obvious interest groups are composed of employees, owners, and consumers. Striking a balance among these three groups alone—to say nothing here about the needs of increased capitalization, of the local community, and of the society beyond—poses basic contradictions of thought and action. In the one sphere of employee interests, for example, the business leader is often torn by the question of whether he should seek to attract labor at minimum cost or whether he should ensure for the organization a pool of quality labor by paying top salaries; whether he should place more or less emphasis on fringe benefits as opposed to wages and salaries; whether he should ensure security of employment to the possible short-term detriment of the corporation or whether he should seek maximum efficiency (which means, to put it bluntly, staff layoffs during periods of lax activity) to the possible long-term detriment of the corporation. Such questions are not completely resolved in the marketplace. The decisions turn more nearly on the system of values within which the corporation functions. These values, in turn, are imposed not so much by the economic function of the corporation as by its culture, traditions, history of recent experience, and by the personal proclivities of its leaders within the current context of the polity, the economy, and the society.

In this same sphere of employee interests, but now in a wider sense, the corporate leader must balance or arbitrate a secondary and often equally important interest: What is to be the share of the corporate resources allocated to each unit? What percentage of the budget will be allotted to manufacturing, research and development, advertising, computerization, the development of staff, and so on? It is a tempting belief that such questions are resolved in the organizational hierarchy solely by considerations of corporate need based on objective analysis and authoritative projections. But this is seldom the case. The business leader is as much circumscribed as the political leader by "political" constraints internal to the organization. And with all the accounting systems of planning, programming, and budgeting now in force and yet to come, one suspects that this will continue.

All this takes us back to the structural and functional aspects of the position of organizational leader. He is, of course and above all else, a maker of decisions; not, be it noted, *the* decision-maker. He differs from all the other makers of decision in the organization he leads in this: his decisions are ordinarily more consequential for the fate of that organization and for those parts of its environment affected by the ramified results of those decisions. He faces with fearsome regularity the need to assess conflicting interests, conflicting sentiments, and conflicting convictions within the organization. In this regard, there can be no rest for the sometimes weary leader. He is structurally located at the very node of conflicting wants and demands within the organization. His role requires him to acknowledge and work on these conflicts, not to deny them or to cover them over with the rhetoric of feigned consensus. He has the task of alerting the others to the sources of the conflict, to define and redefine the situation for them, to have them acknowledge in turn that decisions gauged in the light of the organization as a whole must often override the particular concerns of its parts.

It is no easy matter to discover what is in the best interest of the total organization, and so there is ample leeway for continuing disagreement. A degree of indeterminacy requires the exercise of reasonably confident judgment rather than the demonstration of certain outcomes. The leader may err in his calculated decisions engaging the conflicting interests and beliefs of his constituency. That is bad enough. But his greatest error comes in trying to evade these conflicts. Nothing catches up with an organizational leader so much as a conscientious policy of evasion that seeks the appearance of peace and quiet by avoiding decisions that might alienate this or that sector of the constituency. And *because* of a degree of indeterminacy about the validity of the decision, it is not merely the substance of his decisions that is consequential for the organization but the mode through which he arrives at them and the mode in which he makes them known. Effective leaders arbitrate and mediate the inevitable conflicts within the organization in such fashion that most of the members involved in his decisions feel most of the time that justice has been done. It is the role of the leader to act for the whole while interpreting for the parts. And so it is that even a substantively mistaken decision—as the limiting case—taken in ways that win the respect of associates and presented in ways that enlist their however reluctant assent will be less damaging than decisions that are substantively sound at the time but have little support in the organization because they are taken as arbitrary and inequitable. The reason for this is plain enough. Organizational decisions become transformed into organizational realities only to the extent that they engage the willing support of those who must translate them into day-by-day practice. Without such support, the initially sound decision has a way of becoming converted into a subsequently unsound one.

Social Environment of the Organization

Just as the corporate leader must balance the interests of interest groups within his organization, so he is caught in the even more difficult dilemma of balancing the interests of interest groups outside his organization. The direct relationship between the portions of economic wealth distributed by the corporation to its various primary "publics" is reasonably well understood. Should dividends greatly increase, there will be less under static conditions for distribution to the workers in the form of wages and to consumers in the form of stable or lower prices. But conditions are not static; indeed, it is one of the functions of the private and public sectors alike to see to it—through innovation, cost control, new efficiencies —that they never become static.

As a business grows in its capacity to create economic wealth, two interrelated phenomena occur, both of which establish new contradictions with which the organizational leader must cope. One is the demands of the traditional interest groups (employees, owners, consumers) for the production of wealth that is not essentially economic, that is, social wealth. The other is the rise of new interest groups that make other demands on the organization's resources for both economic and social wealth. A few topical examples will bring each of these developments to mind.

The rise of consumerism can be ascribed, at least in part, to a growing public which, surfeited with material possessions, now demands that these same possessions be imbued with qualities that are not only economically profitable but socially desirable. Thus, in our autos we demand seat belts rather than chrome strips; in our drugs, efficacy rather than palliatives (or worse); in our health care, adequacy for all rather than for the few. In like fashion, the call for "relevance" and "meaning" in work cannot be ascribed only to the altogether alienated few but must be recognized as also representing the deepest drives for self-actualization and self-esteem among those who, already employed, have found a measure of economic security. Finally, we can discern the faint beginnings of social commitment among at least a few of the twenty-eight million stockholders in this country—the clearest example being the voting of church-owned stock in an effort to achieve, in particular companies, the employment and advancement of minorities.

The second phenomenon is a corollary of business success. That success attracts notice and consequently increased demands, of both an economic and social kind. Thus, eleemosynary associations find their way to the corporate doorstep seeking contributions; quasi-public associations of all kinds place demands on the corporation that are not only financial but managerial (the time of staff) and physical (meeting sites); and on occasion entire communities descend on the successful corporation to seek aid in cleaning up the air and water (which, be it noted, the corporation has often helped to pollute), in employing the unemployed, in creating needed public transportation.

But if success brings enlarged demands, it also brings enlarged obligations for the corporation to engage in public service. The corporation, particularly the large and successful one, cannot stand aloof from the society in which it exists, if for no other reason—and there are other reasons—than its own economic health. In the last analysis, in this democratic republic at least, every corporation exists at the sufferance of society. To continue to exist, the corporation must meet its obligations, and not particularly those that it accepts as its own but those that are placed on it by society.

Thus, the leader of a significant business corporation must be both a "local" and a "cosmopolitan." By a local, I mean one who is largely oriented to his organization or immediate community that dominates his interests, concerns, and values. By a cosmopolitan, I mean one who is oriented toward the larger social world beyond his immediate organization or community, with extended interests, concerns, and values. The effective leader of a major business faces the task of combining both orientations and developing capabilities appropriate for putting both into practice. He must be able to look inward at his organization and outward at its concentric zones of environment. Social change has reduced his realistic options. Now, more than ever before, he must be both local and cosmopolitan. For although organizations have always been part of a larger social system and an ecosystem, the extent and character of those linkages were for a long time not widely noticed. With the spread of education—defective as it often is—all this is changing. Awareness of the interrelations involved in the ecosystem and social system is developing in every sector of our society. For leaders of business the enlarged awareness means that they must abandon the spectacular malapropism of not so long ago: "What's good for business is good for society." They must transform it into the countermaxim: "What's good for society is good for business—even when it's seemingly not."

In short, the leaders of business in the morally more sensitive society of our time are coming to recognize that they must pay the price of a growing commitment to the moral purposes of the larger society. Acting in terms of an authentic moral commitment is not cost-free. It comes at a price, a price paid for what that society has been contributing and continues to contribute to its constituent organizations. For, as the economists tell us in their analyses of market externalities, the price system often fails to account for the benefits received or the costs suffered by those who are not directly parties to a transaction. The beneficiaries of technological change, for example, are at best only a small part of those who suffer from their deleterious secondary consequences (as the report on the assessment of technology by the National Academy of Sciences reminds us) and as we observe for ourselves while suffering our polluted environments of air, water, sound, landscape, and society.

Conceding that the private sector of our economy does have a role in helping to solve public problems, regardless of whether its role is in competition or in cooperation with government, it is evident that the traditional concepts of competition, within and among companies, must be redefined in confronting those problems. One reason is that the problems themselves are so immense that their solution will require all of the organizations' competitive energies; another is that the face of the competitive "enemy" has changed: It is the problem itself, rather than, in the first instance, another company or another industry. These competitions continue, of course, but they are caught up in larger purposes. This notion finds analogy in the American mission-to-the-moon project, which was not a triumph of competition alone (if we put aside the jingoistic impetus to the program: "Beat Russia"). It was a triumph of cooperation (for an imperfectly examined objective). Within that, it was a triumph of managerial ability in getting thousands of organizations and millions of individuals to collaborate in the attainment of one overarching goal. Actually, the contradictions apparent in this example are socially generated rather than inevitably imposed. For as behavioral studies have shown—and as every business leader knows from experience in his own organization—the fruits of cooperation are far more abundant than those of competition. The basic contradictions, then, may lie within our institutions, within our social and cultural patterns, and derivatively in our assumed psychological needs and aspirations.

An Emerging Self-Critical Society

Finally, in raising questions about the very purpose of our business organizations, we find basic ambivalences that must at one time or another plague every corporate executive: Does the successful business try first to profit or to serve? The quick, agile answer—it tries to do both—escapes the dilemma by swift flight from it. Leaders of business have only begun to wrestle with the problem of *how* to do both in appropriate scale. For they are at work in a rapidly changing moral environment which requires them to make new assessments of purpose. This is a tough assignment. I have alluded to the increasing moral sensibility of American society, knowing that I cannot actually demonstrate that increase beyond all reasonable doubt, let alone measure its extent. All the same, it seems to me that evidence for it abounds on every side. Most of all, it is found in our national inventory of self-critical diagnoses. In growing numbers, we Americans direct our critical attention to the shortcomings of our society just as we have long directed our admiring attention to its strengths. The more we demand of our society, the more faults we find in this process of collective self-scrutiny. As we raise our sights and enlarge our moral expectations, we become more sensitive to the inequities of our society, its corruptions, and its unrealized potentials for a humane life. Unlike an apathetic society, or a complacent one, a self-critical society represents a heightened moral sensibility. What was good enough before, in the form of convenient compromises with moral principle, is no longer judged good enough. More and more Americans are stirring themselves out of the complacency induced by affluence to ask the harder questions: affluence for what? and for whom? and what beyond affluence?

Leaders of organizations in this changing moral environment are being pressed to become agents for the enlarging of equity and humane life. The range of their options is becoming delimited. For should they choose to believe that *only* the fiscal record of profit can testify to the success of their organizations, they will find this self-defeating. In due course, they will find that even that restricted index of accomplishment will deteriorate as they remain on the periphery of the great social transformations of our time. With a degree of optimism, one can be persuaded that newly emerging orientations in the private sector of the nation's business, with their attendant contradictions, ambiguities, and doubts, will force a fresh examination of the social role of business and of the business leader, and that this examination will result in an extended, enduring place for the ideal of social commitment in this revolutionary society.

6

Dilemmas
in Voluntary Associations

LONG BEFORE and of course ever since Sir Thomas More wrote his *Utopia* in 1516, men and women have conjured up worlds in which all things work together for good. There is something eternally appealing about the vision of a self-contained world that enjoys a perfect social, economic, and political system. But perfection has a way of remaining just that— a vision. That is why More described it as U-topia, or Nowhere, rather than as Eu-topia, a Place of Felicity. He had reason to understand that the imagery of a cost-free world where evil, conflict, and other troubles are absent and where the separate purposes of human beings are wonderfully consolidated into common purposes without loss of freedom was an ideal rather than an attainable reality.

Yet human beings continue to strive for Utopian ideals. In more immediate point, the professions in a democratic society search for an optimum form of organization that will work effectively both in defining and achieving its goals and that will accomplish larger social purposes without the kind of deep-seated conflict that negates those purposes. This may be all to the good. By directing their collective efforts toward ideals that are, strictly speaking, unattainable, people are energized to do much and achieve much that they would otherwise neither do nor achieve.

Reprinted with permission from *The American Journal of Nursing* 66 (May 1966), pp. 1055–61. With its unspoken specifications for the democratic professional association most in view, this piece was written while I was consulting sociologist to the American Nurses' Association. It was one of the papers providing context for my opinion (which developed into conviction during the dozen years of my consultantship) that the ANA would have to improve its position, in terms of influence, respect, and authority accorded it, however grudgingly, by the powerful American Medical Association, if it was to greatly advance the cause of nursing and health care.

The Changing Theory of Democracy

One such Utopian ideal is that of a perfect, frictionless, and cost-free democracy. An early modern conception of democracy formulated this ideal on the basis of several assumptions about man and about organization.

First, the theory took for granted that every person was just as competent as every other person. All were truly equal. What is more, they stayed that way, all apart from differences in experience, training, and education. Next, the theory assumed, everyone had equal access to relevant information. Everybody would make the effort to learn what they should know and would use the information in reasonable and instructed ways. Finally, in this trio of assumptions, uniformly distributed competence, knowledge, and expertise would work in an environment that left the society or organization alone, free to go its own democratic way without disturbance from the outside.

In this country, the doctrine of the omnicompetent citizen led, as early as the Jacksonian period, to the practice of a simple rotation of citizens through public offices. Competence was assumed, not assessed: neither experience nor trained capacity was needed since, according to this doctrine, all men were equally equipped to do the job. Thus, an early theory of democracy was rooted in highly moral and altogether precarious assumptions that made for a kind of democratic complacency.

Walter Lippmann has put all this in a sentence: "The democratic El Dorado has always been some perfect environment, and some perfect system of voting and representation, where the innate good will and instinctive statesmanship of every man could be translated into action."[1]

History has negated these assumptions of democracy, without at all negating the value of democracy as an Utopian ideal to be perpetually sought after. Men and women are *not* equally competent to do the work of a democratic polity. They differ in capacity, in acquired skills, and in knowledge. Complex social systems cannot provide full information to everyone nor, to the extent that it is supplied, does everyone attend equally to it. And not least, in an increasingly complicated and turbulent world, democracies are not isolated, secure from the pressures of the social and political environment.

But if the ideals of perfect and spontaneous democracy cannot be

---

1. Walter Lippmann, *Public Opinion* (New York: Harcourt Brace Jovanovich, 1922), p. 311.

fully realized, they can be variously approximated. This calls for considerable modification of the early assumptions. Pure idealism must be tempered with organizational realism. This can be seen from a summary of structural and functional requirements of democratic organization.

Functional Requirements of Democratic Organizations

In order for an organization to maintain a viable democratic character, it must satisfy at least the following functional requirements.

> It must somehow provide for ways to ascertain and record the will of the majority.

This apparently simple requirement conceals several difficulties. First of all, it is not easy to find out what most people actually want, not least because many of them do not themselves know. Second, the significance of the majority does not rest in its necessarily being right, but in its being determinate. In contrast, when a minority has veto power, it can overrule the indicated will of a larger number of people than can any majority:

> The democratic organization must provide for periodic audits of dissent as well as assent.

The decisions committing a democratically organized association reflect the views of the majority as variously ascertained. (Only direct rather than representative democracy would require these views to be directly ascertained through referenda and plebiscites.) But it must provide for audits of dissent as well as assent. This acquaints the representatives of the organization with the spread of opinion within it and enables them to take this diversity into account in formulating organizational policy. It thus provides occasion for dissenting minorities to modify the thinking of the majority.

Finally, within the framework of an ultimate consensus, the dissenting minorities yield once the decision of the majority has been made. They may remain a critical opposition but must accept the majority decision as binding. Otherwise, there would be a chaos of conflicting decisions rather than organization:

The foregoing functional requirements presuppose that a sufficient flow of organizationally relevant information is provided the membership.

This presupposition of the early theory of democracy remains intact. But it does not assume, as the early theory did, that members of the organization will in fact take possession of this information in the sense of attending to it sufficiently to know what is being communicated. One of the difficult tasks of the democratic organization is to maintain motivation among its members to keep themselves informed:

There must be provision for accountability of policy-making representatives to the membership.

The leaders of a democratic organization are also its servants. They take initiatives within the framework of values and purposes previously set by the organization, but they must also periodically account for their stewardship to those they serve. Accountability permits forward movement in an organization, yet also serves as a restraint on the directions of this movement departing too far from the wishes of the membership.

Other functional requirements of the democratic organization can be itemized but they are not distinctive of it. Rather, they are required for any form of effective organization, including the democratic:

The effective organization must maintain a process of dynamic adaptation for coping with its environment, in part responding to that environment, in part controlling it, in order to acquire and use the resources needed to attain the goals of the organization.

This requirement was omitted from the early theory of democracy which tacitly assumed either insulation of the organization or polity from its environment, or a comparatively unchanging environment which allowed the polity to run its own, internally generated course. But all organizations exist in social environments and these environments themselves are changing. This circumstance requires continuing adaptation to keep the organization from becoming ineffectual and obsolete and to enable it to acquire a measure of control over parts of the environment.

Moreover, owing to the systemic interdependence among parts of the social structure, organizational efforts to cope with one set of problems will introduce new ones.[2] But the succession of problems emerging in the process of adaptive problem-solving does not mean that organizational development is illusory. It reminds us, rather, that human organization is not static and never fully adapts to its internal and external environments. (How dull life would be were it otherwise.) And although new solutions to old problems give rise to new ones, they also provide an enlarged organizational experience that can be utilized for coping with the newly emerging problems:[3]

> The pacing and phasing of new organizational goals is a difficult and essential requirement for an effective organization.

One sign of defective organizational leadership is, in the words of that astute student of large-scale organization, Philip Selznick: ". . . the failure to set goals. Once an organization becomes a 'going concern,' with many forces working to keep it alive, the people who run it can readily escape the task of defining its purposes. This evasion stems partly from the hard intellectual labor involved, a labor that often seems but to increase the burden of already onerous daily operations. In part, also, there is the wish to avoid conflicts with those in and out of the organization who would be threatened by a sharp definition of purpose, with its attendant claims and responsibilities."[4]

The latter part of this observation deserves special emphasis. The formulation of new goals produces a measure of conflict (and brings about a new basis for consensus). For every new goal can be seen by components of the organization to have *differing consequences*, in degree or kind, for them.

Such conflict is the inevitable price of the basic requirement to set new goals—a price that can be afforded only by organizations that embrace a sufficient consensus to be able to endure these newly induced conflicts. Organizational leadership has the difficult task of so pacing the introduction of new goals that the basic consensus is not greatly threatened and the inevitable conflicts are contained within bounds.

2. Robert K. Merton and Robert A. Nisbet, eds., *Contemporary Social Problems* (New York: Harcourt Brace Jovanovich, 1971, 3rd ed.), pp. viii, 802–6; Peter M. Blau and W. Richard Scott, *Formal Organizations* (San Francisco: Chandler Publishing Co., 1961), p. 250; Mary P. Follett, "Process of Control," in *Papers on the Science of Administration*, ed. by Luther Gulick and L. Urwick, (New York: Institute of Public Administration, 1937), p. 166.
3. Blau and Scott, *op. cit.*, p. 250.
4. Philip Selznick, *Leadership in Administration: A Sociological Interpretation* (Evanston, Ill.: Row, Peterson, 1957), pp. 25–26.

These, then, in as small a compass as I can condense them, are the principal functional requirements of the democratic organization. These principles and functions are converted into operating realities by appropriate forms of organizational structure.

Structural Components of Democratic Organizations

The ethos of democracy registers respect for the individual. Everyone matters. This does not mean, of course, that everyone in the polity is equally informed, equally capable of contributing to the work of the whole, or equally influential in affecting what goes on in the organization. It means instead that, however much they may differ in these and kindred respects, all members have in principle equal right to make their voices heard. That is the ultimate force of the doctrine: one person, one vote:

> The democratic organization provides for an inclusive electorate of members and for regularly scheduled elections.

Regular elections open to all in the organization represent a device for meeting several functional requirements of the organization. They enable the wishes of the majority to be identified: they provide, through the choice of officials, for audits of assent and dissent; and they constitute a basic means for holding representatives to account.

Periodic elections require the people who have been temporarily placed in positions of power to listen both to followers who have put them there and to opponents who, by adding disaffected others to their number, may, next time around, remove them from office. Taking account of dissenting groups in the association is a requirement not only for being returned to office but for enjoying the respect of large fractions of the electorate while occupying office.

Crucial to the effective exercise of democracy in voluntary associations is the opportunity for nominations to high office to be made from below. Otherwise there operates what has been called the "iron law of oligarchy": continued control of the organization by a comparatively small band of insiders.[5] Some associations have tried to circumvent this tendency by honoring written or unwritten rules to the effect that top officers may succeed themselves only once or twice or not at all. Such a

5. Robert Michels, *Political Parties* (New York: The Free Press, 1949).

policy, however, does not prevent incumbents in office from co-opting successors drawn from their own circle. A machinery of nomination by more dispersed units of the association is needed to provide better insurance against oligarchic tendencies:

> The democratic organization must provide for initiatives of policy to come from elected representatives and to be evaluated by the membership through recurrent elections of representatives.

In one form or another, a democracy must provide for a legislative body: a Congress, a Parliament, or a House of Delegates. The comparatively limited resources of voluntary associations usually mean that their legislative bodies meet periodically for severely limited periods of time rather than remaining in session for extended periods throughout each administration. It is, therefore, all the more important that a voluntary association's legislative body, which usually represents the near-ultimate authority of the association, be representative of the diverse interests and values of the entire membership.

The democratically selected legislative body contributes to all the principal functions of the association. It decides upon goals and priorities among goals; it provides for enabling resources and the allocation of these resources to the various goals and functions of the association; it reaffirms the ultimate consensus that transcends the immediate conflicts of interest, opinion, and judgment registered in debates; it provides for the release of collective tensions through collective decisions openly arrived at.

In a democracy, stability should not be equated with tranquility. The legislature is a body designed for the open expression of dissent, and heated discussions are bound to come about when individuals feel intensely about the nature and activities of their association. (When members do not feel deeply about these matters, it only means that the association concerns them little or not at all.) But, once these frictions have been openly manifested, they must be followed by an assessment of collective judgment: the legislative vote.

The foregoing expression of conflicts need not weaken but, in the end, can strengthen the organization. For stability of the organization does not depend upon complete consensus about every proposed new goal or about every new means for working toward that goal. Rather, stability rests on the democratic rules of the game which require that, once debate has been closed, the various minority opinions give way to the commitments of the association as a whole:

If it is to be effective as well as democratic, the voluntary association must provide organizational devices that enable executive action to work toward the association's goals.

In all large-scale voluntary associations, there is a potential for conflict between the continuing full-time staff—the civil service, so to speak —and the elected officials, who typically devote only part of their energies to the association. This puts a premium upon effective and continued cooperation between the two.

Beyond this relation is the requirement that the elected representatives —the boards of directors or trustees, for instance—have substantial authority for making decisions during the interims between meetings of the legislative body. Often, these will be far-reaching decisions that commit the organization. But, in the end, they are decisions for which the officers will be held accountable by the legislature. Lacking a body with such interim authority, the association condemns itself to clumsy and self-defeating inertia:

Channels of communication between membership, constituent units, and executive staff must be open for a two-way flow of communication.

This is another of those organizational imperatives seemingly so obvious that they are often neglected in practice. That makes it all the more important that democratic organizations periodically review their structure to see whether this requirement is being adequately met.[6]

That these structural arrangements for effective democratic organization are not exhaustive must be plain to all of us, but they do represent an indispensable minimum.

Voluntary Membership

The members of a voluntary association, unlike those of other kinds of organizations, serve in a double capacity. They are both the principal *clientele* of the association—recipients of services for which they pay in the form of dues or contributions—and, to a greater or lesser extent, the *operating personnel* who intermittently carry on much of the activity of the association. Some members thus contribute both money and services

6. On channels of organizational communication, see C. I. Barnard, *The Functions of the Executive* (Cambridge: Harvard University Press, 1938), pp. 175 ff.

to the association; others, only money. And, as we shall soon observe, there is also the important category of nonmembers who are eligible for membership.

Up to this point, we have to a great extent been referring to members of voluntary associations as though they were all of a piece. True, we have alluded to differences among them in trained capacity, organizational experience, and knowledge about the association. But we must now take more orderly note of other, fairly decisive, differences among them.

Consider only two familiar aspects in which members of an association differ: first, the degree of their commitment to the association and, second, the degree of their participation in its affairs. By degree of commitment we mean the extent to which the association is important to members as compared with the many other competing demands on their attention, energies, and allegiance. By degree of participation we mean the amount and character of actual engagement in the association's work.

At first glance, these would seem to be much the same—and, indeed, they are correlated—but involvement and participation can and do vary independently. By grouping the two attributes in their several possible combinations, we can examine significant differences among them.[7]

Involved and Active

These are the members who typically find their way into one or another part of the working apparatus of the association. Gratification from activities within the organization tends to reinforce their commitment to it and this, in turn, tends to make for even greater participation. They almost always include the top leadership and, often, many of those working at intermediate levels of the association.

Involved and Inactive

This is a strategic, unused resource of voluntary associations. These members are ready to devote themselves to the work of the association but, either because of deficiences in the structure or because of limitations of the individual, their potentials for contributing to the association have

7. The typology is adapted from the analyses by Merton, *Social Theory and Social Structure* (New York: The Free Press, 1968, enlarged ed.), pp. 338–42; J. H. Fichter, *Social Relations in the Urban Parish* (Chicago: University of Chicago Press, 1954), Part 1; Amitai Etzioni, *A Comparative Analysis of Complex Organizations* (New York: The Free Press, 1961), pp. 293–95.

not been realized. Devices for identifying them are needed to enlarge the effective resources of the association.

Uninvolved and Active

These are the reluctant members who have been co-opted by the association even though they do not, at the time, have a deep interest in it. Often, they possess a particular kind of expertise that is badly needed and so can be persuaded to lend their help even though they do not regard the association as holding central interest for them. Some among this type of member later move into the first type: having been co-opted, they become more deeply engaged and develop a basic allegiance to the association.

Uninvolved and Inactive

In every large voluntary association, these comprise by far the largest single aggregate of members. They are passive recipients of the functions performed by the association, peripheral members rather than central ones. Nevertheless, they are indispensable to the association in that they serve important latent functions for the system of democracy. They keep internal conflicts from becoming too intense; they provide a brake on excessive rates of change and thus maintain continuity; they help provide for stability while the first type of member provides for initiative and change.[8]

No systematic data are available as to the proportions of these four kinds of members but there are clues. The principal fact is that only a small proportion of members take an active part in the work of their voluntary associations. One study has found, for instance, that only 19 per cent of the membership of voluntary organizations were "active" in the limited sense of both attending meetings regularly and participating in at least one of the following activities: holding office, being committee members, or doing any work for the association outside of formal meetings.[9] The extent of turnover among such active members is not known. But there are intimations that they tend to be much the same hard core over a period of time, with comparatively few being added to their ranks over short spans of time.

8. Bernard Berelson, Paul F. Lazarsfeld, and William McPhee, *Voting* (Chicago: University of Chicago Press, 1954), Chap. 14.
9. Wendell Bell, Richard J. Hill, and Charles R. Wright, *Public Leadership* (San Francisco: Chandler Publishing Co., 1961), pp. 21–23, 44–47.

All this means that, whatever the ideologies and wishes of the voluntary association, a comparatively small proportion ordinarily do the work of the association and are thrust into positions of continuing leadership. What may be blandly assumed to be a case of the iron law of oligarchy often turns out to be a case of leadership by default. Avenues for progressive movement into topmost levels of leadership remain untraveled, as few make the effort to convert nominal and inactive membership into central and highly active membership. This puts a premium on the process of co-opting new prospects for the cadres of leadership at various levels of the organization.

Nonmembers[10]

Just as members are not all of a kind, neither are nonmembers. It is important to distinguish among them, since some constitute a promise and others a threat to the voluntary association.

Consider first that voluntary associations differ in the degree of their "completeness"—that is, in the proportion of those eligible for membership who actually are members. The higher this proportion, the more nearly complete the membership of the association. And the more nearly complete the association, the greater the authority it exercises and the higher the public standing it enjoys. Completeness is distinct from the actual size of the membership. What counts is the ratio between actual members and potential or eligible members.

Just as members differ in their attitudes toward the association, so do nonmembers: Some aspire to membership, others are indifferent to it, and still others are motivated to remain unaffiliated. Anyone practiced in the work of a voluntary association can identify the several types and recognize that they present distinct challenges, promises, and difficulties for the association.

To take just one example, the individuals eligible for membership who nevertheless expressly reject it pose more of a threat to the association than do the antagonists who are similarly motivated not to belong but who aren't eligible anyway. Rejection by eligibles symbolizes the relative weakness of the association by emphasizing its incompleteness of membership, just as it symbolizes the apparent dubiety of its values and its services which are not accepted by those who should find them good and useful.

Particularly in the case of professional associations, eligible nonmem-

10. Merton, op. cit., pp. 342–51.

bers typically receive an unearned increment of social, moral, and economic gains from the work of their professional colleagues in the association. As I have suggested before, ". . . those who remain outside the organization are the 'freeloaders'; they do not pay their way, either in dues or kind."[11]

But to describe nonmembers who are eligible for membership as freeloaders is not to find fault with them. For it remains to be seen why people who benefit from the activities of a voluntary association do not join it. Often, it is because the organization is defective in its modes of recruitment, especially at the time when prospective members first acquire the criteria for membership; it fails to convey a sense of what it is accomplishing both for its members and for the large collectivity of which the nonmembers form an important part.

Organizational Tensions

In order to prepare ourselves to understand the central dilemma of democratic voluntary organizations, we have examined various aspects of that type of organization: the assumptions upon which it is based, its functional requirements and structural components, and the characteristics of both its members and eligible nonmembers. All this is needed as context to understand the major functional problem that confronts the democratic association: the problem of welding democratic process and expertise into an effective alliance.

For some time now, sociologists have identified a tension that develops in social systems. This is the tension between *instrumental* functions and *group-maintaining* functions, between the funneling of organizational energies into activities aimed principally at attaining goals or at maintaining the organization.[12] This functional problem is likely to become especially acute in the democratic form of organization.

Democratic organizations require an intense commitment to democratic values among their members if they are to retain a democratic form. Otherwise, seemingly more efficient practices will be adopted in place of slower and more cumbrous democratic ones, with the result that

11. R. K. Merton, "The Functions of the Professional Association," *The American Journal of Nursing* 58 (Jan. 1958), pp. 50–54.

12. Talcott Parsons and Edward A. Shils, eds., *Toward a General Theory of Action* (Cambridge: Harvard University Press, 1951), Chapter 5; Talcott Parsons and Neil J. Smelser, *Economy and Society* (New York: The Free Press, 1956), Chapter 1.

democracy becomes eroded. But this deep commitment to democratic values easily becomes excessive and leads to what has been described as the *displacement of goals*: the organizational means become transformed into ends-in-themselves and displace the principal goals of the organization.[13] There develops more concern with maintaining the democratic forms than with achieving the democratically defined goals.

Once the general process of displacement of goals has been identified, we become alerted to its workings. We note that some members develop so deep a passion for democratic processes that they often forget the purposes which these processes were meant to serve. They become absorbed in the minutiae of democratic machinery. Sometimes, they even succeed in mutilating democratically selected purposes by placing principal emphasis upon organizational means rather than upon organizational goals.

But we need to remember that the dilemma of goal-attainment versus organization-maintenance has two horns. At the other extreme, members of the association primarily committed to achieving the organizational goals develop a major concern with moving things ahead in the most effective way possible. They then experience the democratic processes, which ordinarily slow up the movement toward goals, as intolerable restraints. They may want to formulate new goals and policies that run far ahead of the collective assent of the membership.

Process and Expertise

Now it is the nature of a dilemma that it provides no easy choice among conflicting alternatives: one value must be temporarily sacrificed to another.[14] But if the organizational dilemma cannot be fully resolved, once

13. There is now a considerable tradition of work on the "displacement of organizational goals." For a sampling, see Merton, *Social Theory and Social Structure*, pp. 253–55; Merton, "Unanticipated Consequences of Purposive Social Action," reprinted in this volume; Peter Blau, *The Dynamics of Bureaucracy* (University of Chicago Press, 1955), pp. 184–99; Peter Blau, *Bureaucracy in Modern Society* (New York: Random House, 1956), Chapter 5; Blau and Scott, *op. cit.*, pp. 229–31; David L. Sills, *The Volunteers: Means and Ends in a National Organization* (New York: The Free Press, 1957), pp. 63–66; Michel Crozier, *The Bureaucratic Phenomenon* (University of Chicago Press, 1964), pp. 179–201; Robert Presthus, *The Organizational Society* (New York: Knopf, 1962), pp. 8, 186, 195, 322; Marshall W. Meyer, *Bureaucratic Structure and Authority* (New York: Harper & Row, 1972), pp. 2, 63–64.
14. C. I. Barnard, *Organization and Management* (Cambridge: Harvard University Press, 1948).

it is recognized, it can be coped with. To do so, the activities of the democratic association must be phased through a series of alternating emphases upon instrumental functions (getting things done) and system-maintenance functions (maintaining the democratic process).

There are times when the accent must be on the first phase—on action directed toward an organizational goal—even at the risk of approaching the edge of democratic process. As such instrumental action moves a certain distance toward an organizational goal, it will typically turn out that the democratic value of collective assent starts to be infringed. Then is the time for a counteractive phase in which concern centers primarily on the democratic review and possible redirection of organizational action.

In other words, the legitimacy of decisions committing the organization is ultimately vested in the membership who review the proposals of their representatives—for example, in a House of Delegates. But once such collective decisions on goals and on the *broadly defined* character of methods for moving toward the goals are taken, there remain, of course, the interim periods in which specific steps must be taken: the work must be carried forward, if the association is to be effective as well as democratic. During this phase, it becomes the delegated task of qualified, expert personnel to devise effective ways for advancing toward democratically determined goals.

These "experts"—such as the appointed staff, and members of committees—accomplish their purposes not only through their delegated interim authority, but also through their specialized competencies. The rapid growth of specialization and technical complexity in today's society has created a gap between "the right to take a specific action and the knowledge needed to do so."[15] The gap can be bridged by making use of these expert personnel to work on the basic organizational commitments that have been reached by the democratic assembly.

This would appear obvious. And still, in actual practice, associations jealously concerned to safeguard their democratic character will sometimes repudiate the use of experts. Yet just as clinical specialists within medicine or nursing are a necessary response to the growing complexity of knowledge and technique in the health professions, so organizational specialists—knowledgeable and skilled in complex matters of administration or education or professional practice—are needed to achieve the purposes of the association.

The essential point is that, during the principally instrumental phase,

15. Victor A. Thompson, *Modern Organization: A General Theory* (New York: Knopf, 1961), p. 139.

the trained capacities of experts can be harnessed to the purposes of the organization, without impairing those purposes or imposing entirely new ones. It would be a costly misreading of democracy to assume that all are equally qualified to work out the technical details of collective decisions. Democratic equality refers to representation, not to technical competence. It would be ironic if a professional association were to confuse the two. For surely, the professions, more than most other occupations, are dedicated to the belief that the specialized competence of experts is indispensable to our times.

This confronts the association with the big task of finding, recruiting, and retaining the personnel that have the expertise, the special capabilities, to do the organizational job. In voluntary professional associations, those possessing this expertise fall into two large groups: first, the full-time employed staff that is needed to administer the details of organizational decisions and to work out the details of the provisional recommendations reached by members of the association working in teams or committees; and, second, an intermittent "staff" made up of members of the association who meet from time to time to work on next steps in the goal-oriented programs of the association—committees, task forces, and the like.

These unremunerated workers perform many staff functions and, in a voluntary association, make up a great resource available at small cost. They provide specialized and technical advice about appropriate methods of moving toward organizational goals. They pool their knowledge in intensive work sessions of a kind not feasible for large assemblies. They put their expertise into the service of the collectively determined objectives of the association.

Finally, they provide the basis for the exercise of intelligent choice by the democratically elected representatives of the association. Although they do their joint thinking, debate, review, and analysis behind closed doors, their reports and recommendations are subject to the scrutiny and final judgment of the membership through their elected representatives. It is then that the proposed decisions move from the committee room into the democratic forum, and the alternate phase—that of the democratic review—is set in motion.

Minimizing the Dilemma

The alternation of phases will not eliminate but can reduce tension between instrumental and democracy-maintaining functions. In point of fact, effective democratic associations have sometimes hit upon this alternation of phases without full awareness of the organizational techniques they were successfully using.

In the phase focused on the democratic process, emphasis is placed on the right and obligation of the membership to decide upon new organizational goals. This is the *what* of democratic purpose. Then, in the phase focused on action toward these goals, emphasis is placed on the services of experts to determine how best to work toward them. This is the *how* of democratic accomplishment.

This delicate process of alternating phases is a little like walking a tightrope, with all its attendant risks and successes. You start to fall off to one side as you block the advancement toward organizational goals by refusing, in the name of "complete democracy," to make use of needed expertise. Or you start to fall off to the other side by limiting the commitment to democratic decision and turning over to experts the making of significant organizational decisions in order to move more effectively toward established goals. But, difficult as it may be, we know that it is possible to walk a tightrope. And it can be more readily done when a democratic association recognizes that the alternation of instrumental and representational phases can make for both attainment of goals and preservation of democratic process.

Part 2

7

Stuctural Analysis
in Sociology

... Solipsists declare
That no one else is there,
   Yet go on writing—for others.

... Behaviorists affirm
That thinkers don't learn,
   Yet go on thinking—undismayed.

... Subjectivists find
That it's all in the mind,
   Yet go on sitting—on real chairs.

... Popperians deny
That we can verify,
   Yet go on searching—for the truth.[1]

WHEN ALVIN W. GOULDNER, my friend, colleague-at-a-distance, and one-time student, entitled his recent book *The Coming Crisis of Western Sociology*,[2] he rather understated the case. For it can be argued, without

Reprinted with permission from *Approaches to the Study of Social Structure*, Peter M. Blau, ed. (New York: The Free Press, 1975). Written while I was a Fellow at the Center for Advanced Study in the Behavioral Sciences, this paper was supported by a grant from the National Science Foundation to the Program in the Sociology of Science, Columbia University. Helpful criticism was provided by fellow Fellows: Joshua Lederberg, Yehuda Elkana, Arnold Thackray, and Harriet Zuckerman.

1. An imperfect extension of three lines from Auden's lyrical repudiation of social science, "Under Which Lyre: A Reactionary Tract for the Times" in *Collected Shorter Poems 1927–1957*:
        ... existentialists declare
        That they are in complete despair,
           Yet go on writing.
2. New York: Basic Books, 1970.

paradox and with as much persuasiveness, that sociology has been in a condition of crisis throughout its history.

The Chronic Crisis of Sociology

Sociology has typically been in an unstable state, alternating between phases of extravagant optimism and extravagant pessimism among its cultivators about their capacity, then and there or at least very soon, to find abiding solutions to the problems of human society and the problems of human sociology, that is, solutions to the major social problems and the major cognitive ones.

As the population of sociologists attained a critical mass, the rate of such diagnoses quickened. Just about every generation of sociologists has managed to identify *its* time as a decisive moment for better or for worse in the development of the discipline. Those of us who have lived long enough to have observed this behavior over a span of decades can easily bring to mind some of the more striking diagnoses of crisis. For myself, it is enough to select the year 1956, when Georges Gurvitch announced "the crisis of sociological explanation" and Pitirim Sorokin itemized another version of the crisis in his *Fads and Foibles in Modern Sociology*.

Quite understandably, every doctor making the diagnosis prescribes a formally identical but substantively different therapy: See things and do things my way. The grave crisis will take a turn for the better only if the collective patients will adopt the diagnostician's own sociological perspective—be it Gurvitch's dialectical sociology or Sorokin's integralist sociology or, more recently, Gouldner's reflexive sociology. Nor, as we shall see, need this prescription of one's own theoretical commitment be an occasion for cynical amusement. After all, what cognitive basis—not, mind you, social or psychological or political basis—what cognitive basis should there be for subscribing to a theoretical perspective other than believing it to be at once more fruitful, more comprehensive, and more cogent than its rivals?

The aspects of sociology that have been taken to provide the signs and symptoms of crisis are of a familiar kind—a change and clash of doctrine accompanied by deepened tension, and sometimes abrasive conflict, among practitioners of the craft. The clash involves the strong claim that existing paradigms are incapable of handling problems they should, in principle, be capable of handling. It is in this sense that we can describe sociology as having experienced chronic crisis,[3] intermittently broken only by short surprising periods of relative calm. As distinct from the actual ongoing condition of the discipline, the periodic *sense* of crisis erupts at moments when sociologists become particularly aware of conspicuous inadequacies of cognitive or practical performance, typically as gauged by heightened aspirations for larger accomplishment.

On the social plane, this intensified awareness of inadequacy among sociologists (and their far-from-silent observers in the larger society) is occasioned by dynamic social systems generating new major troubles or aggravating old ones, such events undercutting what purported to be acceptable solutions to major social problems. I refer here in particular to those often pesky and, in a world of very imperfect knowledge, inevitably unanticipated consequences[4] of our purposed social action, individual and collective.[5] As social dysfunctions accumulate in society or concentrate in one or another of its sectors, there develops an increasingly acute sense among practitioners of the social sciences that the

3. "Chronic crisis" is not the paradoxical phrase it may seem to be. Beginning at least by the early 1930s, Horkheimer intermittently examined the "contemporary crisis in science." Max Horkheimer, "Bemerkungen über Wissenschaft und Krise," *Zeitschrift für Sozialforschung* 1 (1932), pp. 1–7. And although Raymond Boudon, in his book *La Crise de la Sociologie* (Paris–Geneva: Droz, 1971), remarks that many sociologists have "rightly" spoken of the current "crisis of sociology," he promptly goes on to observe that "sociology is more or less permanently characterized by a situation of latent crises." Apart from its special aptness for describing the condition of sociology through the years, the term "chronic crisis" acquires more general relevance now that, according to Alan Musgrave's article, "Kuhn's Second Thoughts," *British Journal of the Philosophy of Science* 22 (1971), pp. 287–306, T. S. Kuhn has amended his thinking so that periods of "normal science," rather than being "dogmatic periods *between* crises," are now seen to be "full of crises of their own." Compare the original version of Thomas S. Kuhn's *The Structure of Scientific Revolutions* (Chicago: University of Chicago Press, 1962) with later amendments: "Postscript—1969," in *The Structure of Scientific Revolutions* (Chicago: University of Chicago Press, 1970, Second Edition); "Reflections on My Critics," in Imre Lakatos and Alan Musgrave, eds., *Criticism and the Growth of Knowledge* (Cambridge: Cambridge University Press, 1970), pp. 231–78. Thanks to my colleague, Robert Nisbet, I am put back in mind of what I should never have forgotten: the historian Elizabeth L. Eisenstein's heavily documented observation that for our present-day, crisis-minded scholars, "every era once regarded as 'transitional' is now presented as an age of 'crisis.' ... One may read, in chronological sequence, about the political crisis of the early Italian Renaissance and the aesthetic crisis of the late Italian Renaissance; about innumerable crises—including an 'identity crisis'—precipitated by the Reformation; about a general European crisis in the early seventeenth century (1560–1660); about a crisis of the European conscience in the late seventeenth century (1680–

state of their knowledge does not begin to measure up to the requirements of the situation.

On the cognitive plane, the intensified awareness of inadequacy is generated by the dynamics of sociological thinking and inquiry, variously distributed among the aggregates making up the community of sociologists, which open up new problems, also not foreseen, that put back in question some of what had been taken as reasonably settled knowledge. A major crisis in a science develops when inconsistencies of theoretical expectation and actual observation accumulate to the point of becoming notorious among those at work in the field, no longer to be accommodated by a lengthening chain of *ad hoc* hypotheses designed to "save the phenomena."[6] This in turn brings with it *specified ignorance*: the express recognition of what is not yet known but needs to be known in order to lay the foundation for still more knowledge. Paradoxically, then, a sense of crisis can be occasioned by new knowledge, resulting in more exacting demands being made of old knowledge.

The social and cognitive processes within the collectivity of sociologists thus interact with developments in the environing society to produce variability in appraisals of the state of the art. When historical demands coalesce in both cognitive and social domains, as they appear to have done in the late 1960s, they generate an acute sense, in place of the acceptably or even agreeably chronic sense, of less than adequate performance in developing cognitively powerful and socially applicable

---

1715); and about the 'age of crisis' immediately following, during the eighteenth-century Enlightenment (1715–1789). Four centuries of crisis thus have to be traversed even before arriving at those classic late-eighteenth-century points of departure for our present twentieth-century crisis: political revolution in France and Industrial Revolution or the so-called Great Transformation in England." Eisenstein, "Clio and Chronos: An Essay on the Making and Breaking of History-Book Time," *History and Theory* 6 (1966): pp. 36–65, at p. 38. When a composite of historians declares the last four hundred years or so a time of continuing European crisis, perhaps we sociologists looking at our short collective past may be indulged in finding it to be one long crisis.

4. The problem of those residual unanticipated consequences is not really solved by a thoroughgoing rationalism, not even through use of the recipe thoughtfully devised by Bertie Wooster as he sternly advised his man: "Always anticipate everything, Jeeves. It is the only way." But as the immortal Wodehouse makes clear, the trouble is that most of us are less sanguine than Bertie and all of us far less knowing than Jeeves.

5. "Unanticipated Consequences of Social Action," in this volume.

6. Pierre Duhem, *To Save the Phenomena: An Essay on the Idea of Physical Theory from Plato to Galileo* (Chicago: The University of Chicago Press, 1969). Originally published in 1908.

paradigms. Such historical times of trouble transform chronic sociological aches into acute sociological pains. It is then that observant doctors are apt to advance their diagnosis that sociology is in deep crisis.

The sociologists engaged in making that diagnosis are only doing in their own domain what they are called upon to do in other domains of society and culture. After all, a principal task assigned the sociologist and other breeds of social scientists is to identify the character and sources of social discontent. Aggregated discontent signals underlying inadequacies in the structure of the social system or in the values and expectations developing in that system, or both. Not by analogy with medicine, but in their own right, social scientists observe that the processes giving rise to aggregated social complaints are not necessarily known to those expressing them. The same considerations invite analytical sociologists to adopt the role of metasociologist by diagnosing their own collective condition and by prescribing appropriate therapy for the ailments they find.

Were I called in as a consulting physician to diagnose the condition of sociology today, my opinion would be this: that superimposed on the chronic crisis of sociology to which I have referred is an acute crisis of a particular kind. This is the "crisis of prosperity," a general type identified by Tocqueville in his time and by Durkheim, a learned and independent 'student' of Tocqueville in his.[7] Sociology faces a crisis of abundance today partly as the result of an abundance of social crises. The great transformations taking place in much of the world confront sociologists with the immense task of investigating them effectively and of arriving at science-based recommendations for coping.

It is the newly won standing of sociology resulting from *some* advancement of knowledge that leads sociologists to stumble as they think themselves ready to select or to accept the assignment of helping to solve these large practical problems. The effective demand for solution of social problems far exceeds the current capacity of sociological knowledge and the current resources of sociological manpower and womanpower. As an unnecessary but understandable result, that demand far too often meets with nominal approximations to the genuine article. Sociologists who

7. The inverted commas indicate that Durkheim was of course only a close student, not a pupil, of Tocqueville. Nor is there any direct evidence that Durkheim's notion of a crisis of prosperity presented in Book II, Chapter 5 of *Suicide: A Study in Sociology* (New York: The Free Press, 1951; originally published in 1897) is based upon Tocqueville's chapter entitled "Why the Americans Are so Restless in the Midst of Their Prosperity," Book II, Chapter 13 of *Democracy in America* (New York: Vintage Books, 1954; originally published in 1835).

want to believe or who claim that enough is known or is immediately knowable to provide guidelines for coping with this or that massive social problem manage to put the entire discipline on premature trial. Their make-do investigations or off-the-cuff pronouncements of instantly achieved truths gain temporary credibility from the actual but severely limited achievements of scrupulous social science. But this oracular sociology filled with swift answers to tough questions can only lead to disillusionment, not least among students and new recruits to the field. The demands made of a sociology precisely because it has been slowly advancing accelerate at a rate that only widens the gap between expectation and accomplishment, a situation well calculated to produce a deepened sense of cognitive crisis.[8]

Reinforcing the malaise among sociologists deriving from excessive practical demands prematurely accepted and inadequately met is the malaise deriving from developments in neighboring cognitive domains. Chief among these, in my opinion, is the impact of ideas being variously advanced by Popper, Kuhn, Lakatos, Feyerabend, Toulmin, and many another in the philosophy of science. Often poorly understood by sociologists on the periphery of that currently tempestuous discipline, some of these ideas are sometimes taken to indicate that subjectivity reigns supreme in the physical and life sciences and so, it is inferred, it must surely reign in the social and behavioral sciences. Sociologists drawing this gratuitous inference take it as license legitimatizing a total subjectivity in which anything goes since, as they believe they have learned from the philosophers, objectivity in science is only a figment. I say no more about this subject now, as I shall be returning to it later. Here, it is enough to note that current anxieties and acute doubts expressed by those experiencing a "crisis of sociology" are often explicitly connected with ideas much debated in today's philosophy of science.

8. By this point, it must be evident that I consider that the form of malaise expressed by some sociologists about the condition of theoretical sociology today does not constitute a deep crisis in the strong sense of involving basically new controversy over fundamentals. The main lines of argument have a long and easily accessible history. Were that history carefully reviewed, the most recent announcements of crisis in sociology would be recognized as a continuation of theoretical issues long under debate.

Perhaps it is in this sense that the new book by the Polish sociologist Piotr Sztompka entitled *System and Function: Toward a Theory of Society* (New York: Academic Press, 1974) concludes with the judgment: "Finally, I believe that the so-called crisis of contemporary sociology is nothing but a new myth of the discipline, and that in fact there exists a solid foundation on which to base further, much needed theoretical efforts."

This tentative diagnosis of the current sense of crisis in sociology as deriving from developments in both the social and the cognitive domains is not incompatible with the tentative diagnosis advanced by Ben-David.[9] He sees the recent expressions of dissatisfaction with sociological theory by Gouldner,[10] Friedrichs,[11] and Runciman[12] as resulting from a particular change of academic generations since the end of the Second World War. Not that sociological criticism and dissent are new; not that assumed consensus on the substance of sociological theory has been replaced by marked dissensus. Rather, as Ben-David summarizes it (and I quote him at length since many sociologists do not see the journal in which his article appeared):

> This unity of the profession [in the immediate post-war period] was not based on the existence of anything resembling a "paradigm" for theory and research, such as postulated by Thomas Kuhn as the characteristic of a "normal science." There was no paradigm in sociology, and sociologists were often very critical of each other's approach. Consensus existed only in one respect, namely, that all sociologists accepted the scientific method as relevant to sociology, and the scientific morality as binding for sociologists. They clearly demarcated science from ideology, and if, on occasion, they accused each other as crypto-ideologists, this was done in the name of value-free science, not as a denial of the possibility of an objective value-free sociology.
>
> My hypothesis is that the passing of this consensus in the late 1960s was due to a new change of generations. The generation which obtained its Ph.D. in the 1960s consisted of young people for whom the problem of sociology versus ideology did not have the same crucial importance as for their predecessors. The choice between the two did not appear to them as a choice between inevitable intellectual disappointment and moral failure on the one hand, and the reasonable likelihood of solid, though probably slow advance, on the other hand. The lesson of the previous generation was not entirely lost on them, and they were probably more sceptical of ideology than young people used to be in the 1920s and 1930s, but they were also sceptical about social science and sociology. Lacking the experience of liberation from

9. Joseph Ben-David, "The State of Sociological Theory and the Sociological Community," *Comparative Studies in Society and History* 15 (1973), pp. 448–72.
10. Gouldner, *op. cit.*
11. Robert W. Friedrichs, *A Sociology of Sociology* (New York: The Free Press, 1970).
12. W. G. Runciman, *Social Science and Political Theory* (Cambridge: Cambridge University Press, 1963), and *Sociology in Its Place* (Cambridge: Cambridge University Press, 1970).

ideology, they could find in sociology few past achievements or great intellectual opportunities to command their loyalty to the profession. Listening to the self-criticism of the sociologists of the adult generation, they found it difficult to share the loyalty to, and the unshaken belief in, sociology of the latter. Therefore, questioning the very possibility of a scientific sociology, and considering the possibility that the demarcation line between sociology and ideology drawn in the 1950s may not have been final, does not have for them the same meaning of totalitarian threat as for the older generation.

This development, in conjunction with the confusions of present-day sociological theorizing, can explain the outburst and the timing of the dissatisfaction and the radical questioning of the logical basis of sociology which occurred in the late 1960s.[13]

Were I called in as a consulting physician to review not only the diagnosis but also the recommended therapy, my opinion would be this: that the chronic crisis of sociology, with its diversity, competition, and clash of doctrine, seems preferable to the therapy sometimes proposed for handling the acute crisis, namely, the prescription of a single theoretical perspective that promises to provide full and exclusive access to the sociological truth. The reasons for my opinion are clear, if not compelling. No one paradigm has even begun to demonstrate its unique cogency for investigating the entire range of sociologically interesting questions. And given the variety of these questions, the past prefigures the future. Periodic claims to the contrary turn out to be only premature claims to theoretical closure. What's more, were the proposed therapy actually adopted, it would produce something far worse than crisis. It would lead to stasis: the stagnation of sociological inquiry as a result of premature agreement on a single paradigm that is claimed to be an exhaustive guide to investigating the wide range of sociological questions.

In having adopted the medical metaphor of *crisis* through the years, sociologists are, of course, not alone. Practitioners in other intellectual disciplines of a far more exacting kind have long used the same figure of speech to express their reasonable discontent with the condition of this or that part of the discipline. But, as we all know, metaphors are not to be taken literally. To do so is only to mislead or to be misled, since few metaphors are heuristic analogies. In picking up the metaphor of crisis, therefore, I do not intend to push it without limit in order to achieve, or to impute, a *reductio ad absurdum*. The term *crisis* remains

13. Ben-David, *op. cit.*, pp. 471–72.

a faded metaphor: neither a literal meaning nor a close analogy but only a loose, figurative and not especially heuristic meaning transferred from one domain of experience to another.

In the domains of science and scholarship, a sound diagnosis of crisis, chronic or acute, means that the given discipline is found to be incapable of dealing with parts or aspects of the reality with which it does or "should" concern itself. In its strong form, the diagnosis of crisis in science involves unresolved fundamental paradoxes. To identify such paradoxes is itself no small achievement. It requires and signifies considerable scientific development, as with Planck's[14] deep formulation at the turn of the century that was designed to resolve the paradoxes confronting the classical theory of the emission and absorption of light. In a somewhat weaker form, the diagnosis of crisis identifies pertinent problems which, it is claimed, the concepts, ideas, and methods available to practitioners cannot adequately handle. This is the case with Morgenstern's recent account of "thirteen critical points in contemporary economic theory."[15] But in neither the strong nor the weak form does it follow that scientists come through their crises only by collectively inventing a unified theory capable of solving the entire range of problems in their discipline.

The *ideal* of a unified comprehensive theory is not here in question. Like other ideals of the Pareto type T, this one may be functional, even

14. This is the same Max Planck, it will be remembered, who in his youth abandoned the study of economics because of its difficulty and, of course, the same Planck whose observation on the rise of new truths in science is perhaps the most often quoted of its kind. Bernard Barber, "Resistance by Scientists to Scientific Discovery," *Science* 134 (1961), pp. 592–602; Kuhn, *op. cit.*, 1962, p. 150; Daniel S. Greenberg, *The Politics of Pure Science* (New York: New American Library, 1967), p. 45; Warren Hagstrom, *The Scientific Community* (New York: Basic Books, 1965), p. 283; and Harriet Zuckerman and Robert K. Merton, "Age, Aging, and Age-Structure in Science," in Robert K. Merton, *The Sociology of Science: Theoretical and Empirical Investigations*, ed. and with an Introduction by Norman W. Storer (Chicago and London: University of Chicago Press, 1973), p. 514, among sociologists of science have variously drawn upon the remark that "a new scientific truth does not triumph by convincing its opponents and making them see the light, but rather because its opponents eventually die, and a new generation grows up that is familiar with it." Max Planck, *Scientific Autobiography and Other Papers* (New York: Philosophical Library, 1949), pp. 33–34. As Scheffler has noted, it is the sort of aphorism that easily and mistakenly lends itself to an unexamined relativism and subjectivism. Israel Scheffler, *Science and Subjectivity* (Indianapolis: Bobbs-Merrill, 1967), pp. 370–71.

15. Oskar Morgenstern, "Thirteen Critical Points in Contemporary Economic Theory," *Journal of Economic Literature* 10 (1972), pp. 1163–89.

when not attained, for advancing the state of sociological knowledge.[16] But when the ideal is mistaken for the current thing, it becomes dysfunctional to that quest. Taken seriously as a guide to all research programs, the premature claims to theoretical closure in sociology that are the only kind of claims that can be staked out by the theoretical monists among us would only lead to much misguided effort, with disillusionment followed by something like stasis. For however effective some current paradigms may be in their own limited terrain (still to be adequately mapped), they have no sufficient claim to monopolize the search for sociological understanding. As we have briefly noted and will see more fully in this discussion, it is not so much the plurality of paradigms as the collective acceptance by practicing sociologists of a single paradigm proposed as a panacea that would constitute a deep crisis with ensuing stasis.[17]

On the Limited Case for Structural Analysis

All this may explain why I do not consider that the paradigm of structural analysis developing through the years provides the only way out of the periodically announced crisis in sociology. In paraphrase of Win-

16. Vilfredo Pareto, *The Mind and Society*, Vol. III (New York: Harcourt Brace Jovanovich, 1935), pp. 1300–1322. Originally published in 1917.

17. There is apparently a growing body of sociological opinion to this same effect. In January, 1975, while this paper was in press, Shmuel Eisenstadt and I discovered during my visit to Jerusalem that for several years we had been independently developing much the same themes about the plurality of sociological theories, the nature of their interrelations, the recurrent insistence on a *recent* crisis in sociology, and the connections of all this to the structure of the community of sociologists and to critical developments in the environing society. Until now, both of us had developed these ideas in the form of oral publication: Eisenstadt, in lectures at the Hebrew University; I, in lectures at Columbia University. And now we are putting these ideas into print: he, on the large scale, in his forthcoming book with M. Curelaru entitled *Sociological Theory, The Sociology Community and "Crisis" of Sociology*; I, on the small scale, in this paper. For a preliminary paper based upon that book, see Eisenstadt, "Some Reflections on the Crisis in Sociology," *Sociological Inquiry* 44 (1974), pp. 147–57. Too late to have their substance drawn upon for this paper, are two reflective articles by Gallino and Pizzorno in Pietro Rossi (ed.), *Ricerca Sociologica e Ruolo del Sociologico* (Bologna: Società editrice il Mulino, 1972), which Eisenstadt called to my attention.

In February, 1975, while this paper was still in press, Stefan Nowak, of the University of Warsaw, gave me a copy of the paper he had presented to the VIIIth World Congress of Sociology at Toronto a few days before I was presenting

ston Churchill on democracy, I regard the paradigm of this kind of structural analysis as the worst theoretical orientation in sociology—except all those other orientations that have been tried from time to time. Plainly so, or I should not continue to put my effort into it. But that is far from saying that structural analysis, this variant or any other, provides an exclusive and exhaustive theoretical base. Quite otherwise. Structural analysis has generated a problematics I find interesting and a way of thinking about problems I find more effective than any other I know. Moreover, it connects with other sociological paradigms that, the polemics notwithstanding, are anything but contradictory in much of what they suppose or assert. This is no doubt an unbecoming pacifist position to adopt at a time when the arena of sociology echoes with the claims of gladiators championing rival doctrines. Still, recent work in structural analysis leads me to spheres of agreement and of complementarity rather than to the alleged basic contradictions between various sociological paradigms. This is nothing strange. For it is not easy to achieve even mildly plausible sociological doctrines (paradigms, theories, conceptual schemes, models) that contradict one another in basic assumptions, concepts, and ideas. Many ideas in structural analysis and symbolic interactionism, for example, are opposed to one another in about the same sense as ham is opposed to eggs: they are perceptibly different but mutually enriching.

This, then, is the context for my enjoying the autobiographical license that Peter Blau has granted a dozen or so of us in this symposium. As chief architect of the symposium, he evidently decided that the ordinary standards of decorum calling for the disguise of personal ideas in impersonal discourse could be safely relaxed for the occasion, enough for each contributor to engage in the plenary self-indulgence of reflecting in public about some of his own favorite ideas. Or as Blau put it in his charge, each of us is to set forth "the distinctive significance of your

---

this one to the American Sociological Association in Montreal. Again, there is a striking and, to me, comforting parallelism (a fitting response to independent multiples in science and scholarship). Nowak sees the "crisis" as long characteristic of sociology, disposes of "the old dream of systematizing all relevant theoretical knowledge about society into one 'unique' and all-inclusive theory," and notes that "we will have to live for a long time with many *partial theories*—mutually complementary, and cumulative in different senses of the term, applicable to different aspects of social reality, answering to different theoretical questions, and useful for different practical social purposes." Stefan Nowak, "Empirical Knowledge and Social Values in the Cumulative Development of Sociology." Revision of paper prepared for the Round Table, "Is there a Crisis in Sociology?" at the VIIIth World Congress of Sociology, Toronto, August 1974.

approach to providing systematic explanations of social structures and their dynamics."

In my case, the temptation must be resisted—at least in part. For to discuss this aspect of my work would be only to repeat part of what Charles and Zona Loomis, Filippo Barbano (in a series of papers, among them one subtitled "The Emancipation of Structural Analysis in Sociology"), Walter Wallace, M. J. Mulkay, and, most analytically, Arthur Stinchcombe have worked out as the essentials of this mode of structural analysis, more deeply and more critically than I am prepared to do.[18]

In place of these complex, detailed accounts, I only sketch out basic components of this variant of structural analysis in the form of a series of stipulations. Although the term "stipulation" is taken from the adversary culture of the law, I use it here only to indicate provisional agreement on the kind of structural analysis under discussion. With such agreement, I can proceed to the rest of my subject: the place of that mode of theorizing in the cognitive and social structure of sociology and in relation to some current ideas in the sociology and philosophy of science.

Fourteen Stipulations for Structural Analysis

These, then, are fourteen stipulations of this one variant of structural analysis. *It is stipulated*:

1. *That* the evolving notion of "social structure" is polyphyletic and polymorphous (but not, one hopes, polymorphous perverse): that is, the notion has more than one ancestral line of sociological thought, and these differ partly in substance and partly in method.[19]

18. Charles P. and Zona K. Loomis, *Modern Social Theories* (New York: Van Nostrand, 1961), Chap. 5; Filippo Barbano, "L'Opera del Merton nella Sociologia Contemporanea," in R. K. Merton, *Teoria e Struttura Sociale* (Bologna: Il Mulino, 1959), pp. ix–xxvi; Barbano, "R. K. Merton e le Analisi della Sociologia," in R. K. Merton, *Teoria e Struttura Sociale*, 2d ed. (Bologna: Il Mulino, 1966), pp. vii–lviii; Barbano, "Social Structures and Social Functions: The Emancipation of Structural Analysis in Sociology," *Inquiry* 11 (1968), pp. 40–84; Barbano, "La Teorie Sociologiche tra Storicità e Scienza," in R. K. Merton, *Teoria e Struttura Sociale*, 3d ed. (Bologna: Il Mulino, 1971), pp. vii–xxxiv; Walter L. Wallace, ed., *Sociological Theory* (Chicago: Aldine Publishing Co., 1969), pp. 24–59; M. J. Mulkay, *Functionalism, Exchange and Theoretical Strategy* (London: Routledge & Kegan Paul, 1971), Chap. 5; and Arthur Stinchcombe, "Merton's Theory of Social Structure," in Lewis A. Coser, ed., *The Idea of Social Structure* (New York: Harcourt Brace Jovanovich, 1975), pp. 11–33.
19. Boudon adopts the image of a "polymorphism of sociology" in a related but

2. *That* the basic ideas of structural analysis in sociology long ante-dated the composite intellectual and social movement known as "structuralism."[20] Spanning a variety of core disciplines, structuralism has lately become the focus of a popular, sometimes undiscriminating social movement that has exploited through undisciplined extension the intellectual authority of such iconic figures as Ferdinand de Saussure and Roman Jakobson in linguistics, Claude Lévi-Strauss in anthropology, Jean Piaget in psychology and, most recently, François Jacob in biology. In short, although structural analysis in sociology today has been affected by certain communalities of structuralism serving as cognitive context—for example, certain parallels between Saussure and Durkheim—it does not historically derive from these intellectual traditions any more than, say, the input-output form of "structural analysis" developed by Wassily Leontief in economics.[21]

3. *That* structural analysis in sociology involves the confluence of ideas deriving principally from Durkheim and Marx. Far from being contradictory, as has sometimes been assumed, basic ideas drawn from their work have been found to be complementary in a long series of inquiries through the years, ranging from the social-structural sources of deviant behavior and the formation of bureaucratic personality to the growth and institutional structure of science.[22] In a more compact form, a paradigm proposed for functional analysis in the 1930s and published in 1949 drew attention to the overlaps, not identity, of these theoretical orientations. Examples are the basic concepts of "contradictions" in the

---

different sense to refer to various forms of sociological work: a "brilliant essay," "an empirical descriptive study," a verifiable "analytical theory" or a "speculative theory" pointing to directions of inquiry. Raymond Boudon, *op. cit.*, pp. 9–10.

20. The burgeoning literature on structuralism is practically inexhaustible, and no good purpose would be served by supplying a long list of titles here. The works of the masters are easily accessible and require no mention, except, perhaps, for the overview of Jean Piaget, *Structuralism* (New York: Basic Books, 1970), and the masterly history of heredity with its successive disclosure of structures by François Jacob, *The Logic of Life* (New York: Pantheon Books, 1973). Raymond Boudon has made a serious effort to differentiate and formalize the major conceptions of social structure in relation to notions of structure in other disciplines in *The Uses of Structuralism* (London: Heinemann, 1971). For other secondary works, see Jean Viet, *Les Méthodes Structuralistes dans les Sciences Sociales* (Paris: Mouton & Co., 1965); Oswald Ducrot et al., *Qu'est-ce que le Structuralisme?* (Paris: Editions du Seuil, 1968); and David Robey (ed.), *Structuralism: An Introduction* (Oxford: Clarendon Press, 1973).

21. Wassily Leontief, "Some Basic Problems of Structural Analysis," *The Review of Economics and Statistics* 34 (1952), pp. 1–9.

22. Robert K. Merton, *Social Theory and Social Structure* (New York: The Free Press, 1968, enlarged ed.); and *op. cit.*, 1973.

one and of "dysfunctions" in the other; the fundamental place accorded "conditions" of society in Marx and of "structural context" or "structural constraint" in structural analysis and, in the domain of the sociology of knowledge, Marx's postulate that men's changing "social existence determines their consciousness" corresponding to Durkheim's conception that collective representations reflect a social reality.[23]

The intertwining of these strands of thought has not gone unnoticed. Stinchcombe's analyses[24] of the overlapping sets of theoretical ideas generated his term "Marxian functionalism," while Gouldner takes repeated note of my "emphasizing [the] affinities between them, concluding with the compact observation about the analysis in "Social Structure and Anomie" that "Here, in effect, Merton uses Marx to pry open Durkheim."[25] Kalàb[26] describes Marx's method as "dialectically conceived structural analysis" and notes the interdependence of "historical and structural analysis" as did the exemplary historian Herbert Butterfield years ago when he described the major contribution of Marxism to historiography as one of having "taught us to make our history a structural piece of analysis."[27] In one instructive volume, Giddens[28] has recently analyzed congruities in the writings of Marx, Durkheim, and Weber, and in another, Sztompka[29] finds close congruities between functional and Marxian analysis, just as Pierre L. van den Berghe did in short compass more than a decade ago (see also Malewski).[30] Van den Berghe's conclusion states the case pointedly:

> Our central contention is that the two major approaches which have dominated much of social science present partial but complementary views of reality. Each body of theory raises difficulties which can be resolved, either by rejecting certain unnecessary postulates, or by in-

23. Merton, op. cit., 1968, pp. 93–95, 160–61, 516 ff.
24. Arthur Stinchcombe, Constructing Social Theories (New York: Harcourt Brace Jovanovich, 1968), pp. 80–101; and op. cit., 1975.
25. Gouldner, op. cit., pp. 335, 402, 426, 448, and, for the aperçu, p. 477.
26. Miloš Kalàb, "The Marxist Conception of the Sociological Method," Quality & Quantity 3 (1969), pp. 5–23.
27. Herbert Butterfield, History and Human Relations (London and Glasgow: Collins, 1951), pp. 79–80.
28. Anthony Giddens, Capitalism and Modern Social Theory (Cambridge: Cambridge University Press, 1971).
29. Piotr Sztompka, op. cit.
30. Andrezej Malewski, "Der Empirische Gehalt der Theorie des Historischen Materialismus," Kölner Zeitschrift für Soziologie und Sozialpsychologie 11 (1959), pp. 281–305; and Verhalten und Interaktion (Tübingen: J. C. B. Mohr [Paul Siebeck], 1967).

troducing concepts borrowed from the other approach. As functionalism and the dialectic show, besides important differences, some points of convergence and overlap, there is hope of transcending *ad hoc* eclecticism and of reaching a balanced theoretical synthesis.[31]

4. *That* since the confluence of elements of Durkheim and Marx has been evident from at least the 1930s, it cannot be taken, as Gouldner[32] proposes it should be taken, as another sign of the crisis he ascribes to both functional and Marxist sociology in the 1960s.[33] Put more generally, it is being stipulated here that far from necessarily constituting a sign of theoretical crisis or decline, the convergence of separate lines of thought can, and in this case, does involve a process of consolidation of concepts, ideas and, propositions that result in more general paradigms.[34]

5. *That*, like theoretical orientations in the other social sciences, to say nothing of the physical and life sciences, structural analysis in sociology must deal with successively micro- and macro-level phenomena. Like them, it therefore confronts the formidable problem, lately taken up anew by Peter Blau[35] and many another, of developing concepts, methods, and data for linking micro- and macro-analysis.[36]

31. Pierre van den Berghe, "Dialectic and Functionalism: Toward a Theoretical Synthesis," *American Sociological Review* 28 (1963), pp. 695–705.
32. Gouldner, *op. cit.*, pp. 341 ff.
33. In this connection, I must disown Gouldner's avowed conjecture that, in the 1930s and 1940s, I "sought to make peace between Marxism and Functionalism precisely by emphasizing their affinities, and thus make it easier for Marxist students to become Functionalist professors." Gouldner, *op. cit.*, p. 335. Here, Gouldner surely does me too much honor. I had neither the far-seeing intent nor the wit and powers thus to transmogrify my students.
34. This stipulation is of long standing. I have been arguing for the importance of theoretical consolidation in sociology since the 1940s (Merton, *op. cit.*, 1968, Chapter 2, esp. pp. 49–53).
35. Peter Blau, *Exchange and Power in Social Life* (New York: John Wiley & Sons, 1964).
36. It seems safe to stipulate rather than to discuss this conception at length now that it has found its way into that depository of "established knowledge," the textbook. (On the significance of the textbook in different disciplines, see Kuhn, *op. cit.*, 1962, pp. 163–65.) Thus, in discussing Blau's "exchange structuralism," Jonathan Turner writes: "Bridging the Micro-Macro Gap. One of the most important analytical problems facing sociological theorizing revolves around the question: To what extent are structures and processes at micro *and* macro levels of social organization subject to analysis by the same concepts and to description by the same sociological laws? At what levels of sociological [sic] organization do emergent properties require use of additional concepts and description in terms of their own social laws?" Jonathan Turner, *The Structure of Sociological Theory* (Homewood, Ill.: Dorsey Press, 1974), p. 292.

6. *That*, to adopt Stinchcombe's important and compact formulation on the micro-level

the core process conceived as central to social structure is *the choice between socially structured alternatives*. This differs from the choice process of economic theory, in which the alternatives are conceived to have inherent utilities. It differs from the choice process of learning theory, in which the alternatives are conceived to emit reinforcing or extinguishing stimuli. It differs from both of these in that . . . the utility or reinforcement of a particular alternative choice is thought of as socially established, as part of the institutional order.[37]

7. *That*, on the macro-level, the social distributions (i.e., the concentration and dispersion) of authority, power, influence, and prestige comprise structures of social control that change historically, partly through processes of "accumulation of advantage and disadvantage" accruing to people occupying diverse stratified positions in that structure (subject to processes of feedback under conditions still poorly understood).[38]

8. *That* it is fundamental, not incidental, to the paradigm of structural analysis that *social structures generate social conflict* by being differentiated, in historically differing extent and kind, into interlocking arrays of social statuses, strata, organizations, and communities that have

---

And without indulging in easy and misplaced analogizing, sociologists must take a degree of interest in the reminder by the polymathic physicist, Richard Feynman, that in connection with the laws of physics, "we have found that the behaviour of matter on a small scale obeys laws very different from things on a large scale. So the question is, how does gravity look on a small scale? That is called the Quantum Theory of Gravity. There is no Quantum Theory of Gravity today. People have not succeeded completely in making a theory which is consistent with the uncertainty principles and the quantum mechanical principles." Richard Feynman, *The Character of Physical Law* (London: Cox and Wyman, 1965), pp. 32–33.

37. Stinchcombe, *op. cit.*, 1975, p. 12.

38. Since appearing in the sociology of science in 1942, the idea of "accumulation of advantage" (which relates to the notions of "the self-fulfilling prophecy" and "the Matthew-effect") in systems of social stratification has been developed in a series of investigations: Merton, *op. cit.*, 1973, pp. 273, 416, 439–59; Zuckerman and Merton, *op. cit.*, p. 325; Harriet Zuckerman, *Scientific Elite* (New York: The Free Press, in press), Chapter 3; Jonathan R. Cole and Stephen Cole, *Social Stratification in Science* (Chicago: University of Chicago Press, 1973), pp. 237–47, passim; Paul D. Allison and John A. Stewart, "Productivity Differences Among Scientists: Evidence for Accumulative Advantage," *American Sociological Review* 39 (1974), pp. 596–606; Harriet Zuckerman and Jonathan R. Cole, "Women in American Science," *Minerva* 13 (1975), pp. 82–102.

their own and therefore potentially conflicting as well as common interests and values.[39] (I shall have more to say about this presently.)

9. *That* normative structures do not have unified norm-sets. Instead,
that *sociological ambivalence* is built into normative structures in the
form of incompatible patterned expectations and a "dynamic alternation
of norms and counternorms" in social roles, as this "sociological ambivalence" has been identified, for example, in the spheres of bureaucracy,
medicine and science.[40]

10. *That social structures generate differing rates of deviant behavior*, variously so defined by structurally identifiable members of the
society. The behavior defined as deviant results, in significant degree,
from socially patterned discrepancies between culturally induced personal
aspirations and patterned differentials in access to the opportunity structure for moving toward those aspirations by institutional means.[41]

11. *That*, in addition to exogenous events, *social structures generate
both change within the structure and change of the structure* and that
these types of change come about through cumulatively patterned choices
in behavior and the amplification of dysfunctional consequences resulting
from certain kinds of strains, conflicts, and contradictions in the differentiated social structure.[42]

39. Robert K. Merton, "Social Problems and Sociological Theory," in R. K. Mer-
ton and R. A. Nisbet, eds. *Contemporary Social Problems*, Third Edition (New
York: Harcourt Brace Jovanovich, 1971), p. 796; and *op. cit.*, 1968, pp. 424–25.
40. Robert K. Merton and Elinor Barber, "Sociological Ambivalence," in E. A.
Tiryakian, ed., *Sociological Theory, Values, and Sociocultural Change* (New York:
The Free Press, 1963), pp. 91–120 [Reprinted as Chapter 1 of this volume];
Merton, *op. cit.*, 1973, Chap. 18; and Ian Mitroff, "Norms and Counter-Norms in
a Selected Group of the Apollo Moon Scientists: A Case Study in the Ambivalence
of Scientists," *American Sociological Review* 39 (1974), pp. 579–95.
41. Merton, *op. cit.*, 1968, pp. 185–248; and Merton, *op. cit.*, 1971, pp. 793–846.
42. Merton, *op. cit.*, 1968, pp. 176–77. This is stipulated in spite of the recent
critiques by Runciman and Nisbet. Both agree that it is badly misplaced to charge
functional or structural analysis with not having any "theory of social change,"
and they make their case in the best way: by stating that theory and criticizing it.
In a series of works, Nisbet strongly criticizes the idea of structurally or im-
manently generated social change as being theoretically untenable. I remain un-
persuaded. His analysis only shows that sources exogenous to social structure *also*
operate to produce change, a position altogether congenial, as he evidently recognizes, to those of us who do not take structural analysis to exhaust all aspects of
social phenomena. Robert A. Nisbet, "Developmentalism: A Critical Analysis," in
John C. McKinney and Edward A. Tiryakian, eds., *Theoretical Sociology* (New
York: Appleton-Century-Crofts, 1970), pp. 167–294 at pp. 178, 194–96; Nisbet,
Social Change and History (New York: Oxford University Press, 1969); Nisbet,
ed., *Social Change* (New York: Harper & Row, 1972); W. G. Runciman, *op. cit.*,
1963, p. 43.

12. *That*, in accord with preceding stipulations, every new cohort born into a social structure it never made proceeds differentially, along with other age cohorts, to modify that structure, both unwittingly and by design, through its responses to the objective social consequences, also both unanticipated and designed, of previous organized and collective action.[43]

13. *That* it is analytically useful to distinguish between manifest and latent levels of social structure as of social function (with the aside that structuralism as set forth in other disciplines—for example, by Jakobson, Lévi-Strauss, and Chomsky—finds it essential to distinguish "surface" from "deep" structures).[44]

14. And, finally, as will become evident in the rest of the paper, it is stipulated as a matter of theoretical principle (rather than as a stab at conspicuous modesty) *that*, like other theoretical orientations in sociology, structural analysis can lay no claim to being able to account exhaustively for the entire range of social and cultural phenomena.

From these severely condensed stipulations, it must be plain that this variant of structural analysis owes much to the classic mode of structural–functional analysis developed by my teacher, friend, and colleague-at-a-distance, Talcott Parsons.[45] But the variant differs from the standard form in, for me, two major respects—substantive and metatheoretical.

Structural Sources of Conflict and Deviant Behavior

Substantively, the variant doctrine makes a large place for the structural sources and differential consequences of conflict, dysfunctions, and contradictions in the social structure, thus representing, as has been noted,

43. See Chapter 8 in this volume.
44. Cf. Alvin W. Gouldner, "Cosmopolitans and Locals: Toward an Analysis of Latent Social Roles: I and II," *Administrative Science Quarterly* 2 (1957), pp. 281–306, 2 (1958), pp. 444–480; Barbano, *op. cit.*, 1968, pp. 55–57.
45. Parsons has developed his conception of structural–functional analysis in a library of books that cannot be itemized here. A sample would include his first big book, *The Structure of Social Action* (New York: McGraw-Hill, 1937), which is in effect his *Summa contra Utilitarianos*; *Essays in Sociological Theory* (New York: The Free Press, 1949), which amounts to his *Summa Sociologica*, thereafter further developed in several directions, partly represented in *Structure and Process in Modern Societies* (New York: The Free Press, 1960) and *Sociological Theory and Modern Society* (New York: The Free Press, 1967), two collections of papers that live up to the titles of the books in which they are collected.

an intertwining of central strands of thought in Marx and Durkheim. I find it significant that Ralf Dahrendorf, long tagged as a "conflict theorist" in the sometimes demi-mythic classifications of theoretical sociology, noted this basic point years ago. In his chapter, signally entitled "Die Funktionen sozialer Konflikte," Dahrendorf observed that this mode of structural analysis

> enables Merton, in contrast to Mayo, to accept the idea that conflicts may be *systematically produced by social structures.* There are for him circumstances where the structures of roles, reference-groups, and institutions to some degree *necessarily generate conflict.* But where do these conflicts arise, and what is their significance? It is at this point that he introduces the concept of "dysfunction" which has been used so much since. . . . This step forward [in the development of functional analysis] lay above all in its indication of the possibility *of a systematic explanation of conflict* ("on the structural level") [italics inserted].[46]

Much the same observation was made independently by Hans Goddijn in noting that this mode of structural analysis finds "the origins of social conflict within the social structure itself, namely in the antithesis of social positions. For that reason, this analysis can be seen within the context of a sociology of conflict."[47]

Gouldner has made the same kind of historical and analytical observation about the structural analysis of deviant behavior. Easily breaking through the make-believe barricades that would obstruct even restricted passage between theoretical orientations stemming from Marx and Durkheim, he notes the overlap between them. As I cannot improve upon Gouldner's own formulation, I borrow it. He observes that certain theorizing on deviant behavior

> should be seen *historically*, in terms of what it meant when it first appeared and made the rounds. In this context, it needs emphasis that Merton's work on *anomie* as well as Mills's work on "social pathology" was a *liberative* work, for those who lived with it as part of a *living* culture as distinct from how it may now appear as part of the mere *record* of that once-lived culture.
>
> There are several reasons for this. One is that both Merton and Mills kept open an avenue of access to Marxist theory. Indeed both of them

46. Ralf Dahrendorf, *Pfade aus Utopia* (München: R. Piper & Co., 1967), pp. 268–69.
47. H. P. M. Goddijn, *Het Funktionalisme in de Sociologie* (Assen: Van Gorcum, 1963), Chapter 4.

had a kind of tacit *Marxism*. Mills's Marxism was always much more tacit than his own radical position made it seem, while Merton was always much more Marxist than his silences on that question may make it seem. . . . Merton always knew his Marx and knew thoroughly the nuances of controversy in living Marxist culture. Merton developed his generalized analysis of the various forms of deviant behaviour by locating them within a systematic formalization of Durkheim's theory of *anomie*, from which he gained analytic distance by tacitly grounding himself in a Marxian ontology of social contradiction. It is perhaps this Hegelian dimension of Marxism that has had the most enduring effect on Merton's *analytic* rules, and which dispose him to view *anomie* as the unanticipated outcome of social institutions that thwarted men in their effort to acquire the very goods and values that these same institutions had encouraged them to pursue.[48]

These observations on deviant behavior like those on social conflict are sharply at odds with the hackneyed and immutable notion, current in some sociological quarters, which holds that a theoretical orientation called "conflict sociology" is inescapably opposed to the mode of structural analysis under discussion here. In a way, Dahrendorf, Goddijn, Gouldner, and not a few others had falsified that claim before it became current. The fixed claim, made out of whole cloth, imputes to this kind of structural analysis the undisclosed assumption that societies or groups have a *total consensus* of values, norms, and interests. This imputed (rather than documented) assumption presumably contrasts with the assumption that social conflict is somehow indigenous to human society. But, of course, social conflict cannot occur without a clash of values, norms, or interests variously shared by each of the social formations that are in conflict. As we noted in the eighth stipulation, it is precisely that kind of socially patterned differentiation of interests and values that leads structural analysis to hold that social conflict is not mere happenstance but is rooted in social structure.[49]

All apart from the Dahrendorf–Goddijn–Gouldner observations and my own reiterations to the same effect in the development of structural analysis, there is ample evidence to negate the stereotype that describes it as "consensual sociology." After all, it is no accident (as one says) that Lewis Coser, a continuing exponent of the variant tradition of structural analysis, adopted for investigation the twin foci registered in the

48. Alvin W. Gouldner, "Foreword," in Ian Taylor, Paul Walton, and Jock Young, *The New Criminology: For a Social Theory of Deviance* (London: Routledge & Kegan Paul, 1973), pp. ix–xiv at pp. x–xi.
49. Merton, *op. cit.*, 1971, pp. 796–97.

title of his early book, *The Functions of Social Conflict*;[50] then went on to develop *Continuities in the Study of Social Conflict*;[51] and most recently, focused on structural sources of social conflict in his *Greedy Institutions: Patterns of Undivided Commitment*.[52]

Pluralistic Cognitive Structure of Sociology

So much for one substantive aspect of this variant of structural analysis as a theoretical orientation. As we have briefly noted and will now consider at length, this orientation has been associated in its metatheoretical aspect with a particular image of the cognitive map of sociology.

In that image, sociology has a plurality of theoretical orientations—distinct paradigms and theories of the middle range—rather than a single actual or soon-to-be attained comprehensive theory. This imagery relates to the general question of the form of various models of the structure and growth of scientific knowledge generally, which has more recently re-entered the domain of sociology through the gateway provided by the philosophy of science. Popper, Kuhn, Lakatos, Feyerabend, and Naess are among the principal (in some cases, charismatic) figures in the renewed debate between theoretical pluralism and theoretical monism.

The issue is examined here for several reasons. For one thing, it is in direct line of cognitive if not historical continuity with the debate taking place in sociology since the 1940s. That debate contrasted the ideal and prospect of an overarching theoretical system with the image of a multiplicity of occasionally consolidated paradigms. For another thing, the issue is relevant because muddled versions of the Popperian and the Kuhnian doctrines have been seeping into sociology particularly through that neighbor of the philosophy of science, the sociology of science. Not least, inquiry into the issue will help us to locate structural analysis on the cognitive map of sociology.

I begin with the seemingly paradoxical judgment that Talcott Parsons (at least the Parsons of the 1940s) and Thomas Kuhn (at least the Kuhn of 1962), though usually taken to be poles apart, have in fact been nearly of a kind on the question of the cognitive structure, if not the processes of change, of scientific disciplines. They have both been theo-

50. New York: The Free Press, 1956.
51. New York: The Free Press, 1967.
52. New York: The Free Press, 1974.

retical monists, setting out the image of a single, all-encompassing paradigm in mature sciences: Parsons principally in the context of advocacy; Kuhn in the context of his descriptive conceptualization of "normal science."

The ground for this judgment needs to be filled in with a little detail because of the triple relevance of the subject and because it is especially the moving antepenultimate past of a rapidly growing discipline that becomes opaque to successive cohorts of recruits. The more distant past is known to them through prescribed study of the doctrine whereas the institutionally prescribed focus on the moving frontier of investigation leads to studied neglect of the sources of ideas and findings that have been obliterated by incorporation into canonical knowledge.[53]

During the 1940s, when he was plainly emerging as the leader of a school which, as he saw to it, was chiefly made up of critical followers rather than disciples, Talcott Parsons was anticipating and advocating theoretical monism. As he put it, "there is every prospect" that the then-current diversity of theories advanced within the "professional group"—the collectivity of trained sociologists—would "converge in the development of a single conceptual structure."[54] Even in those remote days, as no doubt to excess since, one of Parsons's students countered this monistic orientation by observing the actuality, and advocating the uses, of a plurality of theories. The clash of opinion was no less deep-seated for being expressed in would-be forceful but civil terms such as these:

53. Historians and sociologists of science are obliged to take note of this pattern of "obliteration of source of ideas or findings by their incorporation in currently accepted knowledge" (Merton, *op. cit.*, 1968: pp. 28, 35, 38). *Obliteration of source* in the strict sense of erasing every trace of origins is the limiting case in the lineage of scientific knowledge and even then holds primarily for the journeymen of science. Every scientific discipline has some practitioners who take pleasure in keeping green the memory of developers of ideas though none, to my limited knowledge, more so than Paul Samuelson, master constructor of those freight trains of eponyms that instantly catch up main lines in a genealogy of ideas ("an exact Hume–Ricardo–Marshall model of international trade" can serve as the example of the hyphenated variety although a longer search would surely uncover as long a freight train as the adjacency type exemplified in "the economic theory of index numbers associated with the names of Pigou, Könus, Keynes, Staehle, Leontief, Frisch, Lerner, R. G. D. Allen, Wald, and my own theories of revealed preference"). As I have had occasion to note in *On the Shoulders of Giants* (New York: The Free Press, 1965), pp. 218–19, obliteration of scholarly or scientific source often occurs in the form of palimpsests in which later writings efface earlier ones.
54. Talcott Parsons, "The Position of Sociological Theory," *American Sociological Review* 13 (1948), pp. 156–64 at p. 157.

... when Mr. Parsons suggests that our chief task is to deal with "theory" rather than with "theories," I must take strong exception. The fact is that the term "sociological theory," just as would be the case with the terms "physical theory" or "medical theory," is often misleading. It suggests *a tighter integration of diverse working theories than ordinarily obtains in any of these disciplines.* Let me try to make clear what is here implied. Of course, every discipline has a strain toward logical and empirical consistency. Of course, the temporary co-existence of logically incompatible theories sets up a tension, resolved only if one or another of the theories is abandoned or is so revised as to eliminate the inconsistency. Of course, also, every discipline has basic concepts, postulates, and theorems which are common resources of theorists, irrespective of the special range of problems with which they deal.

Of course, distinct theories often involve partly *overlapping concepts and postulates.* But the significant fact is that the progress of these disciplines consists in working out a large number of theories specific to certain types of phenomena and in exploring their mutual relations, and not in centering attention on "theory" as such.

To concentrate solely on the master conceptual scheme for deriving all sociological theory is to run the risk of producing twentieth-century equivalents of the large philosophical systems of the past, with all their suggestiveness, all their architectonic splendor and all their scientific sterility [italics inserted].[55]

In view of the various pluralistic doctrines now filling the journals of the philosophy of science, it is even more in point that this rudimentary proposal for a plurality of middle-range theories described actual sociological theory as consisting largely of gross, loose-knit "general orientations" rather than having the fine-grained, tight-knit fabric of the "hypothetico-deductive theory" then being widely bruited. For example, it was noted that

> much of what is described in textbooks as sociological theory consists of *general orientations* toward substantive materials. Such orientations involve broad postulates that indicate *types* of variables which are *somehow to be taken into account* rather than specifying determinate relationships between particular variables. Indispensable though these orientations are, they provide only the broadest framework for empirical inquiry [italics inserted].[56]

55. Robert K. Merton, "The Position of Sociological Theory," *American Sociological Review* 13 (1948), pp. 164–68 at pp. 164–65.
56. Robert K. Merton, "Sociological Theory," *American Journal of Sociology* 50 (1945), pp. 462–73.

That was why, from the 1940s onward, some of us took to proposing the terminology of "paradigms" and "theoretical orientations" to refer to the actually operating theoretical structure of sociology. Those were the days when I touched upon the character and functions of paradigms in sociology and worked out paradigms for functional analysis and for the sociology of knowledge designed to identify basic assumptions, concepts, problematics, and types of pertinent evidence.[57] It remained for Raymond Boudon to clarify and explicate the distinction between sociological theory properly so-called and paradigms and, through his typology of paradigms, to indicate their distinctive uses and limitations.[58]

One reason for the ready acceptance of the notion of a plurality of paradigms immediately suggests itself. It depicted the actual state of things, if not the remote ideal, in social science. Although good sized regions of economics and even of psychology were then taken as having developed fairly tight-knit theoretical systems, social scientists generally were chastened enough by actual experience to acknowledge the truly modest character of their theoretical achievements. The notion of paradigm, loose in construction but far better than the bottomless pit of sheer empiricism, provided both description and rationale for what was going on, although not leading one to abandon all hope of developing paradigms into broader and more exacting theoretical constructions.

As mini-structures of basic ideas, concepts, problematics, and findings, paradigms were held to represent unpretentious but organized claims to a limited kind of scientific knowledge. They were taken as intermediate to what Leontief had described in those days as "implicit theorizing" with its absence of theoretical control, and hypothetico-deductive theorizing, with its elaborate sets of logically interdependent and empirically grounded propositions.[59] Finally, in contrast to the scientism of the time deriving from logical empiricism and the "unity of science" movement, the notion of a plurality of loose-knit paradigms insulated sociologists from adopting the comparatively mature sciences of physics, chemistry, and biology as realistically appropriate models rather than as, in some ways, contrasting reference models.

57. Merton, op. cit., 1968, pp. 69–72, 109, 514; and Robert W. Friedrichs, "Dialectical Sociology: An Exemplar for the 1970s," Social Forces 50 (1972), pp. 447–55.
58. Raymond Boudon, "Notes sur la Notion de Théorie dans les Sciences Sociales," Archives Européennes de Sociologie 11 (1970), pp. 201–51.
59. Wassily Leontief, "Implicit Theorizing: A Methodological Criticism of the Neo-Cambridge School," Quarterly Journal of Economics 51 (1937), pp. 337–51.

Kuhn and Structural Analysis

This condition of sociologists diversely working at their lasts in a state of reality-enforced modesty continued recognizably through much of the 1940s and 1950s (as, in spite of some current views to the contrary, the use of multiple paradigms has continued since). Then came 1962 and the public appearance of *The Structure of Scientific Revolutions* by the physicist and historical philosopher of science, Thomas Kuhn.[60] The result of almost 15 years of slowly crystallizing thought, the monograph began to take final shape, appropriately enough, during Kuhn's stay in 1958–1959 at the interdisciplinary Center for Advanced Study in the Behavioral Sciences. It was there, as he reports in the preface to his consequential book, that he was struck by the multiplicity of overt disagreement over fundamentals among social scientists of a kind that seemed to him unlike the controversies in fields such as astronomy, physics, chemistry, and biology. As Kuhn noted, it was

> attempting to discover the source of that difference [which] led me to recognize the role in scientific research of what I have since called "paradigms." These I take to be universally recognized scientific achievements that for a time provide model problems and solutions to a community of practitioners. Once that piece of my puzzle fell into place, a draft of this essay emerged rapidly.[61]

In several respects, the fate of Kuhn's book is self-exemplifying. It exemplifies the influence and the occasionally commanding authority exercised by a well-selected though loosely constructed paradigm of the pre-Kuhnian variety. It provides an array of basic assumptions made explicit, fundamental concepts, an array of problems, and a tacit typology of pertinent evidence, all drawing explicitly upon and also significantly recombining and developing earlier ideas in the historical philosophy and sociology of science. It was, as Kuhn has often remarked since, an effort at codification in this sphere of knowledge.

Kuhn's own concept of "paradigm" was multivalent enough to yield 21 discriminable senses to a sympathetic analyst.[62] Understandably

60. *Op. cit.*, 1962.
61. Kuhn, *op. cit.*, 1962. p. x.
62. As is well known, it was Margaret Masterman who carried out the considerable feat of distinguishing these numerous senses. As is the way with such exercises, they could be reduced to only a few classes: metaphysical paradigms, socio-

enough, the multiplicity of meanings was no bar to the wide diffusion of Kuhn's informing idea. If anything, that great variety of meanings may have contributed to its rapid spread. For as the variegated literature making use of it attests, Kuhn's paradigm about paradigms was taken to mean all manner of things to all manner of practitioners in all manner of scientific and philosophical groups and communities requiring him, on occasion, to disown ideas imputed to him by his more enthusiastic self-appointed disciples. (Confronted with the imputations of these disciples, Kuhn must periodically be tempted to exclaim, after the fashion of that Victorian scholar who spent much of his long exile in the British Museum: "Je ne suis pas Kuhniste.") Above all else for our immediate purposes, the Kuhnian paradigm could be interpreted as asserting that at least the "mature" sciences in their prolonged "normal" puzzle-solving periods were characterized by full consensus on a paradigm. Thus, apparently without Kuhn's intent, though with his powerful inadvertent assistance, the book advanced, if it did not launch, the Doctrine of the Single Paradigm.

Kuhn afforded ample opportunity for this selective reading of his 1962 book. Quickly told examples will serve (especially since they are deliberately taken out of the contexts evidently ignored by critics and, even more significantly, by would-be adherents): "Normally, the members of a mature scientific community work from a single paradigm or from a closely related set."[63] Or again, Kuhn refers more than once to "the reception of a common paradigm" by "the scientific community."[64] It is no doubt this sort of statement[65] strewn throughout *The Structure of Scientific Revolutions* that led the invincible Imre Lakatos to observe with a doubly redundant emphasis on Kuhn's singularity that "In Kuhn's 1962 view major fields of science are, and must be, always dominated by one single supreme paradigm. My (Popperian) view allows for simultaneously growing rival research programmes. In *this* sense—and I

---

logical paradigms, and artifact or construct paradigms. For this careful, even loving, analysis, see Margaret Masterman, "The Nature of a Paradigm," in Imre Lakatos and Alan Musgrave, eds., *op. cit.*, pp. 59–90. As Kuhn himself notes, "The most thoughtful and thorough negative account" of this multiplicity of senses in which he uses the term is provided by Dudley Shapere, "The Structure of Scientific Revolutions," *Philosophical Review* 73 (1964), pp. 383–94.

63. Kuhn, *op. cit.*, 1962, p. 161.
64. *Ibid.*, e.g., p. 162.
65. Yet those wanting to read otherwise can find a plenitude of statements in the 1962 Kuhn (e.g., p. 165) alluding to multiple paradigms even in presumably "mature" scientific communities during their "normal" state given over to "puzzle-solving."

am sure Professor Koertge will agree—no Popperian approach is 'mono-theoretical.' "[66]

That was the Kuhn of 1962—or, at least, it was the 1962 Kuhn as widely perceived. In a style exemplifying institutional norms of science, Kuhn has since gone to some pains to re-examine and clarify his earlier ideas and to communicate—or, put more cautiously, in light of the re-ciprocal misunderstandings pandemically alleged by philosophers of sci-ence, to state—his current ideas.[67] He has done so in response to the strong critical impulse among colleagues of differing (though overlap-ping) theoretical persuasion who were themselves behaving in accord with that institutional norm of science known for some time as "organized (or systematic) skepticism," which calls for mutual criticism and less easily achieved self-criticism in the process of proposing or publicly assessing claims to knowledge.[68]

The vigorous multilateral debates about the Kuhnian paradigm have generated a good-sized library in the recent philosophy of science—and the end is not in sight. But this, surely, is not the place to examine in detail even the sociologically relevant ingredients in those discussions involving Popper and Kuhn, in almost the first instance, but also a goodly company of others including Lakatos, Quine, Feyerabend, Toulmin, Putnam, Agassi, Ayer, Naess, Watkins, Wisdom, Scheffler, Shapere, Mus-grave, and Jonathan Cohen, as well as an unitemized number of still others, all arguing their finely differentiated views in today's tumultuous philosophy of science. That examination must wait for another time. Still,

66. Imre Lakatos, "Falsification and the Methodology of Scientific Research Pro-grammes," in Lakatos and Musgrave, eds., *op cit.*, pp. 91–195; and "History of Science and Its Rational Reconstruction," in Buck and Cohen, eds., *op. cit.*, p. 177. Lakatos is replying here to the "charge" by his onetime student Noretta Koertge that his account of the growth of science is "mono-theoretical," i.e., that it claims that "the most important critical processes take place within the context of a *single* theory or a *single* research programme." Noretta Koertge, "Intra-theoretic Criticism and the Growth of Science," in R. Buck and R. Cohen, eds., *Boston Studies in the Philosophy of Science* Vol. 8 (Dordrecht, Holland: Reidel, 1971). It is symptomatic, of course, that the alleged theoretical monism is treated as un-tenable by both critic and criticized.

67. Thomas S. Kuhn, "Postscript—1969," *op. cit.*; "Reflections on My Critics," *op. cit.*; and "Second Thoughts on Paradigms," in Frederick Suppe, ed., *The Structure of Scientific Theories* (Urbana: University of Illinois Press, 1974), pp. 458–82.

68. Merton, *op. cit.*, 1973, pp. 264–66, 277–78, passim; and Norman Storer, *The Social System of Science* (New York: Holt, Rinehart & Winston, 1966), pp. 77–79, 87–88, 116–26.

it must be noted that the ideas in these discussions have been adapted, often in distorted versions, by sociologists who would find aid and comfort for their total relativism and subjectivism in what they regard as the Kuhnian doctrine, and even in the Popperian and Lakatosian doctrines. Foreclosing discussion at this time, I can only claim that neither the self-described $Kuhn_1$ of 1962 nor the $Kuhn_2$ of the early 1970s but only the reconstructed $Kuhn_3$ wishfully imagined by subjectivistic sociologists can be taken to provide that wanted authoritative support.[69] Beyond that, I note only that Kuhn's recent iterations and reiterations seem to me to be in their sociological aspects, as they evidently seem to him, of a piece with modes of structural analysis developing in the sociology of science over the years.[70]

In place of the much needed detailed examination of the matter, it may be useful to set out some of the principles (and, most spottily, just a few of the principals, Popper and Kuhn being, of course, ubiquitous) caught up in the developing debates. So far as I have been able to dis-

69. This differentiation of selves and of ascribed images of selves only continues what threatens to become a traditional practice among philosophers of science. Lakatos seems to have started it all when, in 1968, he distinguished three Poppers: $Popper_0$, "The dogmatic falsificationist who never published a word"; $Popper_1$, "the naive falsificationist"; and $Popper_2$, "the sophisticated falsificationist." See Imre Lakatos, "Criticism and the Methodology of Scientific Research Programmes," *Proceedings of the Aristotelian Society* 69 (1968), pp. 149–86; and "Falsification and the Methodology of Scientific Research Programmes," *op. cit.* at p. 181. $Feyerabend_2$ picked up the practice in "ironical criticism" of Lakatos in referring to $Feyerabend_1$ (a "Popperian" author). Paul Feyerabend, "Consolations for the Specialist," in Imre Lakatos and Alan Musgrave, eds., *op. cit.*, pp. 197–230 at pp. 214–15. Kuhn then went on to distinguish $Kuhn_1$, author of the essay "Reflections on My Critics" and of a book of now-familiar title published in 1962 by $Kuhn_2$, "the author of another book with the same title ... here cited repeatedly by Sir Karl Popper...." Thomas S. Kuhn, "Reflection on My Critics," *op. cit.*, p. 231. On at least one occasion, Popper himself would have none of this differentiation of selves, "... I do not want to enter here into Professor Lakatos's distinctions between $Popper_0$, $Popper_1$, $Popper_2$." See Popper, "Replies to My Critics" in Paul A Schilpp, ed., *The Philosophy of Karl Popper* (LaSalle, Illinois: Open Court, 1974), pp. 961–1197 at p. 1186, n. 70a. As expositional and polemical tactic, this multiplication of entities is reminiscent of Alfred Korzybski [*Science and Sanity* (Lakeville, Conn.: The International Non-Aristotelian Library Publishing Company, 1949, Third Edition.)]. As behavior, it invites the attention of sociologists of science to the recurrent syndrome, in scientific controversy, of *having been misunderstood*—or, at least, of having been misrepresented. The recurrence of this common complaint among scholars and scientists invites sociological reflection beyond the short work made of it by Merton, *On Theoretical Sociology* (New York: The Free Press, 1967), pp. 21–22. A related problem needing investigation by

cover, these would include at least the following variously linked problems and subproblems:[71]

1. *Theoretical monism and theoretical pluralism*[72]
   (Popper, Kuhn, Feyerabend, Naess, Lakatos, Radnitzky)

2. *Incommensurability of paradigms, disciplinary matrices, exemplars* (Kuhn); *research programs* (Lakatos); *images of science* (Elkana); *themata* (Holton); *paradigms, general theoretical orientatations* (Merton)

3. *Selective accumulation of scientific knowledge (including problem of progressive and degenerating problemshifts)*
   (Childe, 1956; Lakatos, 1970; Agassi, 1963; Kuhn, 1962, 1968; Radnitzky, 1971; Elkana, 1974)

   a. *Whig, anti-Whig and anti-anti-Whig perspectives on the growth and development of science*
      (Butterfield, 1951; Samuelson, 1974 at p. 76)

---

sociologists of science deals with the operation of "organized skepticism." The various disciplines apparently differ in their patterns of cognitive competition and conflict. Sociologists themselves appear forever engaged in hot dispute. Perhaps they are, beyond the generality of other scholars and scientists, but surely no more so than the internecine tribe of today's philosophers of science, each of its members engaged in vigorously announcing his own claims to knowledge while cheerfully denouncing the claims of most others.

70. Thomas Kuhn, "The History of Science," in *International Encyclopedia of the Social Sciences*, Vol. 14 (New York: The Macmillan Co. and The Free Press, 1968), pp. 74–83 at pp. 80–82.

71. For previously uncited works, see appended list of references, pp. 143–44.

72. The term "theoretical pluralism" is adopted here in the broad sense of a plurality of hypotheses, ideas, or, for that matter, theories and paradigms involved in the growth of a scientific discipline. The term is not being employed in the special sense most emphatically and extensively used by Feyerabend and Klima, which not only advocates the "proliferation of hypotheses" but as Naess, Lakatos, and many another point out argues a kind of methodological dadaism. See Paul Feyerabend, "Against Method: Outline of an Anarchistic Theory of Knowledge," in M. Radner and S. Winokur, eds., *Minnesota Studies in the Philosophy of Science*, Number 4 (Minneapolis: University of Minnesota Press, 1970) and Paul Feyerabend, *Against Method: Outline of an Anarchistic Theory of Knowledge*. (London: NLB, 1975); and Rolf Klima, "Theoretical Pluralism, Methodological Dissension and the Role of the Sociologist," *Social Science Information* 69 (1972), pp. 69–108. As Popper himself observes, "The idea of theoretical pluralism is no novelty. Under the name 'The Method of Multiple Hypotheses,' its methodological importance was stressed by the geologist T. C. Chamberlin at the end of the nineteenth century." Popper, *op. cit.*, 1974, p. 1187, n. 80.

b. *Continuities and discontinuities in scientific development*
    (D. T. Campbell, 1970, 1974; Toulmin, 1972; Cohen, 1973)

4. *Demarcation of science and non-science (in particular, pseudo-science)*
    (Popper, 1959, 1962, 1972, 1974; Lakatos, 1974; Musgrave, 1968)

5. *Theory-laden facts and scientific instruments*
    (Kuhn, passim; Norman Campbell, 1920 at pp. 101–112; Henderson, 1932; Parsons, 1937 at pp. 28, 41–42; Hanson, 1958)

6. *Falsification and confirmation in scientific inquiry*
    (Popper, passim; Watkins, 1964; Lakatos, 1970; Musgrave, 1973)

7. *Subjectivism and relativism*
    (Kuhn, Popper, Lakatos, passim; Scheffler, 1967, 1972)

8. *Social substrate of science ("the scientific community")*
    (Polanyi, 1958; Kuhn, passim; Price, 1961, 1963; D. T. Campbell, 1969; Thackray, 1974)

Clearly, a tempting array of problems for sociological and not only philosophical investigation.

The Uses of Diversity

Reverting to my observations on the announced crisis of sociology, I propose that, although the unified consolidation of paradigms remains a useful but distant ideal of the Pareto T-type, a plurality of paradigms has its own uses in an evolving discipline. For as some of us have been monotonously reiterating for decades, paradigms have diverse cognitive functions just as they have diverse social functions for the collectivities of scientists engaged in developing them. Among these uses, I touch upon only two.

First, a plurality of paradigms institutes a great variety of problems for investigation instead of prematurely confining inquiry to the problematics of a single, assumedly overarching paradigm. That is one reason, for example, why Keynes deeply regretted that Malthus's unpublished line of approach to the connections between savings, outputs, and profits was ignored while Ricardo's prevailed, describing that century-long domination as no less than "a disaster to the progress of economics."[73] The

73. John Maynard Keynes, *Essays in Biography*, Vol. X of *The Collected Writings of John Maynard Keynes* (London: The Macmillan Press Ltd., 1972) pp. 98–99. Originally published in 1933.

disaster lay rather in the failure to ask certain questions than in the answers to the questions that were raised. Or, turning from great matters to small ones, it was in the difficult 1940s (not the difficult 1960s or 1970s) that a paradigm included this observation under the caption of "Concepts of Dynamics and Change":

> Functional analysts *tend* to focus on the statics of social structure and to neglect the study of structural change. This emphasis upon statics is not, however, *inherent*.

and further:

> The concept of dysfunction, which implies the concept of strain, stress and tension on the structural level, provides an analytical approach to the study of dynamics and change.

And, still addressing itself to the focus of a particular line of thought, this statement of the 1940s continues with a basic question about the pattern of preemption of interest in the course of theoretically oriented inquiry:

> Does the prevailing concern among functional analysts with the concept of *social equilibrium* divert attention from the phenomena of *social disequilibrium*?[74]

In cases such as this, the question is not one of detecting substantive contradictions between paradigms but of considering their problematics. Paradigms differ in focusing upon distinctive ranges of problems of investigation. As a result, the exclusive adherence of a scientific community to a single paradigm, whatever it might be, will preempt the attention of scientists in the sense of having them focus on a limited range of problems at the expense of attending to others. Through such preemption, monistic theory becomes dysfunctional for the advancement of other types of knowledge in that field. Manifestly, therefore, conscientious advocates of theoretical monism will heed the warning: *caveat praeemptor*.[75]

74. Merton, *op. cit.*, 1968, pp. 107–8. Originally published in 1949.
75. A current investigation by Joshua Lederberg, Harriet Zuckerman, Yehuda Elkana, and myself has identified this process of the preemption of interest as probably involved in patterns of "prematurity, maturity, and postmaturity" of contributions to science. On the dysfunctions of monopolistic orthodoxies in science resulting in "accumulative imbalances" of research attention and on the functions of regulated cognitive conflict for correcting those imbalances, see Merton, *op. cit.*,

This formulation leads directly to a second use of diverse paradigms with their more-or-less differing problematics: they direct the attention of research workers to differing kinds of *phenomena* through which each array of problems can be investigated to good advantage. This is no small or incidental matter. It is not happenstance, for example, that structural analysis of the Marxian variety elects to center on historical change in class structures rather than on routines of everyday social interaction, just as it is not happenstance that ethnomethodology centers on tacit rules exhibited in the routine interactions of individuals getting through their day rather than on the dynamics of changing class structure. The set of problematics imbedded in differing paradigms directs attention toward differing strategic research sites, objects or materials that will best exhibit the processes, mechanisms, or structural arrangements to be investigated. Thus, knowledge becomes unwittingly confined to the understanding of limited materials exhibiting the phenomena of theoretical interest.[76] To the extent that the paradigms are intellectually disciplined and not merely an adventitious assortment of personal interests generating little cognitive power, diversity leads to the illuminating of quite distinct aspects of human action and society, including aspects that a single paradigm would leave unnoticed.

The diversity of aspects requiring investigation provides another reason why paradigms are often in social rather than cognitive competition.

1973, pp. 57–58; Gerard Radnitzky, "Philosophy of Science in a New Key," *Methodology and Science* 6 (1973), pp. 134–78 at p. 136; for analysis of "the imbalance between psychological and sociological orientations to the subject of ambivalence," see Merton and Elinor Barber, *op. cit.*, pp. 93–94 (in this volume, pp. 4–6).

76. As Frank Beach has reported, for example, for a time more than half of American experimental psychologists had focused on one species, the rat, as their experimental organism. See Frank Beach, "The Snark Was a Boojum," *American Psychologist* 5 (1950), pp. 115–24. Ernst Mayr notes certain implications of such a focus on research objects and research interests: "Much of the recent controversy in the literature on animal behavior can be better understood now that we are aware of the important differences between behaviors controlled by closed and by open genetic programs. Ethologists have been primarily interested in species-specific signals and in their evolution. Comparison of different species has been of great concern to them. The classical experimental psychologists, who were principally interested in the neurophysiological and developmental aspects of behavior, almost invariab., worked with only a single species. Their primary interest was in learning, conditioning and other modifications of behavior. They approached behavior with the interests of the physiologist, and the phenomena thus studied were, to a large extent, aspects of noncommunicative behavior, such as maze running or food selection." Ernst Mayr, "Behavior Programs and Evolutionary Strategies," *American Scientist* 62 (1974), pp. 650–59 at p. 657.

Exponents of particular sociological paradigms compete for the interest of new cohorts of recruits to move ahead with their line of work just as they compete, one surmises less effectively, for old cohorts of veterans who have been using other paradigms to transfer their allegiance. In short, exponents of paradigms compete in the allocation of all resources that affect the distribution of attention by sociologists to the broad spectrum of sociological work. More often than might be supposed, co-existing paradigms, conspicuously so in a laboriously evolving discipline such as sociology, involve competition for cognitive *attention* rather than cognitive contradictions and confrontations, although the disagreeable and, to some, alluring noise of polemics may suggest otherwise.[77]

Although often obscured by polemics, the cognitive problems of co-existing paradigms call for discovering the capabilities and limitations of each. This involves identifying the kinds and range of problems each is good for (and identifying those for which it is incompetent or irrelevant), thus providing for potential awareness of the respects in which they are complementary or contradictory. It is within this sort of context that the stipulations for one variant of structural analysis have indicated a range of problems for which it seems particularly suited; the detailed expansion of those hints is hardly the work of an evening. But even in condensed form, the stipulations may suggest why this kind of structural analysis continues to hold a certain interest and why, at the same time, even sociologists dedicated to structural analysis must recognize that it remains only one, albeit a most inviting one, among the plurality of sociological paradigms now being energetically worked with.

Examining this same circumstance from the perspective of the sociology of science, I must report that variations in the number and variety of paradigms in scientific disciplines remain poorly understood. So far, no model of the growth of science has managed to account for the extent of doctrinal pluralism in different disciplines or in the same discipline at differing times. Long before the subject of growth of knowledge became a renewed focus for inquiry, the older metaphors carried with them suggestions of one or another model. The metaphor of a "marketplace of ideas" suggested processes of production, distribution, and exchange under conditions ranging from monopoly to open competition; the "forum of ideas" suggested an image of free discussion subject to processes of persuasion and the exercise of types of authority; the "arena of ideas" conveyed the image of combat to the desperate end, rejecting

---

77. On the general process, especially that of cognitive agreement and value disagreement, see Merton, *op. cit.*, 1973, Chapter 3.

the possibility, except for rare indulgent moments, of coexistence or complementarity of paradigms; and, to go no further, the metaphor of "a population of ideas" suggests a population–genetics model of variation and selection in evolutionary development. But whether one adopts Popper's falsification model or Kuhn's matrix model or Lakatos's model of research programs or the evolutionary models of Donald Campbell, Gerald Holton, and Stephen Toulmin, the models of scientific growth are all as one in maintaining that a plurality of paradigms in competitive and sometimes conflictful interaction are subject to more or less common criteria and rules of evidence that transcend other differences among the contending intellectual traditions.[78] Thus, after Kuhn had rejected the total relativism that many held to be implicit in the 1962 version of his doctrine, Radnitzky taxed even his far more restrained version with being unable to deal with the strategically important issue of whether shifts in paradigms represent, in given instances, an advance or a retrogression, a question that Imre Lakatos makes central to his idea of "research programmes."[79] Once again, the exponents of the total subjectivism that is here and there finding its way into today's sociology, who expressly seek legitimation in today's philosophy of science, are being left behind to fend for themselves. Even in the last third of the twentieth century, push-pin is not as good as poetry.[80]

It should be plain, then, that in describing and advocating a plurality of theoretical orientations in sociology in the form of a "disciplined eclecticism," I neither describe nor advocate a kind of theoretical anarchism in which anything goes.[81] Nor does this stance rest upon the dictum from Peking: "Let a hundred flowers blossom and let a hundred schools of thought contend." After all, as the concept of hyperexis teaches us, there really can be too much of a good thing (as Chairman Mao has

78. In any case, the strong impression of substantial underlying agreement on this assumption is gained from long-continued examination of the vigorous debates that I have barely touched upon in the preceding part of this paper.
79. Gerard Radnitzky, "From Logic of Science to Theory of Research," *Communication and Cognition* 7 (1974), pp. 110–11; Imre Lakatos, *op. cit.*, 1970 and "Popper on Demarcation and Induction," in Paul A. Schilpp, ed., *op. cit.*, pp. 241–73.
80. The allusion is, of course, to Bentham's almost unforgettable affirmation: "Prejudice apart, the game of push-pin is of equal value with the arts and sciences of music and poetry." *Rationalist Review*, (1825), p. 206.
81. Cf. Paul Feyerabend, "Problems of Empiricism," in R. Colodny, ed., *Beyond the Edge of Certainty* (Englewood Cliffs, N.J.: Prentice-Hall, 1965), pp. 145–260; Feyerabend, *Against Method: Outline of an Anarchistic Theory of Knowledge, op. cit.*; and Arne Naess, *The Pluralist and Possibilist Aspects of the Scientific Enterprise* (Oslo: Universitetsforlager, 1972).

evidently concluded since his pronouncement of 1957). It is among a much smaller plurality of theoretical orientations that structural analysis in sociology must find its evolving place. It seems safe to conclude from what has gone before that, in the interactive process of cognitive and social selection among sociological ideas, structural analysis will continue to link up with complementary ideas in other paradigms and thus continue to make modest theoretical consolidations toward the ultimate and still very remote ideal of a unified comprehensive theory.

Additional References

Joseph Agassi, *Towards an Historiography of Science, History, and Theory*, Beiheft 2 of *History and Theory* ('S-Gravenhage: Mouton & Co., 1963).

Herbert Butterfield, *The Whig Interpretation of History* (New York: Charles Scribner's Sons, 1951).

Donald T. Campbell, "Ethnocentrism of Disciplines and the Fish-Scale Model of Omniscience," in Muzafer Sherif and Carolyn Sherif, eds., *Interdisciplinary Relationships in the Social Sciences* (Chicago: Aldine Publishing Co., 1969), pp. 328–48.

———, "Natural Science as an Epistemological Model," in R. Naroll and R. Cohen eds., *A Handbook of Method in Cultural Anthropology* (Garden City, New York: The Natural History Press, 1970), pp. 51–85.

———, "Evolutionary Epistemology," in Paul A. Schilpp, ed., *op. cit.*, pp. 413–63.

Norman R. Campbell, *Physics: The Elements* (Cambridge: Cambridge University Press, 1920).

V. Gordon Childe, *Society and Knowledge* (London: Allen and Unwin, 1956).

L. Jonathan Cohen, "Is the Progress of Science Evolutionary?" *British Journal of the History of Science* 24 (1973), pp. 41–61.

Yehuda Elkana, "Scientific and Metaphysical Problems: Euler and Kant," in R. S. Cohen and M. W. Wartofsky, eds., *Methodological and Historical Essays in the Natural and Social Sciences. Boston Studies in the Philosophy of Science*, Number 14 (Dordrecht, Holland: D. Reidel Publishing Co., 1974), pp. 277–305.

———, *The Discovery of the Conservation of Energy* (London: Hutchinson International, 1974).

——— ed., *The Interaction between Science and Philosophy* (Atlantic Highlands, N.J.: Humanities Press, 1974).

N. R. Hanson, *Patterns of Discovery* (Cambridge University Press, 1958).

L. J. Henderson, "An Approximate Definition of Fact," *University of California Publications in Philosophy* 14 (1932), pp. 179–99.

Alan Musgrave, "On a Demarcation Dispute," in I. Lakatos and A. Musgrave, eds., *Problems in the Philosophy of Science* (Amsterdam: North-Holland Publishing Co., 1968), pp. 78–85.

————, "Falsification and Its Critics," in P. Suppes et al., eds., *Logic, Methodology, and Philosophy of Science* (Amsterdam and London: North-Holland Publishing Company, 1973), pp. 393–406.

Talcott Parsons, *The Structure of Social Action* (New York: McGraw-Hill, 1937).

Michael Polanyi, *Personal Knowledge* (London: Routledge & Kegan Paul, 1958).

Karl R. Popper, *The Logic of Scientific Discovery* (New York: Basic Books, 1959). Originally published in 1935.

————, *Conjectures and Refutations: The Growth of Scientific Knowledge* (London: Routledge & Kegan Paul, 1962).

————, *Objective Knowledge: An Evolutionary Approach* (New York: Oxford University Press, 1972).

Derek J. de Solla Price, *Little Science, Big Science* (New York: Columbia University Press, 1963).

Gerard Radnitzky, *Contemporary Schools of Metascience* (Göteborg: Akademiförlaget, 1970).

————, "Theorienpluralismus-Theorienmonismus," in Alwin Diemer, ed., *Der Methoden- und Theorienpluralismus in den Wissenschaften* (Meisenheimam Glan: Hain, 1971).

Paul A. Samuelson, "Merlin Unclothed, a Final Word," *Journal of Economic Literature* 12 (1974), pp. 75–77.

Israel Scheffler, "Vision and Revolution: A Postscript on Kuhn," *Philosophy of Science* 39 (1972), pp. 366–74.

Arnold Thackray, "Natural Knowledge in Cultural Context: The Manchester Model," *American Historical Review* 79 (1974), pp. 672–709.

————, *Atoms and Powers* (Cambridge, Mass.: Harvard University Press, 1970).

————, *John Dalton* (Cambridge, Mass.: Harvard University Press, 1972).

Stephen Toulmin, *Human Understanding*, Vol. 1 (Princeton: Princeton University Press, 1972).

J. W. N. Watkins, "Confirmation, the Paradoxes, and Positivism," in M. Bunge, ed., *The Critical Approach to Science and Philosophy* (New York: The Free Press, 1964), pp. 92–115.

8

The Unanticipated Consequences
of Social Action

IN SOME ONE of its numerous forms, the problem of the unanticipated consequences of purposive action has been touched upon by virtually every substantial contributor to the long history of social thought.[1] The diversity of context[2] and variety of terms[3] by which this problem has been known, however, have tended to obscure any continuity in its consideration. In fact, this diversity of context—ranging from theology to technology—has been so pronounced that not only has the substantial identity of the problem been overlooked, but no systematic, scientific analysis of it has as yet been made. The failure to subject the problem to thorough-going investigation has perhaps resulted in part from its having been linked historically with transcendental and ethical considerations. Obviously, the ready solution provided by ascribing uncontemplated consequences of action to the inscrutable will of God or Providence or Fate precludes, in the mind of the believer, any need for scientific analysis. Whatever the actual reasons, the fact remains that although the process has been widely recognized and its importance appreciated, it still awaits systematic treatment.

Reprinted with permission from *American Sociological Review* 1 (December 1936), pp. 894–904.
1. Some of the theorists, though their contributions are by no means of equal importance, are: Machiavelli, Vico, Adam Smith (and some later classical economists), Marx, Engels, Wundt, Pareto, Max Weber, Graham Wallas, Cooley, Sorokin, Gini, Chapin, von Schelting.
2. This problem has been related to such heterogeneous subjects as: the problem of evil (theodicy), moral responsibility, free will, predestination, deism, teleology, fatalism, logical, illogical and non-logical behavior, social prediction, planning and control, social cycles, the pleasure- and reality principles, and historical "accidents."
3. Some of the terms by which the whole or certain aspects of the process have been known are: Providence (immanent or transcendental), Moira, *Paradoxie der Folgen*, *Schicksal*, social forces, heterogony of ends, immanent causation, dialectical movement, principle of emergence and creative synthesis.

Formulation of the Problem

Although the phrase, unanticipated consequences of purposive social action, is in a measure self-explanatory, the setting of the problem demands further specification. In the first place, the greater part of this paper deals with isolated purposive acts rather than with their integration into a coherent system of action (though some reference will be made to the latter). This limitation is prescribed by expediency; a treatment of systems of action would introduce further unmanageable complications. Furthermore, *unforeseen* consequences should not be identified with consequences which are necessarily *undesirable* (from the standpoint of the actor). For though these results are unintended, they are not upon their occurrence always deemed axiologically negative. In short, undesired effects are not always undesirable effects. The intended and anticipated outcomes of purposive action, however, are always, in the very nature of the case, relatively desirable to the actor, though they may seem axiologically negative to an outside observer. This is true even in the polar instance where the intended result is "the lesser of two evils" or in such cases as suicide, ascetic mortification and self-torture which, in given situations, are deemed desirable relative to other possible alternatives.

Rigorously speaking, the *consequences* of purposive action are limited to those elements in the resulting situation that are exclusively the outcome of the action, that is, that would not have occurred had the action not taken place. Concretely, however, the consequences result from the interplay of the action and the objective situation, the conditions of action.[4] We shall be primarily concerned with a pattern of results of action under certain conditions. This still involves the problems of causal imputation (of which more later) though to a less pressing degree than consequences in the rigorous sense. These relatively concrete consequences may be differentiated into (a) consequences to the actor(s), (b) consequences to other persons mediated through the social structure, the culture, and the civilization.[5]

4. Cf. Frank H. Knight, *Risk, Uncertainty and Profit* (Boston and New York: Houghton Mifflin Co., 1921), pp. 201–2. Professor Knight's doctoral dissertation represents by far the most searching treatment of certain phases of this problem that I have yet seen.
5. For the distinction between society, culture and civilization, see Alfred Weber, "Prinzipielles zur Kultursoziologie: Gesellschaftsprozess, Civilisationsprozess und Kulturbewegung," *Archiv für Sozialwissenschaft und Sozialpolitik*, 47, 1920, pp. 1–49; R. K. Merton, "Civilization and Culture," *Sociology and Social Research* 21 (1936), pp. 103–13.

In considering *purposive* action, we are concerned with "conduct" as distinct from "behavior," that is, with action that involves motives and consequently a choice between alternatives.[6] For the time being, we take purposes as given, so that any theories that "reduce" purpose to conditioned reflexes or tropisms, which assert that motives are simply compounded of instinctual drives, may be considered as irrelevant. Psychological considerations of the source or origin of motives, although undoubtedly important for a more complete understanding of the mechanisms involved in the development of unexpected consequences of conduct, will be ignored.

Moreover, it is not assumed that social action always involves clear-cut, explicit purpose. Such awareness of purpose may be unusual, the aim of action more often than not being nebulous and hazy. This is certainly the case with habitual action which, though it may originally have been induced by conscious purpose, is characteristically performed without such awareness. The significance of habitual action will be discussed later.

Above all, it must not be inferred that purposive action implies "rationality" of human action (that persons always use the objectively most adequate means for the attainment of their end).[7] In fact, part of my analysis is devoted to identifying those elements which account for concrete deviations from rationality of action. Moreover, rationality and irrationality are not to be identified with the success and failure of action, respectively. For in a situation where the number of *possible* actions for attaining a given end is severely limited, one acts rationally by selecting the means which, on the basis of the available evidence, has the greatest probability of attaining this goal[8] even though the goal may actually *not* be attained.[9] Contrariwise, an end may be attained by action that, on the basis of the knowledge available to the actor, is irrational (as in the case of "hunches").

Turning now to *action*, we differentiate this into two kinds: unorganized and formally organized. The first refers to actions of individuals considered distributively out of which may grow the second when like-minded individuals form an association in order to achieve a common

6. Knight, *op. cit*, p. 52.
7. Max Weber, *Wirtschaft und Gesellschaft* (Tübingen: J. C. B. Mohr, 1925), pp. 3 ff.
8. See J. Bertrand, *Calcul des probabilités* (Paris, 1889), pp. 90 ff.; J. M. Keynes, *A Treatise on Probability* (London: The Macmillan Co., 1921), Chap. XXVI.
9. [For a specific application of this general observation, see the discussion of "discrepant appraisals of role-performance" on pp. 28–30 of this volume.]

purpose. Unanticipated consequences follow both types of action, although the second type seems to afford a better opportunity for sociological analysis since the processes of formal organization more often make for explicit statements of purpose and procedure.

Before turning to the actual analysis of the problem it is advisable to indicate two methodological pitfalls that are, moreover, common to all sociological investigations of purposive action. The first involves the problem of causal imputation, the problem of ascertaining the extent to which "consequences" can justifiably be attributed to certain actions. For example, to what extent has the recent increase in economic production in this country resulted from governmental measures? To what extent can the spread of organized crime be attributed to Prohibition? This ever-present difficulty of causal imputation must be solved for every empirical case.

The second problem is that of ascertaining the actual purposes of a given action. There is the difficulty, for instance, of discriminating between rationalization and truth in those cases where apparently unintended consequences are *ex post facto* declared to have been intended.[10] Rationalizations may occur in connection with nation-wide social planning just as in the classical instance of the horseman who, on being thrown from his steed, declared that he was "simply dismounting." This difficulty, though not completely obviated, is significantly reduced in cases of organized group action since the circumstance of organized action customarily demands explicit (though not always "true") statements of goal and procedure. Furthermore, it is easily possible to exaggerate this difficulty since in many, if indeed not in most, cases, the observer's own experience and knowledge of the situation enables him to arrive at a solution. Ultimately, the final test is this: does the juxtaposition of the overt action, our general knowledge of the actor(s) and the specific situation and the inferred or avowed purpose "make sense," is there between these, as Weber puts it, a "verständliche Sinnzusammenhang?" If the analyst self-consciously subjects these elements to such probing, conclu-

---

10. This introduces the problem of "chance," which will be treated in another connection. It should be realized that the aim of an action and the circumstances that actually ensue may coincide without the latter being a consequence of the action. Moreover, the longer the interval of time between the action and the circumstances in view, the greater the probability (in the absence of contrary evidence) that these circumstances have happened "by chance." Lastly, if this interval is greatly extended, the probability that the desired circumstances will occur fortuitously may increase until virtually the point of certainty. This reasoning is perhaps applicable to the case of governmental action "restoring prosperity." Compare V. Pareto, *Traité de sociologie générale* (Paris: Payot, 1917), II, par. 1977.

sions about purpose can have evidential value. The evidence available will vary, and the probable error of the imputation of purpose will likewise vary.

Although these methodological difficulties are not discussed further in this paper, an effort has been made to take them into account in the substantive analysis.

Last, a frequent source of misunderstanding will be eliminated at the outset if it is realized that the factors involved in unanticipated consequences are—precisely—factors, and that none of these serves by itself to explain any concrete case.

Sources of Unanticipated Consequences

The most obvious limitation to a correct anticipation of consequences of action is provided by the existing state of knowledge. The extent of this limitation can be best appreciated by assuming the simplest case where the lack of adequate knowledge is the *sole* barrier to a correct anticipation.[11] Obviously, a very large number of concrete reasons for inadequate knowledge may be found, but it is also possible to summarize several classes of factors that are most important.

Ignorance

The first class derives from the type of knowledge—usually, perhaps exclusively—attained in the sciences of human behavior. The social scientist usually finds stochastic, not functional relationships.[12] This is to

11. Most discussions of unanticipated consequences limit the explanation of unanticipated consequences to this one factor of ignorance. Such a view either reduces itself to a sheer tautology or exaggerates the role of only one of many factors. In the first instance, the argument runs in this fashion: "if we had only known enough, we could have anticipated the consequences which, as it happens, were unforeseen." The evident fallacy in this *post mortem* argument rests in the word "enough" which is implicitly taken to mean "enough knowledge to foresee" the consequences of our action. It is then no difficult matter to uphold the contention. This viewpoint is basic to several schools of educational theory, just as it was to Comte's dictum, *savoir pour prevoir, prevoir pour pouvoir*. This intellectualist stand has gained credence partly because of its implicit optimism and because of the indubitable fact that sheer ignorance does actually account for the occurrence of some unforeseen consequences *in some cases*.

12. Cf. A. A. Tschuprow, *Grundbegriffe und Grundprobleme der Korrelationstheorie* (Leipzig: B. G. Teubner, 1925), pp. 20 ff., where he introduces the term "stochastic." It is apparent that stochastic associations are obtained because we have not ascertained, or having ascertained, have not controlled the other variables in the situation that influence the final result.

say, in the study of human behavior, there is found a set of different values of one variable associated with each value of the other variable(s), or in less formal language, the set of consequences of any repeated act is not constant but there is a range of possible consequences, *any one of which may follow the act in a given case.* In some instances, we have sufficient knowledge of the limits of the range of possible consequences, and even adequate knowledge for ascertaining the statistical (empirical) probabilities of the various possible consequences, but it is impossible to predict with certainty the results in any particular case. Our classifications of acts and situations never involve completely homogeneous categories nor even categories whose approximate degree of homogeneity is sufficient for the prediction of particular events.[13] We have here the paradox that whereas past experiences are the guide to our expectations on the assumption that certain past, present and future acts are sufficiently alike to be grouped in the same category, these experiences are in fact different. To the extent that these differences are pertinent to the outcome of the action and appropriate corrections for these differences are not adopted, the actual results will differ from the expected. As Poincaré has put it, ". . . small differences in the initial conditions produce very great ones in the final phenomena. . . . Prediction becomes impossible, and we have the fortuitous phenomenon."[14]

However, deviations from the usual consequences of an act can be anticipated by the actor who recognizes in the given situation some differences from previous similar situations. But insofar as these differences can themselves not be subsumed under general rules, the direction and extent of these deviations cannot be anticipated.[15] It is clear, then, that the partial knowledge in the light of which action is commonly carried on permits a varying range of unexpected outcomes of conduct.

Although we do not know the *amount* of knowledge necessary for foreknowledge, one may say in general that consequences are fortuitous when an exact knowledge of many details and facts (as distinct from general principles) is needed for even a highly approximate prediction.

13. A classification into completely homogeneous categories would, of course, lead to functional associations and would permit successful prediction, but the aspects of social action which are of practical importance are too varied and numerous to permit such homogeneous classification.

14. Henri Poincaré, *Calcul des probabilités* (Paris, 1912), p. 2.

15. The actor's awareness of his ignorance and its implications is perhaps most acute in the type of conduct which Thomas and Znaniecki attribute to the wish for "new experience." This is the case where unforeseen consequences actually constitute the purpose of action, but there is always the tacit assumption that the consequences will be desirable.

In other words, "chance consequences" are those occasioned by the interplay of forces and circumstances that are so numerous and complex that prediction of them is quite beyond our reach. This area of consequences should perhaps be distinguished from that of "ignorance," since it is related not to the knowledge actually in hand but to knowledge that can conceivably be obtained.[16]

The importance of ignorance as a factor is enhanced by the fact that the exigencies of practical life frequently compel us to act with some confidence even though it is manifest that the information on which we base our action is not complete. We usually act, as Knight has properly observed, not on the basis of scientific knowledge, but on that of opinion and estimate. Thus, situations that demand (or what is for our purposes tantamount to the same thing, that appear to the actor to demand) immediate action of some sort, will usually involve ignorance of certain aspects of the situation and will the more likely bring about unexpected results.

Even when immediate action is not required there is the *economic* problem of distributing our fundamental resources, time and energy. Time and energy are scarce means and economic behavior is concerned with the rational allocation of these means among alternative wants, only one of which is the anticipation of consequences of action.[17] An economy of social engineers is no more practicable than an economy of laundrymen. It is the fault of the extreme antinoetic activists who promote the idea of action above all else to exaggerate this limit and to claim (in effect) that practically no resources be devoted to the acquisition of knowledge. On the other hand, the grain of truth in the anti-intellectualist position is that there are decided economic limits to the advisability of not acting until uncertainty is eliminated, and also psychological limits since, after the manner of Hamlet, excessive "forethought" of this kind precludes any action at all.

16. Cf. Keynes, *op. cit.*, p. 295. This distinction corresponds to that made by Keynes between "subjective chance" (broadly, ignorance) and "objective chance" (where even additional wide knowledge of general principles would not suffice to foresee the consequences of a particular act). Much the same distinction appears in the works of Poincaré and Venn, among others.
17. Cf. Knight, *op. cit.*, p. 348. The reasoning is also applicable to cases where the occupation of certain individuals (e.g., social engineers and scientists) is devoted solely to such efforts, since then it is a correlative question of the distribution of the resources of society. Furthermore, there is the practical problem of the communicability of knowledge so obtained, since it may be very complex; the effort to assimilate such knowledge leads back to the same problem of distribution of resources [and costs of information].

Error

A second major factor in unexpected consequences of conduct, perhaps as pervasive as ignorance, is error. Error may intrude itself, of course, in any phase of purposive action: we may err in our appraisal of the present situation, in our inference from this to the future objective situation, in our selection of a course of action, or finally in the execution of the action chosen. A common fallacy is frequently involved in the too-ready assumption that actions which have in the past led to the desired outcome will continue to do so. This assumption is often fixed in the mechanism of habit and there often finds pragmatic justification. But precisely because habit is a mode of activity that has previously led to the attainment of certain ends, it tends to become automatic and undeliberative through continued repetition so that the actor fails to recognize that procedures which have been successful *in certain circumstances* need not be so *under any and all conditions.*[18] Just as rigidities in social organization often balk and block the satisfaction of new wants, so rigidities in individual behavior block the satisfaction of old wants in a changing social environment.

Error may also be involved in instances where the actor attends to only one or some of the pertinent aspects of the situation that influence the outcome of the action. This may range from the case of simple neglect (lack of thoroughness in examining the situation) to pathological obsession where there is a determined refusal or inability to consider certain elements of the problem. This last type has been extensively dealt with in the psychiatric literature. In cases of wish-fulfilment, emotional involvements lead to a distortion of the objective situation and of the probable future course of events; action predicated upon imaginary conditions must have unexpected consequences.

Imperious Immediacy of Interest

A third general type of factor, the "imperious immediacy of interest," refers to instances where the actor's paramount concern with the foreseen

18. Similar fallacies in the field of thought have been variously designated as "the philosophical fallacy" (Dewey), the "principle of limits" (Sorokin, Bridgman) and, with a somewhat different emphasis, "the fallacy of misplaced concreteness" (Whitehead). [For an application of the general idea to the case of organizations, see pp. 74–75 of this volume and "Bureaucratic Structure and Personality," in Merton, *Social Theory and Social Structure* (New York: The Free Press, 1968, enlarged ed.), pp. 249–60.]

immediate consequences excludes consideration of further or other consequences of the same act. The most prominent elements in such immediacy of interest range from physiological needs to basic cultural values. Thus, Vico's imaginative example of the "origin of the family," which derived from the practice of men carrying their mates into caves to satisfy their sex drive out of the sight of God, might serve as a somewhat fantastic illustration of the first. Another kind of example is provided by that doctrine of classical economics in which the individual endeavoring to employ his capital where most profitable to him and thus tending to render the annual revenue of society as great as possible is, in the words of Adam Smith, led "by an invisible hand to promote an end which was no part of his intention."

However, after the acute analysis by Max Weber, it goes without saying that action motivated by interest is not antithetical to an intensive investigation of the conditions and means of successful action. On the contrary, it would seem that interest, if it is to be satisfied, requires objective analysis of situation and instrumentality, as is assumed to be characteristic of "economic man." The irony is that intense interest often tends to preclude such analysis precisely because strong concern with the satisfaction of the immediate interest is a psychological generator of emotional bias, with consequent lopsidedness or failure to engage in the required calculations. It is as much a fallacious assumption to hold that interested action necessarily entails a rational calculation of the elements in the situation[19] as to deny rationality any and all influence over such conduct. Moreover, action in which the element of immediacy of interest is involved may be rational in terms of the values basic to that interest but irrational in terms of the life organization of the individual. Rational, in the sense that it is an action which may be expected to lead to the attainment of the specific goal; irrational, in the sense that it may defeat the pursuit or attainment of other values not, at the moment, paramount but which nonetheless form an integral part of the individual's scale of values. Thus, *precisely because a particular action is not carried out in a psychological or social vacuum, its effects will ramify into other spheres of value and interest.* For example, the practice of birth control for "economic reasons" influences the age-composition and size of sibships with profound consequences of a psychological and social character and, in larger aggregations, of course, affects the rate of population growth.

19. The assumption is tenable only in a normative sense. Obviously such calculation, within the limits specified in our previous discussion, *should* be made if the probability of satisfying the interest is to be at a maximum. The error lies in confusing norm with actuality.

Basic Values

Superficially similar to the factor of immediacy of interest, but differing from it in a significant theoretical sense, is that of basic values. This refers to instances where further consequences of action are not considered because of the felt necessity of the action enjoined by fundamental values. The classical analysis is Weber's study of the Protestant Ethic and the spirit of capitalism. He has properly generalized this case, saying that active asceticism paradoxically leads to its own decline through the accumulation of wealth and possessions entailed by the conjunction of intense productive activity and decreased consumption.

The process contributes much to the dynamic of social and cultural change, as has been recognized with varying degrees of cogency by Hegel, Marx, Wundt, and many others. The empirical observation is incontestable: activities oriented toward certain values release processes that so react as to change the very scale of values which precipitated them. This process can come about when a system of basic values enjoins certain *specific* actions, and adherents are concerned not with the objective consequences of these actions but with the subjective satisfaction of duty well performed. Or, action in accordance with a dominant set of values tends to be focused upon that particular value-area. But with the complex interaction that constitutes society, action ramifies. Its consequences are not restricted to the specific area in which they are intended to center and occur in interrelated fields explicitly ignored at the time of action. Yet it is because these fields are in fact interrelated that the further consequences in adjacent areas tend to *react* upon the fundamental value-system. It is this usually unlooked-for reaction that constitutes a most important element in the process of secularization, of the transformation or breakdown of basic value-systems. Here is the essential paradox of social action—the "realization" of values may lead to their renunciation. We may paraphrase Goethe and speak of "Die Kraft, die stets das Gute will, und stets das Böse schafft."

Self-Defeating Predictions

There is one other circumstance, peculiar to human conduct, that stands in the way of successful social prediction and planning. Public predictions of future social developments are frequently not sustained precisely because the prediction has become a new element in the concrete situation, thus tending to change the initial course of developments. This is not true of prediction in fields that do not pertain to human conduct. Thus, the prediction of the return of Halley's comet does not in any way influence the orbit of that comet; but, to take a concrete social example, Marx's prediction of the progressive concentration of wealth and increasing misery of the masses did influence the very process predicted. For at least one of the consequences of socialist preaching in the nineteenth century was the spread of organization of labor, which, made conscious of its unfavorable bargaining position in cases of individual contract, organized to enjoy the advantages of collective bargaining, thus slowing up, if not eliminating, the developments that Marx had predicted.[20]

Thus, to the extent that the predictions of social scientists are made public and action proceeds with full cognizance of these predictions, the "other-things-being-equal" condition tacitly assumed in all forecasting is not fulfilled. Other things will not be equal just because the scientist has introduced a new "other thing"—his prediction.[21] This contingency may often account for social movements developing in utterly unanticipated directions, and it hence assumes considerable importance for social planning.

The foregoing discussion represents no more than the briefest exposition of the major elements involved in one fundamental social process. It would take us too far afield, and certainly beyond the compass of this paper, to examine exhaustively the implications of this analysis for social prediction, control, and planning. We may maintain, however, even at this preliminary juncture, that no blanket statement categorically affirming or denying the practical feasibility of *all* social planning is warranted. Before we may indulge in such generalizations, we must examine and classify the *types* of social action and organization with reference to the elements here discussed and then refer our generalizations to these essentially different types. If the present analysis has served to set the problem, even in only its paramount aspects, and to direct attention toward the need for a systematic and objective study of the elements involved in the development of unanticipated consequences of purposive social action, the treatment of which has for much too long been consigned to the realm of theology and speculative philosophy, then it has achieved its avowed purpose.

20. Corrado Gini, *Prime linée di patologia economica* (Milan: A. Giuffrè, 1935), pp. 72–75. John Venn uses the picturesque term "suicidal prophecies" to refer to this process and properly observes that it represents a class of considerations which have been much neglected by the various sciences of human conduct. See his *Logic of Chance* (London, 1888), pp. 225–26.
21. [For the correlative process, see the paper, "The Self-Fulfilling Prophecy" first published a dozen years after this one, and reprinted in Merton, *op.cit.*, 1968, pp. 475–90.]

9

Social Knowledge
and Public Policy

Historical Preliminaries

COMMISSIONS—in the broad sense of a collegial body of persons charged by an authority with designated activity and purpose—have long been an element in governance. Perhaps the most famous and the most effective commissions have been the Royal Commissions of Inquiry in Britain, which came into their own in the nineteenth century as "favored instruments leading to major advances in social legislation, such as the Factory Acts."[1] And perhaps the most generous and surely the most notable tribute to the character and accomplishments of the royal commissions is found in these familiar words:

> The social statistics of Germany and the rest of Continental Western Europe are, by comparison with those of England, wretchedly compiled. But they raise the veil just enough to let us catch a glimpse of the Medusa head behind it. We should be appalled at the state of things at home, if, as in England, our governments and parliaments appointed periodically commissions of inquiry into economic conditions; if these commissions were armed with the same plenary powers to get at the

Reprinted with permission from Mirra Komarovsky, ed., *Sociology and Public Policy: The Case of Presidential Commissions* (New York & Amsterdam: Elsevier, 1975).

The writing of this chapter was supported in part by a grant from NSF to the Center for Advanced Study in the Behavioral Sciences and in part by an NSF grant to the Program in the Sociology of Science, Columbia University. Helpful criticism was given me by Robert Dahl, Cynthia Epstein, and fellow Fellows at the Center: Graham Allison, Robert Darnton, Irving Janis, Martin Krieger, James March, Arnold Thackray, Edward Tufte, and Harriet Zuckerman.

1. Charles J. Hanser, *Guide to Decision: The Royal Commission* (Totowa, N.J.: The Bedminster Press, 1965); see also Harvey C. Mansfield. "Commissions, Government." *International Encyclopedia of the Social Sciences* (New York: Macmillan Co. and The Free Press, 1968), Vol. III, pp. 13–18.

truth; if it was possible to find for this purpose men as competent, as free from partisanship and respect of persons as are the English factory-inspectors, her medical reporters on public health, her commissioners of inquiry into the exploitation of women and children, into housing and food.[2]

This unstinted praise of the composite integrity, truth-telling, and capability for social investigation of commissions of inquiry appears in Karl Marx's *Capital*—in the celebrated preface to the first German edition. Evidently, the founder of modern Communism, the prime contributor to an early sociology of knowledge, and the pitiless critic of bourgeois society, thought it possible for men "to get at the truth" about social and economic conditions obtaining in that society and to record part of that truth in the form of "social statistics." As Marx explains, the truth was being searched out by royal commissions and others at work in the service of that dispossessing instrument of the ruling class, the bourgeois English State.

Not, of course, that Marx ascribed the integrity of these critical investigators to lofty motives. What is more interesting and more nearly in accord with his general doctrine is that he saw this institutionalized pattern of truth-telling as itself socially induced. It is identified as an expression of class interest in a particular historical context. The American Civil War had "sounded the tocsin for the European working class," just as the American War of Independence had done for the European middle class.

In England the progress of social disintegration is palpable.... Apart from higher motives, therefore, their own most important interests dictate to the classes that are for the nonce the ruling ones, the removal of all legally removable hindrances to the free development of the working-class.[3]

In short extension and paraphrase, Marx is, in effect, advancing the interesting idea that under certain conditions, self-interest, collective and individual, can make for truth-seeking and truth-telling just as, under other conditions, it can and notoriously does make for deliberate lying as well as unwitting deception, both of self and of others.

Commissions of inquiry have not been confined to England. From the beginning, Presidents of the United States have also had their commissions. Washington began with a commission to look into the Whiskey Re-

2. Karl Marx, *Capital* (Moscow: Foreign Languages Publishing House, 1959), Vol. I, p. 9.
3. *Ibid.*, p. 9.

bellion; ever since, Presidents or Congress have instituted one or another kind of commission, at first sporadically and then, in this century, at a greatly quickened pace.[4]

Mansfield has instructively proposed three conjoint criteria for sorting out types of commissions. First, in terms of duration, ranging from "bodies convened *ad hoc* to deal with a specific situation" to those permanently established. Second, in terms of their varying overt purposes, among them arbitration, regulation, operation of public enterprise, advice-giving, investigation of a major historical event (e.g., assassination of a president), and, of most immediate interest to us, commissions charged with the study, planning, and recommendation of public policy. Third, commissions can be considered in terms of their "latent functions, notably, bargaining [among disparate interests], public education, delay, patronage, appeasement, frustration of opposition to current policy, and rubber-stamping."[5] From the standpoint of structure, as Mansfield also notes, the commission form is admirably suited to serving a representational function, by providing for voice in its deliberations to a diversity of distinct and often opposed interests. The extent to which commissions have actually been made up of members strongly opposed in interests and values is quite another, politically significant matter.

This paper deals with a quartet of American Presidential Commissions, appointed for a limited time within the last years for the announced purpose of formulating plans and recommendations for public policy bearing on four distinct sets of socially defined problems in American society. Beyond their announced purpose, as we will see, these *ad hoc* commissions had a variety of latent functions and dysfunctions for diverse

4. No exhaustive counts exist, but it is said that Hoover appointed about 60 commissions and advisory boards during the first year-and-a-half of his presidency; Franklin Roosevelt, more than a hundred in his first two terms; Truman, a mere twenty or so during nearly eight years in office with Eisenhower proceeding at a Truman-like rate during his first term. As we might suppose, the commissions were of varying scope, duration, intensity and consequence but little is known about them through systematic investigation. The estimates of numbers are assembled by Alan L. Dean, "*Ad hoc* Commissions for Policy Formulation?" in Thomas E. Cronin and Sanford D. Greenberg, *The Presidential Advisory System* (New York: Harper & Row, 1969), pp. 101–116. However, the estimates evidently include a good many advisory bodies other than Presidential Commissions, strictly so-called. Popper has compiled a list of these in recent administrations: 11 for Truman, 4 for Eisenhower, 4 for Kennedy, 20 for Johnson, and 5 during Nixon's first two years in office. Frank Popper, *The President's Commissions* (New York: Twentieth Century Fund, 1970), Appendix 1.

5. Mansfield, *op. cit.*, pp. 13–14; see also Daniel Bell, "Government by Commission," *The Public Interest* No. 3 (Spring 1966), pp. 3–9.

social formations. To meet its charge, each of the commissions arranged for research projects and programs, consisting principally of social research of one description or another.

This practice of social investigation is in direct continuity with what had become a tradition for the British Royal Commissions. These regularly provided for inquiry that would "make for a definitive determination of controversial facts and [so it was said] for a trustworthy judgment on a complex public problem."[6] In turn, the Royal Commissions had an emerging tradition of empirical social investigation to draw upon. As Stephen Cole has shown, the statistical and social science associations in Britain that had come into being before the middle of the nineteenth century were largely activated by concern with social reform. With increasing regularity, they fostered or actually mounted empirical investigations of crime, poverty, prison life, factory conditions, and kindred problems. Even before applied social research became more fully institutionalized in the form of providing for a trained full-time paid staff, such research was being carried forward by a variety of (sometimes voluntary and often self-taught) investigators: actuaries, army officers, businessmen, civil servants, clergy, physicians, and, tellingly enough, early in the period, only a sprinkling of professors. Cole goes on to observe that the great bulk of these *de facto* social researchers were in professions that provided them with access to statistics institutionally generated by hospitals, philanthropic organizations, the courts, prisons, and various other agencies of government.[7]

6. Hanser, *op. cit.*, p. 220. It should be emphasized that Royal Commissions and Presidential Commissions have only a cousinly resemblance, structural and functional. For contrasts as well as similarities between them, see Popper, *op. cit.*, pp. 50–54.
7. Stephen Cole, "Continuity and Institutionalization in Science: A Case Study of a Failure," in Anthony Oberschall, ed., *The Establishment of Empirical Sociology: Studies in Continuity, Discontinuity, and Institutionalization* (New York: Harper & Row, 1972), pp. 73–129; see also the paper by David Elesh, pp. 31–72 in the same volume, "The Manchester Statistical Society: A Case Study of Discontinuity in the History of Empirical Social Research." As Paul F. Lazarsfeld reports in his Foreword to that volume, these and other historical and sociological studies of the early period of empirical social research derived from a graduate seminar at Columbia which he and I gave jointly in the 1960s. But what Lazarsfeld characteristically does not go on to report, his conviction about the potential significance of this subject ran deeper than mine. It was he, rather than I, who instituted a series of investigation of one or another aspect of the subject by Oberschall, Bernard-Pierre Lécuyer, Terry Clark, Suzanne Shad, and others. For two other instructive inquiries, see Nathan Glazer, "The Rise of Social Research in Europe," in Daniel Lerner, ed., *The Human Meaning of the Social Sciences* (New York:

Marx was thus merely being observant when he praised the social statistics and other social data being compiled before his eyes in England. It was these data that would enable him and others to reconstruct crucial aspects of the English social reality, to get "upon the right track for the discovery of the natural laws of its movement." It was for reasons such as this, writes Marx, that "I have given so large a space in this volume to the history, the details, and the results of English factory legislation."[8] And an abundant space it is. No one has yet inventoried the whole of the official reports by commissions of inquiry, factory inspectors, public health inspectors, and the other Blue books, which Marx drew upon in the *Capital*. But his careful citation practices, more meticulous than those adopted by most of us pedantically inclined academicians, afford a clue to the scale on which he made use of the researches stemming from these sources. A small sampling of his liberal citations is enough to serve us here.

The 60,000-word monograph entitled "Machinery and Modern Industry," which constitutes the celebrated Chapter XV of the first volume of *Capital*, contains some 240 footnotes. About a sixth of these are given over to developing points in the text or to demolishing *bêtes noires* (such as Malthus and Ure); the remaining 200 or so are used to indicate the sources of the evidence and ideas that he introduces in the text.[9] The arithmetic of these citations summarizes the copious extent to which Marx drew upon the investigations recorded in those reports of parliamentary

---

Meridian, 1959); and Philip Abrams. *The Origins of British Sociology, 1834–1914* (Chicago: University of Chicago Press, 1968).

8. *Capital*, pp. 9–10.

9. His collaborator and editor was altogether aware of the diverse functions served by Marx's use of quotations and citations, principally in footnotes. In his Preface to the English edition of *Capital*, Engels itemizes these functions, hinting at Marx's interest in what was to become the sociology of knowledge and at his deep commitment to the rights of private intellectual property. Following the style of Marx's own practice, one should fully quote Engels's observations to this effect: "A word respecting the author's [this being, of course, Marx's] method of quoting may not be out of place. In the majority of cases, the quotations serve, in the usual way, as documentary evidence in support of assertions made in the text. But in many instances, passages from economic writers are quoted [n.b.] in order to indicate when, where, and by whom a certain proposition was for the first time clearly enunciated. This is done in cases where the proposition quoted is of importance as being a more or less adequate expression of the conditions of social production and exchange prevalent at the time, and quite irrespective of Marx's recognition, or otherwise, of its general validity. These quotations, therefore, supplement the text by a running commentary taken from the history of the science." *Capital*, *op. cit.*, p. 5. Marx's practice generalized would greatly extend the current use of citation analysis for tracing genealogies of ideas.

commissions and other official bodies, known from their dark blue paper covers simply as the Blue books.

Of the approximately 200 citations of all sources, including ancient, medieval, and modern writings, 138 (or more than two-thirds) were to Blue books of one sort or another: 70 referred to Reports of Inspectors of Factories; 45 to Reports of Royal Commissions; 11 to Reports on Public Health; 9 to the Census (primarily of 1861); and 3 to other Blue books (such as the Statistical Abstract of the United Kingdom).[10]

Never before, surely, and probably never since, have the reports of governmental commissions been put to more consequential use.

These few scattered observations on commissions of inquiry in an earlier time and another place are perhaps enough to provide perspective and distance as we examine the use of research by commissions in our own time and place. The observations remind us of the following:

1. Governmental commissions of inquiry are themselves a historically evolving social form for discovering or systematically describing selected aspects of a social reality.

2. Commissions are both producers and consumers of social research.

3. The institutionalization of procedures for undertaking research on behalf of commissions engaged in recommending public policy began some time ago and is presumably still in process.

4. The use of that research need not be confined to its utilization by the commissions inaugurating it.

5. As the historic case of Marx emphatically proclaims, the results of authentic social inquiry can be utilized by people sharply differing in political commitments from those of the commissioners or the investigators.

10. England, taken by Marx as "the classic ground" of "the capitalist mode of production" and therefore "used as the chief illustration in the development of my theoretical ideas," provided other sources of data about its social reality that could be utilized both by critics and defenders of that society. On a half-dozen occasions in the same Chapter XV, Marx drew upon papers and publications by the emerging societies for the advancement of social science. He notes in a "Report of the Social Science Congress, at Edinburgh," October 1863, that "In England women are still occasionally used instead of horses for hauling canal boats." (*Capital*, p. 394). Similarly, he refers the reader to "the speech of N. W. Senior at the seventh annual congress of The National Association for the Promotion of Social Science," 1863, which deals with "the very advantageous results of combining gymnastics . . . with compulsory education for factory children and pauper scholars." Marx thus provides eloquent testimony to the ways in which authentic social reportage and social science can provide subversive evidence about the social reality, a secular version of the doctrine that the truth shall help to make you free.

Four Presidential Commissions
of Inquiry

As a sociological understanding of social institutions and collective behavior would lead us to expect, national commissions of inquiry are created by the President or the Congress or both in response to their reading of the social and political temper of the times, current and prospective. Commissions are usually established in Times of Trouble. (That is, one supposes, why there have been so many of them.) The public troubles are sometimes acute, sometimes chronic, and the one kind is frequently superimposed upon the other.

Acute troubles often lead to the formation of commissions to investigate the unique event (as in the case of the Warren Commission). Occasionally, specific events trigger the appointment of a commission to inquire into the enduring problem dramatized by the particular event, as with the National Commission on Violence, instituted in the grim hours after the assassination of Robert Kennedy. When commissions are created to formulate new policies on chronic problems even though there has been no sudden, visible change in actual circumstances, this presumably represents a threshold phenomenon of accumulated troubles (as, for example, with the belated public and institutionalized response to the deterioration of our human and natural environments). Finally, it seems to have been a combination of chronic and acute troubles that led to a commission to examine the socially defined problems of obscenity and pornography, when that age-old continuity of interest in matters judged unchaste was coupled with a conspicuous growth in scale. In all cases, it appears, national commissions are in origin and outcome deeply affected by both actual and perceived climates of public opinion and action.

Whatever their historical origins and their manifest and latent functions, commissions of inquiry are—commissions of inquiry. That is, they are publicly committed to make a search or investigation directed toward uncovering germane information and knowledge; they are, in short, institutionally committed to research. The research may turn out to be sound or specious, wide-ranging or parochial, deeply significant or inconsequential, inspired or pedestrian. But the public commitment being what it is, research there must be. Yet, surprisingly little seems to be systematically known about the ways in which research programs and projects are brought into being by these policy-formulating commissions, how the research is conducted, and most of all, how the results of research relate to the formulation of proposed policy.

It is therefore a rare opportunity to have circumstantial accounts about these matters prepared by sociologists who have played a major role as members of recent Presidential Commissions: Otto Larsen, Lloyd Ohlin, James Short, and Charles Westoff.

Their accounts, written from the perspective of participant-observers, exhibit an interesting symmetry, with a methodological aesthetic all their own. In their role as *participants*, the authors deal principally with sociology *in* the Commissions (i.e., with the use, nonuse, misuse, or pointed absence of sociological knowledge). In their role as *observers*, they deal principally with the sociology *of* the Commissions (i.e., with their origins, structure, dynamics, evolution, and aftermath). That division of the subject provides a ready format for my own observations on what they have reported to us.

The Sociology of Commissions

It appears throughout that the variety of social processes, structures, and functions observed in the behavior of the commissions can be related to the variegated problematics of the sociological discipline itself.

Plainly, the commissions exhibit the operation of power structures in the production, use, abuse, and nonuse of sociological knowledge. Composed of representatives of various (not, of course, all) constituencies, each commission was bound to experience some degree of internal conflict. From the standpoint of structural analysis, this observed pattern of conflicting perspectives among the commissioners is no mere happenstance. For in a society structurally differentiated as ours is, conflict *must* result from the groundplan of a commission that authentically represents people located in diverse strata and sectors of the social structure, with their distinctive and often incompatible interests and values.

To the extent that the membership of a commission represents the spectrum of major interest groups, this would seem to guarantee a structurally induced strain toward initial conflict and subsequent compromise or continuing stasis. Apparently, it is with commissions as it is with food: the effort to cater to all tastes makes for blandness. Yet, on more than one occasion, through a sociologically interesting process of trade-offs, the commissions came out with strong collective recommendations that individual commissioners were surprised to find themselves endorsing. Some of the recommendations of the Commission on Pornography, for example, were in this special sense spicy rather than bland.

In part, this results from small group processes in continuing or intermittent operation. Processes of polarization, conflict, and mutual accommodation were at work under varying, sometimes ill-understood conditions. But the principal group-induced pressures were generally for compromise. As one observer summed this up, there is apparently nothing like an implacable deadline, as distinct from an ideology, to move a *task-oriented group* toward consensus. In seeming paradox, the commission format providing for minority reports may make for wider consensus than would otherwise obtain. Knowing that the minority can openly dissent, the visible majority may be more agreeable to modifying their position to avoid a scatter of contested recommendations. In turn, the minority report as an avenue of public expression becomes a structural device for avoiding the stasis condition of a hung jury.

Another aspect of the behavior of commissions can be identified from the perspective of a structural sociology focused on organizational constraints and processes of differentiation in groups. One constraint derives from what some of us take to be important variables in group structure and individual membership in groups. These variables can be described as the *expected* (not only the actual) *duration* of a group or organization and the expected duration of the occupancy of a status within a group or organization. Groups differ significantly in this aspect; many have an expectation of indefinitely continuing duration; some have an assigned life span. Memberships in groups differ in the same way: some, as in the case of tenure positions, carry the expectation of indefinitely continued duration; others, as in the case of statutory limits on the holding of office, have a known pending termination. Such socially shared expectations of duration greatly affect the orientations and behavior of members of the group, the workings of authority and power within it, and not least, the social environment in which the group finds its place.[11]

Consequences of the two types of expected duration are repeatedly implied and sometimes expressed in the description of the commissions' behavior. Thus, Lloyd Ohlin notes of the Commission on Law Enforcement and Administration of Justice that "The Chairman, Executive Director . . . and many staff members were acutely conscious of the fact that a Presidential Commission has no enduring life and must rely on other established institutions and agencies to implement the results of its

11. I have long argued that this is so. See R. K. Merton, *Social Theory and Social Structure* (New York: The Free Press, 1968, enlarged edition), pp. 365–66; and three of us found it to be so in a study of "planned communities" conducted some time ago: R. K. Merton, P. S. West, and M. Jahoda. *Patterns of Social Life: Explorations in the Sociology of Housing* (Columbia University Bureau of Applied Social Research, 1948, mimeo.).

work." This sense of the short, more-or-less unhappy life of the Crime Commission, this sense of its expected brief duration, led to a strategy of attempting to involve states and localities in a continuing program. In another connection, Otto Larsen reports that "confidentiality began to disappear completely toward the end of the [Pornography] Commission's life as drafts of reports were circulated," a result that might follow as much from the stage of the work as from the short, remaining duration of the Commission. James Short refers to the substantial effects on the Commission on Violence of Lyndon Johnson's lame-duck incumbency, requiring the research to be carried out and a progress report to be submitted before a new President was inaugurated. The lame-duck pattern is the classical archetype in which the known duration of occupancy of a status operates to affect policy formation and to make for the decreasingly effective exercise of authority.

Still, if it produces a body of research, the socially consequential life of a commission can extend well beyond its existence as a formally convened body. Long after it has been discharged with presidential (or parliamentary) thanks, the inquiries mounted by the commission can remain consequential, as we noted in the case of the Blue books that the British Museum made available to Marx, and as we can note now, for example, in the case of the Crime Surveys made available by the Crime Commission.

Another important constraint upon the utilization of social research by the commissions was the discordant pacing of empirical social inquiry and of decision making. The participant-observers uniformly note that the comparatively slow pace of much social research was out of phase with the urgent timetable by which national commissions work. In this regard, nothing much seems to have happened since at least the 1940s (and, one suspects, long before) when a study of policy-oriented research reported that "the tempo of policy decisions and action is often more rapid than the tempo of applied [social] research."[12]

This temporal disjuncture between research and policy formation sets severe limits upon the possibility that the commissions could draw upon social research for many pertinent problems emerging in their delibera-

12. R. K. Merton, "The Role of Applied Social Science in the Formation of Policy," *Philosophy of Science* 16 (July 1949), pp. 161–81, reprinted in Merton, *The Sociology of Science* (Chicago: University of Chicago Press, 1973), pp. 70–98, the quotation on p. 88. Since the organizers of this symposium have asked me to draw upon my longstanding (and, I like to think, evolving) perspectives on the connections of social knowledge to the formation of policy, I shall continue to refer to my writings throughout this paper.

tions. All this raises several questions about current practices involving the relations of commissions to research programs. As we have seen, *ad hoc* commissions of inquiry are usually appointed in Times of Trouble. They are to seek out the sources of one or another of the currently defined troubles and to tell us what to do about them. For both manifest and latent political functions, commissions tend to be instituted in politically expedient or politically inevitable times. This should lead us to ask whether those are the best times for investigating (not necessarily recommending modes of coping with) the problems in and of our society. It may be, as Edward Tufte has suggested, that the most effective political strategy is to exploit short-run pressures for long-run improvement; the so-called crisis may provide the only chance that will present itself. But although a crisis mentality about a chronic problem provides a politically feasible basis for establishing a Presidential Commission, the same sense of urgency works against doing the careful and considerable research needed then and there. As we learn from the testimony of participant-observers of the research brought into being by an urgent commission, much of it must be piecemeal or otherwise limited by the exigencies of the public business to be transacted.[13]

Since considerations of political expediency—implying political feasibility—are bound to affect the timing of governmentally established commissions, there is reason to argue for the more frequent creation of national commissions by other institutions and associations in the society. Foundations do occasionally provide for such commissions and for programs of research, extending over a period of years, oriented to their requirements. Beyond that, there would seem to be a place for learned societies and professional associations in the social sciences to develop proto-commissions of their own, which would define public issues from their theoretical stance and provide for associated programs of ongoing research oriented to those issues.

I take up only one more item in this incomplete inventory of observations on the sociology *of* commissions which also links up with the role of sociology *in* commissions. Problems in both the microsociology and the macrosociology of scientific knowledge are implicated in the work of commissions.

The participant-observer accounts are rich in detail about the divergence of moral and intellectual perspectives of commissioners and staff

13. James March has suggested that research does not always lag behind the knowledge and information requirements for formulating public policy. Research on the genetic effects of radiation, for example, apparently outruns the pace of policy formation which takes that research into account.

drawn from different sectors of the society. Consider only the most conspicuous case: the interaction of the lawyers and the social scientists in trying to shape a knowledge-related set of recommendations.

As has always been the case since it became our capital, Washington is densely populated by lawyers. Presidential Commissions are generally even more so. The Commission on Population is a rare exception. Of its 24 members, only a handful were lawyers, and these gained entry chiefly as members of Congress. The other three Commissions more nearly reverted to type. Although the Commission on Pornography also had an unusual number of sociologists—Otto Larsen, Joseph Klapper, Marvin Wolfgang—a third of the 18 Commissioners had law degrees. Fifteen of the 19 members of the Crime Commission were lawyers, as were 15 of 25 of the Task Force Directors of the Commission on Violence.

The preponderance of lawyers should come as no surprise: Max Weber had long since remarked on the special availability of lawyers for every arm and function of government. Nor is this merely a result of their lawyerly skills. It also has to do with the structure of their occupation. Far more than, say, physicians or even academics, lawyers can readily detach themselves from their ordinary jobs to take on extraordinary assignments for longer or shorter periods. This eventuates in a tradition of public service within the guild of lawyers that becomes self-perpetuating, in no little part because it is at times greatly rewarded. Lawyers also experience something of role-congruence between the requirements of their occupational roles and the demands of such *ad hoc* units as national commissions.

However, it is not the contrast in detachability of lawyers and academic social scientists, but the differences between them in styles of work, intellectual perspectives, and, specifically, conceptions of evidence that must be noted here. The modes and loci of diverse and sometimes rival professional expertise are themes running throughout the reported behavior of staffs and commissioners. These are perhaps best crystallized in the preference of lawyers for use of sworn eyewitness depositions, and the contrasting preference of sociologists for interviews, social surveys, and other quantitative evidence. These preferences are sustained by a considerable professional apparatus and a not inconsiderable academic apparatus by which the evidence is evaluated. The reward system of science and learning, centered in peer review, reinforces the differential attachment to types of evidence.

An applied sociology of knowledge must take note of such structurally patterned differences in conceptions of what constitutes adequate evidence. It would be of no little interest to mount a research program that systematically compares the scope, relevance, validity, and utility of data that, collected in diverse ways, bear upon the same public issues considered by public commissions and other groups. A next step into the sociology of knowledge would require us to compare the evaluation of these methods by experts drawn from disciplines that have institutionalized distinct methods of gathering and distinct criteria for assessing evidence on the subject.

At any rate, we can earmark the micro- and macrosociology of knowledge as another basic context for that investigation of the behavior and consequences of commissions which constitute the sociology *of* commissions.

Sociology in the Commissions

Sociology *in* the Commissions—that is, the actual role of sociological knowledge in the work and the conclusions of the Commissions—provides its own microcosm of the discipline at large.

To the extent that the commissions drew upon sociological knowledge at all, that knowledge was evidently diverse in both general perspective and specific findings. None of the commissions, or their research staffs, confined itself to a single comprehensive and tight-knit paradigm that defined the range of problems and subjects to be investigated in detail and determined how they were to be investigated. Instead, the Commissions, or at least their staffs, were tacitly committed to a pluralistic theoretical orientation. In some degree, this pluralism was probably built into the structure of the Commissions through the appointment of members representing different constituencies with differing cognitive as well as value perspectives. But, in any case, it is apparent that the sociological research for the Commissions did not uniformly or primarily derive from a single theoretical orientation—not functional analysis, symbolic interactionism, or social ecology; not structural analysis, exchange theory, or social dramaturgy. Indeed, not even Marxism.

This kind of theoretical pluralism only reproduces in microcosm the actual and the cognitively appropriate state of the field of sociology itself —and of the behavioral sciences generally. Even to signal the grounds for this statement of preference for a pluralistic rather than monistic structure of sociological knowledge would require us to move far beyond our immediate subject.[14] But it can be argued that differing theoretical

14. For a statement of these grounds, see R. K. Merton, "Structural Analysis in Sociology," in Peter M. Blau, ed., *Approaches to the Study of Social Structure* (New York: The Free Press, 1975). [Reprinted as Chapter 7 of this volume.]

orientations are useful for an understanding of differing kinds and aspects of sociological and social problems. Whatever the claim to the contrary by advocates of this or that theoretical stance, actual inquiry (and conspicuously so for inquiry aimed at dealing with concrete social problems) requires the use of complementary paradigms and conceptions.

I am aware that, in some quarters, "eclecticism" is an abusive epithet used to designate a shabby, incoherent collection of *ad hoc* interpretations of aspects of reality. The modifier, "mere," is unthinkingly introduced with such frequency that expression becomes telescoped into the composite—"mereclecticism." Yet, the controlled and systematic use of complementary ideas drawn from differing orientations in the form of what can be called "disciplined eclecticism" characterizes much of social science today.[15]

Just as the aggregate of sociologists doing the research for the Commissions adopted a plurality of theoretical orientations, so they also adopted a plurality of methods of inquiry. I shall not dwell here upon the circumstance that different sorts of questions, derived from theoretical constructions or stimulated by empirical observations, call for different sorts of data acquired through diverse methods. It is perhaps enough to note that the plurality of methods employed by the Commissions' research staffs for the collection of data and for their ordering and interpretation also provides a replica of what is the collective practice in sociology at large.

The research program of the Commissions provides a miniaturized replica of our discipline in still another aspect: the basic presuppositions involved in the imagery of the sociological knowledge thought necessary for formulating grounded recommendations for action. So far as one can tell, that imagery of the ambiguous relations between knowledge and the formulation of policy entertained by the researchers was not dominated by any of the various, at times simple-minded, positivisms: neither the scriptural version, "the truth shall make you free," nor the Comtean version, "science provides foresight and foresight provides the power to act" (which somehow sounds rather more compelling when translated back into French). Nor did they adopt the positivistic slogan set out by Friedrich Engels in his nominally antipositivistic tract, *Anti-Dühring*, when he wrote of the "leap of mankind from the realm of necessity into the realm of freedom."

15. Joseph J. Schwab has dealt with the "arts of Eclectic" in a series of evocative papers, among them: "The Practical Arts of Eclectic," *The School Review* 79 (August 1971), pp. 493–542; "What Do Scientists Do?" *Behavioral Sciences* 5 (January 1960), pp. 1–27.

There are, in the reports on the Commissions, few signs of such assumptions. Instead, there are more than hints of concern with the basic and more modest question: Which forms of sociological and behavioral science knowledge made which kinds of difference to the recommendations adopted or rejected by the Commissions? In place of reveling in an orgy of unconnected facts, the researchers focused on strategic concepts and facts that sometimes affected the formulation of policy. Consider only these examples in Westoff's report on the Population Commission:

Item: One study concluded that "population growth played a minor role in the short run" as demographic time is counted (thirty to fifty years) when "compared with technological, economic, and governmental policy considerations." Why did this broad factual conclusion prove to be strategic? Because it seemed to have an almost direct policy implication calling for specified contingency analysis and indicating that, for the time being, population control is a comparatively "indirect and ineffectual policy lever for environmental problems."

Item: Another strategic finding was the demonstration that "if women averaged 2.0 rather than 2.1 births [and, of course, anyone can see that this minute average difference could scarcely matter], zero population growth could be achieved near the same level and in almost the same time with immigration continued at the current volume. Although not a world-shaking scientific discovery, this bit of demographic intelligence was extremely important in the debate over immigration policy and was influential in defeating a recommendation to reduce the volume."

These examples should not be taken to imply that there is typically a direct passage from sociological knowledge to social policy.[16] But to say more here about the gap between the two would only be redundant in view of Paul Lazarsfeld's close and informed analysis of the problem.

This brings us to a series of more detailed observations on the place

16. In his review of this chapter, Irving Janis noted that the uses of pluralism could be formulated at this point in terms of the quality of the planning and decision-making process: the extensiveness of search; openness to a variety of kinds of relevant information concerning the consequences of proposed solutions; the range of possible solutions considered; alertness to contingencies that require special planning; and other factors. For an extensive analysis of decision-making in these terms, see Irving Janis and Leon Mann, Decision Making: A Psychological Analysis of Conflict, Choice and Commitment (New York: The Free Press, 1977).

of theoretical sociology in the research of the Commissions. These observations will take us somewhat afield to consider theoretical issues in the discipline at large that are implied in that research.

Theoretical Orientations

A Focus on Consequences

Throughout much of their work, we are told, the Commissions focused on consequences: the consequences of existing practices and structures and the consequences anticipated from putting proposed policies into effect.

> *Charles Westoff*: The Population Commission "focused on the economic, environmental, political, and social consequences of population growth."
>
> *Otto Larsen*: The "fateful" decision was taken in the Congressional Act establishing the Commission on Pornography to adopt the position that "knowledge about *the effects* [i.e., the consequences] of exposure to explicit sex material [might be] relevant for making decisions about the forms of control that a society might exercise over obscenity."
>
> *Lloyd Ohlin*: "The most important inputs of social science knowledge to the Crime Commission were probably in the documentation of the harmful consequences of existing practices and policies and suggestions of a variety of persuasive theories and justifications for pursuing an alternative course."

The focus on consequences should come as no surprise to sociologists aware of the pervasive character of functional analysis in sociology, not least those sociologists busily engaged in repudiating that mode of analysis. After all, research bearing upon general policies dealing with socially defined problems in and of society *must* focus on multiple functional and dysfunctional consequences of alternative courses of action for a variety of social units (e.g., varied groups, strata, regions) and the more comprehensive social systems. This is the case even though no scientific calculus of course exists for assessing, choosing among, and integrating such diverse consequences.

The four Commissions can be thought of as having played out a scenario composed of tacit and explicit theoretical orientations calling for them to examine the probable outcomes of alternative policies. What produced and maintained the reported conflicts in the Commissions were principally the differences of interests, values, and ideologies affecting the weights to be assigned to selected consequences. So far as policy-oriented research is concerned, the critical conflict of interests and values centers on the question:

Which evidence of which consequences for which social systems, strata, and groups should be taken into account in the research?

In all of the Commissions, the inescapable decision to select some, rather than other, expected consequences for investigation was basic to both the research program and the evolving rationale for alternative policies. To take only one instance, in the Population Commission it was this kind of value-charged, perspective-bound decision that divided the subgroup advocating the "unwanted fertility" perspective from the subgroup advocating the "ecological perspective."

Such conflicts highlight the untenable character of that long-forgotten positivism which, these days, is being revived by a small army of critics who promiscuously attribute caricatured versions of it to sociologists engaged in the empirical investigation of human problems in society. The research staffs of the Commissions evidently did not adopt the easygoing assumption that the sociological truth shall itself make it easy to choose among various courses of social action. Apart from much else, what makes such choices fundamentally underivable from sociological knowledge is the incommensurability of consequences that are in the interest of some sectors of the society and are dysfunctional for others. It is this basic feature of comprehensive decisions, most marked in a highly differentiated society, that leads to their inescapably acquiring a political character.

Thus, the overview of Presidential Commissions in action teaches us once again that when it comes to the formulation of public policy, one of the enduring problems facing sociologists is that of clarifying and working out some way of analyzing "the aggregate of humanly relevant consequences." That problem has long been on the agenda of a certain kind of functional and structural analysis.

What Harold Lasswell presciently, and in a sense prematurely, described as "the policy sciences" in the 1940s, referred chiefly to *social* research that is oriented to public and private policy.[17] Lasswell recog-

17. Daniel Lerner and Harold D. Lasswell, eds., *The Policy Sciences* (Stanford: Stanford University Press, 1951) provides an early summary of the Lasswellian perspective; Lasswell provides a more recent statement in *Pre-View of Policy*

nized that almost the entire spectrum of science could be drawn upon for investigations bearing upon the formation of policy, but he centered on the subset of the social sciences. Since his pioneering formulations, it has become possible to identify more of the distinctive contributions that social science can make to the formation of policy. Among these, I single out the sociological perspective that deals with latent social problems rather than with the manifest problem defined for investigation by the institutional powers that be.

Latent Social Problems

By latent social problems, I mean those unwanted social conditions that are at odds with some of the (often declared) values and interests of groups and strata in the society but are not generally recognized as being so. Sociologists do not impose their values upon others when they undertake to supply knowledge about latent problems that makes them generally manifest. Thus, when demographers working for the Commission on Population, for example, try to identify the social, economic, and cultural consequences of various rates of population growth, they in effect call the advocates of differing population policies to account for the results of putting one or another policy into practice. The demonstrated consequences of uncontrolled birth rates, for example, can then be seen as the aggregated result of people acting in accord with some of their values to produce outcomes that conflict with some of their other values.

This kind of latent social problem constitutes an important special case of the generic pattern of the unanticipated consequences of (individual or collective) social action.[18] Total commitments to values of every

Sciences (New York: Elsevier, 1971). For most recent formulations of the field, see James F. Reynolds, "Policy Sciences: A Conceptual and Methodological Analysis," *Policy Science* 6 (1975), pp. 1–27; Laurence H. Tribe, "Policy Science: Analysis or Ideology?" *Philosophy and Public Affairs*, No. 2 (Fall, 1972), pp. 66–110; and Wehezkel Droer, *Design for Policy Sciences* (New York: Elsevier, 1971).

18. The interest in unintended and unrecognized outcomes of social action has a long, discontinuous history from at least the time of Machiavelli, with contributions by such scholars as Vico, Adam Smith, Marx, Wundt, and to approach our own time, Pareto. The problematics is sketched out in R. K. Merton, "The Unanticipated Consequences of Purposive Social Action," *American Sociological Review* 1 (1936), pp. 894–904 [Reprinted as chap. 8 of this volume]; is renewed and developed in the special case of "The Self-Fulfilling Prophecy," *The Antioch Review*, (Summer 1948), pp. 193–210; is linked up with concepts of "Manifest and Latent Functions" in *Social Theory and Social Structure, op. cit.*,

kind—whether these be the value set on rapid economic expansion ("growth"), or rapid technological advance, or rule-free communities or the value set on that full expression of self in which anything goes (analyzed by Lionel Trilling in the notion of "authenticity")—have cumulative consequences that, if not counteracted, in due course undercut the originating values themselves.

This sociological perspective turns up repeatedly in the research programs of the several Commissions. The same perspective is inherent in the newly popular intellectual and social movement known as technology assessment. In effect, technology assessment focuses on the latent consequences of actual or proposed technological developments. It is designed to search out previously unknown or unconsidered social, ecological, and other humanly relevant consequences of existing or proposed technological complexes.[19]

The implications of all this are significant for an evolving theory of policy-oriented social research because the emphasis upon discovering latent consequences of existing or contemplated arrangements, institutional or technological, puts the current sociological accent on the subjective component of social action in its appropriate context.

The Hazards of Subjectivism

The idea of the subjective component in human action has a long history in sociology and had an even longer history before we sociologists arrived on the historical scene. It is an idea, moreover, that has been formulated in various traditions of sociological thought: in the notion of *Verstehen* (roughly: intuitive understanding) advanced by Max Weber (and many others influenced by him), Robert MacIver's "dynamic assessment," Florian Znaniecki's "humanistic coefficient," Talcott Parsons's "voluntaristic theory of action," and Schutz's "phenomenological perspective." The idea was succinctly formulated by W. I. Thomas in what is probably the single most consequential sentence ever put in print by an American sociologist:

1968 (originally published in 1949), and is brought to bear on "latent social problems" in *ibid.*, pp. 104 ff. and in R. K. Merton and R. A. Nisbet, eds., *Contemporary Social Problems* (New York: Harcourt Brace Jovanovich, 1976, Fourth Edition), pp. 11–13.
19. A recent penetrating paper by one of the chief architects of a basic report on technology assessment can also serve as a root reference to the rapidly growing library on the subject: Laurence H. Tribe, "Technology Assessment and the Fourth Discontinuity: The Limits of Instrumental Rationality," *Southern California Law Review* 46 (June 1973), pp. 617–660.

If men define situations as real, they are real in their consequences.[20]

Now, it is one thing to maintain, with Weber, Thomas, and the other giants of sociology, that to understand human action requires us to attend systematically to its subjective component: what people perceive, feel, believe, and want. But it is quite another thing to exaggerate this sound idea by maintaining that action is *nothing but* subjective. That extravagance leads to sociological Berkeleyanism (the allusion being, of course, to the English champion of philosophical idealism, not to an American geographic or academic place). Such total subjectivism conceives of social reality as consisting *only* in social definitions, perceptions, labels, beliefs, assumptions, or ideas, as expressed, for example, in full generality by the criminological theorist, Richard Quinney, when he writes that "We have no reason to believe in the objective existence of anything."[21] A basic idea is distorted into error and a great injustice is visited upon W. I. Thomas whenever his theorem is thus exaggerated.

Exaggeration of a seminal truth produces its own brand of error. Total subjectivism, which maintains that only social definitions of the situation (or other subjective equivalents) determine the character of human action and its consequences, in effect manages to transform the Thomas Theorem into this fallacious maxim:

If men do *not* define situations as real, they are not real in their consequences.

When the sufficient is thus transformed into the necessary, sociological error replaces sociological insight. Total subjectivism leads us astray by failing to provide a theoretical place for *systematic* concern with objective constraints upon human action. Those social, demographic, economic, technological, ecological, and other constraints are not always caught

20. What we may call the Thomas Theorem appears just once in the corpus of W. I. Thomas's writings: on page 572 of the book he wrote with Dorothy Swaine (Thomas) Thomas entitled *The Child in America* (New York: Knopf, 1928). I ascribe the theorem to W. I. Thomas alone rather than to the Thomases jointly not because of his gender or great seniority but only because Dorothy Thomas has confirmed for me what many have supposed: that the sentence and the paragraph in which it is encased were written by him. There is thus nothing in this attribution that smacks of "the Matthew Effect," which in cases of collaboration between scholars of decidedly unequal reputation has us ascribe all credit to the prominent scholar and little or none to the other collaborator(s). On the Matthew effect, see Merton, *op. cit.*, 1973, Chapter 20.

21. Richard Quinney, *The Social Reality of Crime* (Boston: Little, Brown, 1970), p. 4.

up in social definitions. To ignore those constraints is mistakenly to imply that they do not significantly affect both the choices people make and the personal and social consequences of those choices. It is to pave the road to Utopianism with bad assumptions. For, in the pithy phrasing by the sociologist Arthur Stinchcombe, which tempers the subjective emphasis of W .I. Thomas with the objective emphasis of Karl Marx, "People define situations, but do not define them as they please."[22]

The theoretical hazard of total subjectivism did not first turn up in exaggerations of the recent labeling perspective on deviant behavior.[23] It was potentially there in any voluntaristic paradigm of action and was skirted by Parsons a quarter-century ago. Then, as now, the position taken on total subjectivism seemed to me fundamental to sociological theorizing:

> When Mr. Parsons notes that the "social situation" must be analyzed with respect to "the various types of significance of situational facts to the actor," there is need for further strict clarification. Does this mean that sociology takes into account *only* those aspects of the objective situation to which the acting individual [or group] is oriented (cognitively, affectively, or through goal-definitions)? Does it imply that observable aspects of the situation of which the acting individual [or

22. Audible in Stinchcombe's aphorism is the echo of Marx's famous second paragraph of *The Eighteenth Brumaire of Louis Bonaparte*: "Men make their own history but they do not make it just as they please." As Marx goes on to explain: "They do not make it under circumstances chosen by themselves, but under circumstances found, given and transmitted from the past." Arthur L. Stinchcombe, "Merton's Theory of Social Structure," in Lewis A. Coser, ed., *The Idea of Social Structure* (New York: Harcourt Brace Jovanovich, 1975), pp. 11–33, quoted at pp. 15–16; on the sociological significance of the same passage from Marx, see Rose Laub Coser, "The Complexity of Roles as a Seedbed of Individual Autonomy," *ibid.*, pp. 239 ff.

23. As is often the case with the fate of ideas in the course of their diffusion, it is not so much in the work of the principal initiators of the labeling perspective as in that of their epigoni that extreme subjectivism appears. The seminal works include: Edwin M. Lemert, *Human Deviance, Social Problems and Social Control* (Englewood Cliffs, N.J.: Prentice-Hall, 1967); Howard S. Becker, *The Outsiders* (New York: The Free Press, 1973, Second Edition); Kai T. Erikson, "Notes on the Sociology of Deviance," *Social Problems* 9 (1962), pp. 307–14 and *Wayward Puritans* (New York: John Wiley, 1966); J. I. Kitsuse, "Societal Reaction to Deviant Behavior," *Social Problems* 9 (1962), pp. 247–56; A. V. Cicourel, *The Social Organization of Juvenile Justice* (New York: John Wiley, 1968). For a thoroughgoing critical review, see Edwin M. Schur, *Labeling Deviant Behavior: Its Sociological Implications* (New York: Harper & Row, 1971); Nanette J. Davis, "Labeling Theory in Deviance Research: A Critique and Reconsideration," *The Sociological Quarterly* 13 (Fall 1972), pp. 447–74.

group] is *wholly unaware* are at once eliminated from the realm of facts pertinent for the sociologist? If so, one must register dissent ... it is all the more important to clarify this formulation, else one might suppose that he [Parsons] advocates a basically idealistic or subjectivistic approach to sociological theories, in which *only* those aspects of the situation somehow taken into account by individuals are considered pertinent to the sociological analysis.[24]

To understand social life, we must indeed take account of how people perceive and define situations. But sociological theory can provide an adequate place for such perceptions without falling into the fallacy of total subjectivism. As formulated in the concept of the self-fulfilling prophecy,[25] for example, social definitions common in groups and collectivities *make up an important dynamic part of the social environment* in which anticipations help to create the anticipated social reality. Thus, when schoolteachers decide that children from certain ethnic or economic origins are apt to be substandard *and treat them accordingly*, they help bring about the retarded learning which they had anticipated. Subjective definitions of the situation therefore matter, and can matter greatly. But they do not alone matter.

To correct the imbalance that comes with total subjectivism and to restore the objective components of social situations to their indispensable place, we plainly need this counterpart to the Thomas Theorem:

And if men do *not* define real situations as real, they are nevertheless real in their consequences.

The paired theorems[26] serve as a continuing reminder of a truth that the sociologist must acknowledge (despite the idiomatic expression to the contrary): In society, as in other domains, what you don't know (or don't notice) *can* hurt you.

Indeed, it is precisely what you do not know that will often hurt you most, since you cannot take appropriate measures against the unknown. Whether their causes were socially defined as real or not, tuberculosis and Asiatic cholera managed to decimate many populations before Robert

24. Robert K. Merton, "The Position of Sociological Theory," *American Sociological Review* 13 (April 1948), p. 167.
25. Robert K. Merton, "The Self-Fulfilling Prophecy," *The Antioch Review*, (Summer 1948), pp. 193–210, reprinted as Chapter 13 in Merton, *Social Theory and Social Structure, op. cit.*
26. As James March has pointed out on reading this proposed pairing, taken together they plainly imply the simpler theorem: real situations have consequences. But, of course, information is lost in the more general formulation.

Koch discovered their pathogenic agents and laid the basis for their control.

A major function of science, and not only of research directly oriented toward public policy, is to provide an improved understanding of socially induced situations that are *not* generally defined as real, simply because of (sometimes motivated) ignorance. The geneticist Joshua Lederberg has noted that it is ironic, but not surprising, that science comes to be penalized in the public estimation as the bearer of evil tidings about the dysfunctional consequences of economically or culturally preferred behaviors. Thus, as he recently observed, there may be

> some who wish we didn't know that radiation is mutagenic and carcinogenic. We could then use our atmosphere and other resources as sinks for our waste in that sphere, and get at least a short-term advantage of the economic utility of the procedures. Unfortunately, you cannot play those kinds of games with nature for very long. Those costs will be incurred to the extent that they are real . . . to the extent that there are actual health hazards . . . connected with them *whether you know about them or not.* Merely to be ignorant of them is simply to defer your recognition of them into the future—in no way to blunt . . . the actual impact.[27]

From the theoretical perspective being advanced here, it is of more than passing interest to learn of the emphasis on the interplay between subjective and objective aspects of the social reality found in the policy-oriented research conducted for the four Commissions, which they variously used or ignored in arriving at their recommendations. Whatever else requires change in the future programs of research for national commissions and other policy-formulating groups, such an orientation does not.

Coda

The accounts by participant-connoisseurs of the national Commissions advance the continuing effort to clarify the character and workings of policy-oriented sociological knowledge. They alert us to problems and prospects that we may not have previously considered. Among these are

27. Joshua Lederberg, in *A Tenth Anniversary Event: Remarks on the Tenth Anniversary of the National Institute of General Medical Sciences*, Washington: U.S. Department of Health, Education and Welfare Publication No. (NIH) 74–274, 1974, p. 16.

implications for concerted research programs that might be mounted by the national and international communities of sociologists.

All four observers report a common circumstance confronting the Commissions. In each sphere of inquiry, there was a conspicuously insufficient backlog of the needed social research. Some of the new research had to be produced under forced draft; much of the rest could not be carried through at all within the time available.

This condition of *ad hoc* research under urgent pressure need not continue to be the typical condition. As sociologists attuned to structural and functional alternatives, we might remember that there really are other public institutions besides governmental ones. Among these are the composites of professional association and learned society—the American Sociological Association, for example, and many another of like kind. Perhaps these organizations should take it upon themselves, separately or in concert, to initiate continuing research programs designed for use by functional equivalents of governmental commissions. Independent commissions centered upon social problems on the grand scale could be instituted—say, by the Social Science Research Council—without regard to the immediacies of political expediency. They, in turn, could generate terms of reference for programs of policy-oriented research in the particular sphere of problem, without the strong pressures of urgency that have typically limited work done directly for Congressional and Presidential Commissions.

In a word, it is not really necessary to wait upon invitations from the White House or Congress to undertake continuing programs of policy-focused research of the kinds required by governmental commissions. Independent action by the community of social scientists in this domain would give added meaning to the social role of social science in the last quarter of our difficult century.

10

The Canons
of the Anti-Sociologist

ONCE AGAIN the season of the anti-sociologists is upon us. The academic year has ended and professors are ready to turn from talking to writing. A self-selected few will dust off and publish yet again the litany that fiercely imprecates sociology and all its works. This year, the avowed conservative professor of political science, Russell Kirk, got in first. His version will serve to exhibit the curious admixture of illogic and sentiment that makes up the creed and canons of anti-sociology.

Some sociologists find these assaults tiresome. To me, they have the peculiar charm of testifying to the need for the very kind of sociological inquiry they caricature. For each jaded version reads as though it were written by a sociologist-*manqué*. Each purports to describe the behavior of sociologists, to explain that behavior and, even more ambitiously, to describe and explain the responses to it.

With practiced ease, for example, Mr. Kirk reviews the work of thousands of social scientists and promulgates the first canon that "the representative" specimen is an "empiricist of the positivist variety; emotionally, he is often a secular evangelist." Had Mr. Kirk allowed himself to profit from the introductory course in sociology he so deplores, he might have learned of the danger of creating out of his private impressions a stereotype of the aims and behavior of large numbers of people, all the while pretending to have caught hold of the representative reality. But amateur sociologizing has no place for disciplined inquiry. Rather, it assumes that statements become authoritative simply by being put into the black and white magic of print.

The second canon declares the absurdity and impiety of statistics

Reprinted by permission from *New York Times*, July 16, 1961, © 1961 by The New York Times Company. Reprinted from time to time, this piece nevertheless remains largely inaccessible. It is included here since much the same tired and misplaced attacks on sociology, as distinct from amply applicable and thoughtful criticism of it, continue to find periodic expression in the popular press.

dealing with the behavior of men in society. For nothing significant about human behavior can be counted. If it could be counted, it would be immoral to do so. Everyone knows that no good can come of it.

To support this canon, Mr. Kirk cites Carlyle, who knew little about the primitive statistical methods of his own day and nothing, obviously, about the mathematical bases of modern statistics. As further proof, he quotes the attack by the sociologist Pitirim A. Sorokin on "quantophrenia" or an uncritical devotion to faulty statistics. Unlike myself, Mr. Kirk has not had the benefit of having been Professor Sorokin's student, and so does not know, apparently, that Sorokin used vast arrays of social statistics in every one of his major works and, in "Social and Cultural Dynamics," states that "quantitative judgments . . . in verbal form" are inevitable in any substantial work of history.

No doubt it is more inviting to assume statistics of human behavior. The amateur sociologist will explain, for example, why it is that we have such high rates of mental illness in what Mr. Kirk feels free to describe as our age of "twentieth-century social disintegration." But while the amateur sociologist explains *why* this is so, the disciplined sociologist proceeds first to find out whether it really *is* so. Only through painstaking analysis of the statistics of mental illness—as in the work of Herbert Goldhamer and Andrew Marshall—do we find that we had best postpone our ready-to-hand explanations, if only because it now seems probable that the rate of confinement for mental illness is no higher today than it was during the past century.

Turning up like death and taxes, the third canon of the anti-sociologists declares the sociologists to be both perpetrators and victims of jargon. Here, the anti-sociologist knows himself to be on altogether safe ground, for just about everyone can be counted on to be "against jargon" in the same penetrating sense that President Coolidge's minister declared himself against sin.

Perhaps it is time to distinguish between jargon and that essential of all disciplined thought, technical language. Technical language is a more precise and condensed form of thought and communication than colloquial language. It is designed to fix definite meanings in which each word has ideally only one denotation and is deliberately deprived of connotations. Jargon, in contrast, is a muddled and wordy imitation of technical language.

The mere unfamiliarity or unesthetic quality of language is no criterion. Jargon and technical language sound alike to someone untrained in the discipline where the language is employed.

All this is only prologue to the pair of canons central to the anti-sociologists' creed. Briefly put, these hold, first, that sociological truths cannot be discovered, for there are no detectable uniformities in human behavior, since man is incorrigibly unpredictable. And second, that sociologists constitute a danger to society, for they provide the knowledge through which men can be molded to fit a new and obnoxious social order. I need not burlesque the logic of the anti-sociologists, for they have preceded me here. I need only review it.

It would seem clear that if there are no discoverable uniformities about man in society, there can be no sociological knowledge employed to regiment him. Should anti-sociologists admit that there are such uniformities, they can scarcely argue that these uniformities can be discovered by the defective sociology of today, with its inapplicable statistics, its tattered jargon, and its total misunderstanding of human nature.

Forced to acknowledge that there are discoverable uniformities in social life and that modern sociology, for all its limitations, discovers some of them, would they then propose to exorcise this knowledge for fear that it might be used to violate civilized values? On this last line of retreat, the anti-sociologists would join forces with the anti-intellectuals and totalitarian regimenters of thought they ostensibly combat. They would declare themselves guardians of us all, alone able to distinguish dangerous from undangerous knowledge.

The remaining canons of the anti-sociologists are transparently trivial. Criticism among sociologists, for example, is described by the anti-sociologists in the militant metaphors of "warring camps" and "internecine warfare." Perhaps they should pause before advocating monolithic agreement on intellectual issues. It would be a curious reading of the history of thought to suggest that the absence of disagreement testifies to a developing discipline.

As for the anti-sociologists' canon that gives them alone access to the recorded wisdom of the past—from Plato to Montesquieu and Burke—this need only be stated to refute itself.

Since the anti-sociologists impose their grotesque versions of the methods of sociological inquiry upon a public too busy to look for themselves, a few words should be said about those methods. Social scientists believe it no longer sufficient to describe the behavior, attitudes, values and social relations obtaining in a complex society simply on the basis of a large but scattered array of documents, both public and private, and on educated guesses about what people are thinking and feeling. Studies of the historical past, of course, have no alternative. But in the study of present-day societies, these procedures are giving away to systematic, though far from perfected, methods.

One such method is the "sample survey," which sounds out the practices and attitudes of a group selected as representative of the larger population from which they are drawn. This type of survey is now part of the intellectual landscape. However, the "opinion polls" in the popular press do not begin to reproduce the analytical uses to which such surveys are put by academic sociologists.

Furthermore, it is with this instrument as with the rest: the most devastating criticisms of its misuse have come, not from the anti-sociologists who know about it only through casual inspection, but from the professional sociologists who are prepared to study their sometimes disappointing experience with it. For they, at least the best of them, know that, whatever the worth of one or another tool of inquiry, it is the questions put into the inquiry that determine the significance of the results. If the questions are trivial, then the answers will be trivial.

For sociology as for most other scientific disciplines, the electronic computer has emerged as a new resource. Contrary to the imagery of the anti-sociologists, this machine is not the universal mind of our day. It must be told what to do. But, as with most technical creations, the computer has a capacity for deflecting men from the pursuit of purposes that genuinely matter. It tempts its tenders to cast all manner of raw data into its maw and wait for the thoroughly digested product that will itself be senseless if the thought of its managers is without sense. The potential victims, by their professional training, are best qualified to recognize and to counter this danger.

With or without the computer, today's sociology makes no attempt to substitute science for ethics and esthetics or to displace humanism with scientism. Every responsible sociologist, and there are not a few, knows that his knowledge is no substitute for humanistic thought.

The thinking humanist, for his part, recognizes that the social scientist who knows his business seeks only to provide an understanding of certain, not all, aspects of the behavior of men and the organization of human society. The intellectual gulf between humanist and social scientist has begun to be bridged. The late Gilbert Murray, critic and classical scholar, said that sociology is "destined to bear abundant and ever-increasing fruit." The political journalist Richard Rovere, has observed that "those of us who have been educated in the twentieth century habitually think in sociological terms, whether or not we have had any training in sociology."

After all this, it is only natural to ask: what is going on in sociology and what does it all amount to? It would be foolish to answer this question by staking out the boundaries of sociology, as though it were a piece of real estate. That is not the character of intellectual property. But we can, in this short space, at least hint at the answer.

In the large, sociology is engaged in finding out how man's behavior and fate are affected, if not minutely governed, by his place within particular kinds, and changing kinds, of social structure and of culture. This means that sociology moves across a wide, varied and, to the layman, often bewildering range of topics and problems.

In doing so, one of its principal functions is to subject popular beliefs about man and his works to responsible investigation. As I have implied, the sociologist asks about many of these beliefs, "Is it really so?" The popular assumption, for example, that the rate of social mobility in America has recently declined has been put in question by systematically assembled data.

The alleged breakdown of the American family, with obsequies read regularly over the remains by those who should know better, has been found to be specious; thorough analyses of data on divorce and death find American marriages remaining intact more often now than they once did. Or, to tackle one last widespread assumption, people who reject orthodox religious beliefs are not more apt to engage in crime than people who hold fast to such beliefs.

Some of the findings of sociology take a considerable time to enter the public domain. For more than a generation, sociologists have found that complex organizations of widely different kinds—economic, political, military, educational—exhibit the same tendencies. These tendencies make for the "bureaucratic man," who is shaped by organizationally induced pressures to conform to the rules even when this means that conformity gets in the way of doing the job effectively. How far this is inevitable remains to be seen, and inquiries are now under way to find out how these tendencies can be counteracted.

Basic to sociology is the premise that, in the course of social interaction, men create new conditions that were not part of their intent. Short-run rationality often produces long-run irrationality. Public health measures may go awry; financial incentives may lead to decline rather than an increase in production; intensified punishment may aggravate rather than curb crime. Growing recognition of this has become one of the sources of an enlarged use of sociological research in such fields as medicine and public health, social work, law, education, the ministry, architecture and city planning, business, organized labor and agriculture.

Yet it must be added, that sociologists, perhaps better than the anti-sociologists, know they are just beginning to acquire the knowledge needed to cope with the many social ills man has the inveterate capacity to contract.

We sociologists need to be saved from the anti-sociologists only in respect to the exaggerated claims they make for our prowess and accomplishments. It is they, not we, who say that "sociology is a power in the land." It is they, not we, who make the absurd claim that sociology has the power and the intent to turn men into robots and to construct a new technocratic order. The men and women at work in sociological inquiry have more modest and less sadistic hopes. Like their colleagues in other scholarly and scientific disciplines, they recognize that this "very new science of an ancient subject" has still a long way to go. And undisturbed by the cannonades of the anti-sociologists, they are methodically proceeding on their way.

Part 3

11

Discrimination
and the American Creed

A PRIMARY FUNCTION of sociologists is to search out the determinants and consequences of diverse forms of social behavior. To the extent that they succeed in fulfilling this role, they clarify options available to organized social actions in given situations and of the probable outcome of each. To this extent, there is no sharp distinction between pure research and applied research. Rather, the difference is one between research with direct implications for particular problems of social action and research that is remote from these problems.[1] Not infrequently, basic research that has succeeded only in clearing up previously confused concepts may have an immediate bearing upon the problems of society to a degree not approximated by applied research oriented exclusively to these problems. At least, this is the assumption underlying the present paper: the clarification of apparently unclear and confused concepts in the sphere of race and ethnic relations is a step necessarily prior to the devising of effective programs for reducing intergroup conflict and for promoting equitable access to economic and social opportunities.

In an effort toward such clarification, I shall consider first the place of the creed of equitable access to opportunity in American culture; second, the relations of this creed to the beliefs and practices of Americans; third, the diverse types of orientation toward discrimination *and* prejudice, considered jointly; fourth, the implications for organized action of recognizing these diverse types; and fifth, the expectable consequences of alternative lines of action in diverse social contexts.

Reprinted with permission from *Discrimination and National Welfare*, R. M. MacIver, ed. (New York: Harper & Brothers, 1948), pp. 99–126.

1. [Implications of this idea have been elucidated in a paper published 15 years after this one: R. K. Merton, "Basic Research and Potentials of Relevance," *American Behavioral Scientist* 6 (May, 1963), pp. 86–90.]

The American Creed: As Cultural Ideal,
Personal Belief, and Practice

Set forth in the Declaration of Independence, the preamble of the Constitution, and the Bill of Rights, the American creed has since often been misstated. This part of the cultural heritage does *not* include the patently false assertion that all human beings are created equal in capacity or endowment. It does *not* imply that an Einstein and a moron are equal in intellectual capacity or that Joe Louis and a small, frail Columbia professor (or a Mississippian Congressman) are equally endowed with brawny arms harboring muscles as strong as iron bands. It does *not* proclaim universal equality of innate intellectual or physical endowment.

Instead, the creed asserts the indefeasible principle of the human right to full equity—the right of equitable access to justice, freedom, and opportunity, irrespective of race or religion or ethnic origin. It proclaims further the universalist doctrine of the dignity of the individual, irrespective of the groups of which he is a part. It is a creed announcing full moral equities for all, not an absurd myth affirming the equality of intellectual and physical capacity of all people everywhere. And it goes on to say that although individuals differ in innate endowment, they do so as individuals, not by virtue of their group memberships.

Viewed sociologically, the creed is a set of values and precepts embedded in American culture to which Americans are expected to conform. It is a complex of affirmations, rooted in the historical past and ceremonially celebrated in the present, partly enacted in the laws of the land and partly not. Like all creeds, it is a profession of faith, a part of cultural tradition sanctified by the larger traditions of which it is a part.

It would be a mistaken sociological assertion, however, to suggest that the creed is a fixed and static cultural constant, unmodified in the course of time, just as it would be an error to imply that as an integral part of the culture, it evenly blankets all subcultures of the national society. It is indeed dynamic, subject to change and in turn promoting change in other spheres of culture and society. It is, moreover, unevenly distributed throughout the society, being institutionalized as an integral part of local culture in some regions of the society and rejected in others.

Nor does the creed exert the same measure of control over behavior in diverse times and places. Insofar as it is a "sacred" part of American culture, hallowed by tradition, it is largely immune to direct attack. But it may be honored simply in the breach. It is often evaded, and the evasions themselves become institutionalized, giving rise to what I have described as the "institutionalized evasion of institutional norms." Where the creed is at odds with local beliefs and practices, it may persist as an empty cultural form partly because it is so flexible. It need not prove overly obstructive to the social, psychological, and economic gains of individuals, because there are still so many avenues for conscientiously ignoring the creed in practice. When necessary for peace of mind and psychological equilibrium, individuals indoctrinated with the creed who find themselves deviating from its precepts may readily explain how their behavior accords with the spirit of the creed rather than with its sterile letter. Or the creed itself is re-interpreted. Only those of equal endowment should have equal access to opportunity, it is said, and a given race or ethnic group manifestly does not have the requisite capacity to be deserving of opportunity. To provide such opportunities for the inferior of mind would be only wasteful of national resources. The rationalizations are too numerous and too familiar to bear repetition. The essential point is that the creed, though invulnerable to direct attack in some regions of the society, is not binding on practice. Many individuals and groups in many areas of the society systematically deny through daily conduct what they periodically affirm on ceremonial or public occasions.

This gap between creed and conduct has received wide notice. Learned men and men in high public positions have repeatedly observed and deplore the disparity between ethos and behavior in the sphere of race and ethnic relations. In his magisterial volumes on the American Negro, for example, Gunnar Myrdal called this gulf between creed and conduct "an American dilemma," and centered his attention on the prospect of narrowing or closing the gap. President Truman's Committee on Civil Rights, in their report to the nation, and President Truman himself, in a message to Congress, have called public attention to this "serious gap between our ideals and some of our practices."

But valid as these observations may be, they tend so to simplify the relations between creed and conduct as to be seriously misleading both for social policy and for social science. All these high authorities notwithstanding, the problems of racial and ethnic inequities are not expressible as a discrepancy between high cultural principles and low social conduct. It is a relation not between two variables, official creed, and private practice, but between three: first, the cultural creed honored in cultural tradition and partly enacted into law; second, the beliefs and attitudes of individuals regarding the principles of the creed; and third, the actual practices of individuals with reference to it.[2]

2. [Some implications of this threefold distinction are elucidated in a paper published some 10 years later than this one: R. K. Merton, "Social Conformity, Deviation, and Opportunity-Structures," *American Sociological Review* 24 (April, 1959), pp. 177–189. They have been considerably extended by Rose Laub Coser,

Once we substitute these three variables of cultural ideal, belief, and actual practice for the customary distinction between the two variables of cultural ideals and actual practices, the entire formulation of the problem becomes changed. We escape from the virtuous but ineffectual impasse of deploring the alleged hypocrisy of many Americans into the more difficult but potentially effectual realm of analyzing the problem actually in hand.

To describe the problem and to proceed to its analysis, we must consider the official creed, individuals' beliefs and attitudes concerning the creed, and their actual behavior. Once stated, the distinctions are readily applicable. Individuals may *recognize* the creed as part of a cultural tradition, *without having any private conviction of its moral validity or its binding quality*. Thus, so far as the beliefs of individuals are concerned, we can identify two types: those who genuinely believe in the creed and those who do not (although some of these may, on public or ceremonial occasions, profess adherence to its principles). Similarly, with respect to actual practices: conduct may or may not conform to the creed. And further, this being the salient consideration: *conduct may or may not conform with individuals' own beliefs concerning the moral claims of all people to equal opportunity.*

Stated in formal sociological terms, this asserts that attitudes and overt behavior vary independently. *Prejudicial attitudes need not coincide with discriminatory behavior.* The implications of this statement can be drawn out in terms of a logical syntax whereby the variables are diversely combined, as can be seen in the following typology.

A TYPOLOGY OF ETHNIC PREJUDICE AND DISCRIMINATION

	Attitude Dimension:* Prejudice and Non-prejudice	Behavior Dimension:* Discrimination and Non-discrimination
Type I: Unprejudiced non-discriminator	+	+
Type II: Unprejudiced discriminator	+	−
Type III: Prejudiced non-discriminator	−	+
Type IV: Prejudiced discriminator	−	−

* Where (+) = conformity to the creed and (−) = deviation from the creed. For a brief note on the uses of paradigms such as this, see the appendix to this paper.

"Insulation from Observability and Types of Social Conformity," *American Sociological Review* 26 (February, 1961), pp. 28–39, and "Complexity of Roles as a Seedbed of Individual Autonomy," in Lewis A. Coser, ed., *The Idea of Social Structure* (New York: Harcourt Brace Jovanovich, 1975), pp. 237–63, esp. at pp. 252–59.]

By exploring the interrelations between prejudice and discrimination, we can identify four major types in terms of their attitudes toward the creed and their behavior with respect to it. Each type is found in every region and social class, although in varying numbers. By examining each type, we shall be better prepared to understand their interdependence and the appropriate types of action for curbing ethnic discrimination. The folk-labels for each type are intended to aid in their prompt recognition.

Type I: The Unprejudiced Non-Discriminator or All-Weather Liberal

These are the racial and ethnic liberals who adhere to the creed in both belief and practice. They are neither prejudiced nor given to discrimination. Their orientation toward the creed is fixed and stable. Whatever the environing situation, they are likely to abide by their beliefs: hence, the *all-weather* liberal.

These make up the strategic group that *can* act as the spearhead for the progressive extension of the creed into effective practice. They represent the solid foundation both for the measure of ethnic equities that now exist and for the future enlargement of these equities. Integrated with the creed in both belief and practice, they would seem most motivated to influence others toward the same democratic outlook. They represent a reservoir of culturally legitimatized goodwill that can be channeled into an active program for extending belief in the creed and conformity with it in practice.

Most important, as we shall see presently, the all-weather liberals comprise the group that can so reward others for conforming with the creed as to transform deviants into conformers. They alone can provide the positive social environment for the other types who will no longer find it expedient or rewarding to retain their prejudices or discriminatory practices.

Although ethnic liberals are a *potential* force for the successive extension of the American creed, they do not fully realize this potentiality in actual fact, for a variety of reasons. Among the limitations on effective action are several fallacies to which the ethnic liberal seems peculiarly subject. First among these is the *fallacy of group soliloquies*. Ethnic liberals are busily engaged in talking to themselves. Repeatedly, the same groups of like-minded liberals seek each other out, hold periodic meetings in which they engage in mutual exhortation, and thus lend social and psychological support to one another. But however much these unwittingly self-selected audiences may reinforce the creed among themselves, they do not thus appreciably diffuse the creed in belief or practice to groups that depart from it in one respect or the other.

More, these group soliloquies in which there is typically wholehearted agreement among fellow-liberals tend to promote another fallacy limiting effective action. This is the *fallacy of unanimity*. Continued association with like-minded individuals tends to produce the illusion that a large measure of consensus has been achieved in the community at large. The unanimity regarding essential cultural axioms that obtains in these small groups provokes an overestimation of the strength of the movement and of its effective inroads upon the larger population, which does not necessarily share these creedal axioms. Many also mistake participation in the groups of like-minded individuals for effective action. Discussion accordingly takes the place of action. The reinforcement of the creed for oneself is mistaken for the extension of the creed among those outside the limited circle of ethnic liberals.

Arising from adherence to the creed is a third limitation upon effective action, the *fallacy of privatized solutions* to the problem. The ethnic liberal, precisely because he is at one with the American creed, may rest content with his own individual behavior and thus see no need to do anything about the problem at large. Since his own spiritual house is in order, he is not motivated by guilt or shame to work on a collective problem. The very freedom of the liberal from guilt thus prompts him to secede from any *collective* effort to set the national house in order. He essays a *private* solution to a *social* problem. He assumes that numerous individual adjustments will serve in place of a collective adjustment. His outlook, compounded of good moral philosophy but poor sociology, holds that each individual must put his own house in order and fails to recognize that privatized solutions cannot be effected for problems that are essentially social in nature. For clearly, if every person *were* motivated to abide by the American creed, the problem would not be likely to exist in the first place. It is only when a social environment is established by conformers to the creed that deviants can in due course be brought to modify their behavior in the direction of conformity. But this "environment" can be constituted only through collective effort and not through private adherence to a public creed. Thus we have the paradox that the clear conscience of many ethnic liberals may promote the very social situation that permits deviations from the creed to continue unchecked. Privatized liberalism invites social inaction. Accordingly, there appears the phenomenon of the inactive or passive liberal, himself at spiritual ease, neither prejudiced nor discriminatory, but in a measure tending to contribute to the persistence of prejudice and discrimination through his very inaction.[3]

The fallacies of group soliloquy, unanimity, and privatized solutions thus operate to make the potential strength of the ethnic liberals unrealized in practice.

It is only by first recognizing these limitations that the liberal can hope to overcome them. With some hesitancy, one may suggest initial policies for curbing the scope of the three fallacies. The fallacy of group soliloquies can be removed only by having ethnic liberals enter into organized groups not comprised merely of fellow liberals. This exacts a heavy price of liberals. It means that they face initial opposition and resistance rather than prompt consensus. It entails giving up the gratifications of consistent group support.

The fallacy of unanimity can in turn be reduced by coming to see that American society often provides large rewards for those who express their ethnic prejudice in discriminatory practice. Only if the balance of rewards, material and social, is modified will behavior be modified. Sheer exhortation and propaganda are not enough. Exhortation verges on a belief in magic if it is not supported by appropriate changes in the social environment to make conformity with the exhortation rewarding.

Finally, the fallacy of privatized solutions requires the militant liberal to motivate the passive liberal to collective effort, possibly by inducing in him a sense of guilt for his unwitting contribution to the problems of ethnic inequities through his own systematic inaction.

One may suggest a unifying theme for the ethnic liberal: goodwill is not enough to modify social reality. It is only when this goodwill is harnessed to psychological and social realities that it can be used to reach cultural objectives.

Type II: The Unprejudiced Discriminator or Fair-Weather Liberal

The fair-weather liberal is the man of expediency who, despite his own freedom from prejudice, supports discriminatory practices when it is the

3. [Owing to a recent paper by Paul F. Lazarsfeld in Lewis A. Coser, ed., *The Idea of Social Structure* (New York: Harcourt Brace Jovanovich, 1975), pp. 35–66, esp. at pp. 52–53, I am alerted to this "fallacy" being parallel to the "narcotizing dysfunction" of the mass media in which people conscientiously "mistake *knowing* about problems of the day for *doing* something about them." See Paul F. Lazarsfeld and R. K. Merton, "Mass Communication, Popular Taste and Organized Social Action," in Lyman Bryson, ed., *The Communication of Ideas* (New York: Harper & Row, 1948), pp. 95–118, esp. at pp. 105–106.]

easier or more profitable course. Expediency may take the form of holding his silence and thus implicitly acquiescing in expressions of eth-nic prejudice by others or in the practice of discrimination by others. This is the expediency of the timid: the liberal who hesitates to speak up against discrimination for fear he might lose esteem or be otherwise penalized by his prejudiced associates. Or his expediency may take the form of grasping at advantages in social and economic competition de-riving solely from the ethnic status of competitors. Thus the expediency of the self-assertive: the employer, himself not an anti-Semite or Negro-phobe, who refuses to hire Jewish or Negro workers because "it might hurt business"; the trade union leader who expediently advocates racial discrimination in order not to lose the support of powerful Negrophobes in his union.

In varying degrees, fair-weather liberals suffer from guilt and shame for departing from their own effective beliefs in the American creed. Each deviation through which they derive a limited reward from passively acquiescing in or actively supporting discrimination contributes cumu-latively to this fund of guilt. They are, therefore, peculiarly vulnerable to the efforts of the all-weather liberals who would help them bring con-duct into accord with beliefs, thus removing this source of guilt. They are the most amenable to cure, because basically they want to be cured. Theirs is a split conscience that motivates them to cooperate actively with people who will help remove the source of internal conflict. They thus represent the strategic group promising the largest returns for the least effort. Persistent reaffirmation of the creed will only intensify their conflict but a long regimen in a favorable social climate can be expected to transform fair-weather liberals into all-weather liberals.

Type III: The Prejudiced Non-Discriminator
or Fair-Weather Illiberal

The fair-weather illiberal is the reluctant conformist to the creed, the man of prejudice who does not believe in the creed but conforms to it in practice through fear of sanctions that might otherwise be visited upon him. You know him well: the prejudiced employer who discrimi-nates against racial or ethnic groups until a Fair Employment Practice Commission, able and willing to enforce the law, puts the fear of punish-ment into him; the trade-union leader, himself deeply prejudiced, who does away with Jim Crow in his union because the rank-and-file demands that it be done away with; the businessman who forgoes his own prejudices when he finds a profitable market among the very people he hates, fears, or despises; the timid bigot who will not express his prejudices when he is in the presence of powerful men who vigorously and effectively affirm their belief in the American creed.

It should be clear that the fair-weather illiberal is the precise counterpart of the fair-weather liberal. Both are men of expediency, to be sure, but expediency dictates different courses of behavior in the two cases. The timid bigot conforms to the creed only when there is danger or loss in deviations, just as the timid liberal deviates from the creed only when there is danger or loss in conforming. *Superficial similarity in behavior of the two in the same situation should not be permitted to cloak a basic difference in the meaning of this outwardly similar behavior*, a difference that is as important for social policy as it is for social science. Whereas the timid bigot is under strain when he conforms to the creed, the timid liberal is under strain when he deviates. For ethnic prejudice has deep roots in the character structure of the fair-weather bigot, and this will find overt expression unless there are powerful countervailing forces—institutional, legal, and interpersonal. He does not accept the moral legitimacy of the creed; he conforms because he must, and will cease to conform when the pressure is removed. The fair-weather liberal, on the other hand, is effectively committed to the creed and does not require strong institutional pressure to conform; continuing interpersonal relations with all-weather liberals may be sufficient.

This is one critical point at which the traditional formulation of the problem of ethnic discrimination as a departure from the creed can lead to serious errors of theory and practice. *Overt behavioral deviation (or conformity) may signify importantly different situations, depending upon the underlying motivations.* Knowing simply that ethnic discrimination is rife in a community does not therefore point to appropriate lines of social policy. It is necessary to know also the distribution of ethnic prejudices and basic motivations for these prejudices as well. Communities with the same amount of overt discrimination may represent vastly different types of problems, dependent on whether the population is comprised of a large nucleus of fair-weather liberals ready to abandon their discriminatory practices under slight interpersonal pressure or a large nucleus of fair-weather illiberals who will abandon discrimination only if major changes in the local institutional setting can be effected. Any statement of the problem as a gulf between creedal ideals and prevailing practice is thus seen to be overly simplified in the precise sense of masking this decisive difference between the type of discrimination exhibited by the fair-weather liberal and by the fair-weather illiberal.

That the gulf between ideal and practice does not adequately describe the nature of the ethnic problem will become more apparent as we turn to the fourth type in our inventory of prejudice and discrimination.

Type IV: The Prejudiced Discriminator or the All-Weather Illiberal

This type, too, is not unknown to you. He is the confirmed illiberal, the bigot pure and unashamed, the man of prejudice consistent in his departures from the American creed. In some measure, he is found everywhere in the land, though in varying numbers. He derives large social and psychological gains from his conviction that "any white man (including the village idiot) is 'better' than any nigger (including George Washington Carver)." He considers differential treatment of Negro and white not as "discrimination," in the sense of unfair treatment, but as "discriminating," in the sense of showing acute discernment. For him, it is as clear that one "ought" to accord a Negro and a white different treatment in a wide diversity of situations as it is clear to the population at large that one "ought" to accord a child and an adult different treatment in many situations.

This illustrates anew my reason for questioning the applicability of the usual formula of the American dilemma as a gap between lofty creed and low conduct. For the confirmed illiberal, ethnic discrimination does *not* represent a discrepancy between *his* ideals and *his* behavior. His ideals proclaim the right, even the duty, of discrimination. Accordingly, his behavior does not entail a sense of social deviation, with the resultant strains that this would involve. The ethnic illiberal is as much a conformist as the ethnic liberal. He is merely conforming to a different cultural and institutional pattern that is centered, not on the creed, but on a doctrine of essential inequality of status ascribed to those of diverse ethnic and racial origins. To overlook this is to overlook the well-known *fact* that our national culture is divided into a number of local subcultures that are not consistent among themselves in all respects. And again, to fail to take this fact of different subcultures into account is to open the door for all manner of errors of social policy in attempting to control the problems of racial and ethnic discrimination.

This view of the all-weather illiberal has one immediate implication with wide bearing upon social policies and sociological theory oriented toward the problem of discrimination. The extreme importance of the social surroundings of the confirmed illiberal at once becomes apparent.

For as these surroundings vary, so, in some measure, does the problem of the consistent illiberal. The illiberal, living in those cultural regions where the American creed is widely repudiated and is no effective part of the subculture, has his private ethnic attitudes and practices supported by the local mores, the local institutions, and the local power structure. The illiberal in cultural areas dominated by a large measure of adherence to the American creed is in a social environment where he is isolated and receives small social support for his beliefs and practices. In both instances, the *individual* is an illiberal, to be sure, but he represents two significantly different *sociological types*. In the first instance, he is a *social conformist*, with strong moral and institutional reinforcement, whereas in the second, he is a *social deviant*, lacking strong social corroboration. In the one case, his discrimination involves him in further integration with his network of social relations; in the other, it threatens to cut him off from sustaining interpersonal ties. In the first cultural context, personal change in his ethnic behavior involves alienating himself from people significant to him; in the second context, this change of personal outlook may mean fuller incorporation in groups significant to him. In the first situation, modification of his ethnic views requires him to take the path of greatest resistance whereas in the second, it may mean the path of least resistance. From all this, we may surmise that any social policy aimed at changing the behavior and perhaps the attitudes of the all-weather illiberal will have to take into systematic account the cultural and social structure of the area in which he lives.

Some Assumptions Underlying Social Policies for Reduction of Racial and Ethnic Discrimination

To diagnose the problem, it appears essential to recognize these several types of people and not to obscure their differences by general allusions to the "gulf between ideals and practice." Some of these people discriminate precisely because their local cultural ideals proclaim the duty of discrimination. Others discriminate only when they find it expedient to do so, just as still others fail to translate their prejudices into active discrimination when *this* proves expedient. It is the existence of these three types of people, in a society traditionally given over to the American creed, who constitute "the racial problem" or "the ethnic problem." Those who practice discrimination are *not* people of one kind. *And because they are not all of a piece, there must be diverse social therapies, each directed at a given type in a given social situation.*

Were it not for widespread social policies to the contrary, it would be unnecessary to emphasize that there is no single social policy that will be adequate for all these types in all social situations. So far as I know, sociological science has not yet evolved knowledge for application to this problem sufficient to merit great confidence in the results. But it has reached the point where it can suggest, with some assurance, that different social types in different social contexts require different social therapies if their behavior is to be changed. To diagnose these several types, there-fore, may not be an "academic" exercise, in the too frequent and dolorous sense of the word "academic." However scanty our knowledge, if action is to be taken, such diagnoses represent the first step toward pragmatic social therapy. The unprejudiced discriminators will respond differently from the prejudiced non-discriminators and they, in turn, differently from the prejudiced discriminators or all-weather illiberals. And each of these will respond according to the social composition of the groups and com-munity in which they are involved.

In setting forth my opinions on the strategy of dealing with ethnic and racial discrimination, I hope it is plain that I move far beyond the adequately accredited knowledge provided by sociology to this point. In 1948, neither the rigorous theory nor many needed data are at hand to "apply" sociological science to this massive problem of American society. But moving from the slight accumulation of sociological knowledge at my disposal, it may be possible to suggest some considerations that it seems wise to take into account. For at scattered points, our knowledge may be sufficient to detect probably erroneous assumptions, although it is not always adequate to set out probably sound assumptions.

It is sometimes assumed that discrimination and its frequent though not invariable adjunct, prejudice, are entirely the product of ignorance. To be sure, ignorance *may* support discrimination. The employer un-familiar with the findings of current anthropology and psychology, for example, may discriminate against Negroes on the ground of the honest and ignorant conviction that they are inherently less intelligent than whites. But, in general, there is no indication that ignorance is the major source of discrimination. The evidence at hand does not show that ethnic and racial discrimination is consistently less common among those boast-ing a college education than among the less well educated.[4]

To question the close connection between ignorance and discrimina-tion is to raise large implications for social policy. For if one assumes that ignorance and error are alone involved, obviously all that need be

4. [An obviously dated statement, somewhat misleading even at the time it was put forward.]

done by way of curbing prevalent discriminatory practices is to introduce a program of education concerning racial and ethnic matters, on a scale yet unimagined. Mass education and mass propaganda would at once become the sole indicated tools for action. But there are few who will accept the implications of this assumption that simple ignorance is a major or exclusive source of discrimination and will urge that formal education alone can turn the trick. If some seem to be saying this, it is, I suspect, because they are begging the question; they are using the phrase "education on racial and ethnic matters" in an equivocal sense to mean "eradication of racial and ethnic prejudices." But, of course, that is precisely the question at issue: what *are* the procedures most likely to eradicate prejudice and discrimination?

If the assumption of ignorance as the root source of discrimination is put to one side, then *we must be prepared to find that discrimination is in part sustained by a socialized reward system.* When a population is divided into subgroups, some of which are set apart as inferior, even the lowliest member of the ostensibly superior group derives psychic gains from this institutionalized superiority of status. This system of discrimination also supplies preferential access to opportunity for the more favored groups. The taboos erect high tariff walls restricting the importation of talent from the ethnic outgroups. But we need not assume that such psychic, social, and economic gains are *sufficient* to account for the persistence of ethnic discrimination in a society that has an ideal pattern proclaiming free and equal access to opportunity. To be sure, these rewards supply motivation for discrimination. But people favor practices that give them differential advantages only so long as there is a moral code that defines these advantages as "fair." In the absence of this code, special advantage is not typically exploited. Were this not the case, the doctrine of Hobbes would stand unimpaired: everyone would cheat—in personal, economic, and other institutional relations. Yet the most cynical observer would not suggest that chicanery and cheating are the typical order of the day in all spheres, even where fear of discovery is at a minimum. This suggests that discrimination is sustained not only by the direct gains to those who discriminate but also by cultural norms that legitimatize discrimination.

To the extent that the foregoing assumptions are valid, efforts to minimize discrimination must take into account at least three sets of factors sustaining discriminatory practices. And each of these points toward distinct, though interrelated, lines of attack on the forces promoting discrimination. First, mass education and propaganda would be directed toward the reduction of sheer ignorance concerning the objective attributes of ethnic groups and of the processes of intergroup relations and attitudes. Second, institutional and interpersonal programs would seek to reduce the social, psychic, and economic gains presently accruing to those who discriminate. And third, long-range efforts would be required to reinforce the legitimacy of the American creed as a set of cultural norms applicable to all groups in the society.

One gains the impression that certain secular trends in the society are slowly affecting each of these three fronts. On the educational front, we find an increasing proportion of the American population receiving higher schooling. And in the course of schooling, many are exposed for the first time to salient *facts* regarding ethnic and racial groups. Preconceptions notwithstanding, higher educational institutions even in the Deep South do not teach discredited myths of race superiority; if race is treated at all, it is in substantially factual terms countering the cognitive errors now sustaining race discrimination. Without assuming that such education plays a basic role, I suggest that insofar as it is at all effective, it undermines erroneous conceptions of racial and ethnic qualities.

On the economic front, secular change moves with geological speed but consistently in the same positive direction. This secular trend is represented in slow shifts in the occupational composition of Negroes and other ethnic groups toward a perceptibly higher average level. Again, the importance of these slight shifts should not be exaggerated. As everyone knows, prejudice and its frequent corollary in action, discrimination, are resistant, if not entirely immune, to the coercion of sheer facts. Yet the white agricultural laborer does recognize, at some level of his self, the improbability of his "superiority" to the Negro physician or university president. *The discrepancy between achieved occupational status and ascribed caste status introduces severe strains upon the persistence of rationalized patterns of social superiority.* As occupational and educational opportunity expands for Negroes, the number of Negroes with class status higher than that of many whites will grow and with it the grounds for *genuinely believing*, no matter what one's protestations, that "any white man is better than any nigger" will be progressively eroded. This secular change is, of course, a two-edged sword: every economic advance of the Negro invites increased hostility and resentment. *But no major change in social structure occurs without the danger of temporarily increased conflict (though it is a characteristic of the liberal to want the rose without the thorn, to seek major change without conflict).* In any event, it seems plausible that the secular trend of occupational change presently militates against the unimpeded persistence of discrimination.

On the third front of the reinforcement of the American creed, the impressionistic picture is not so clear. But even here, there is one massive fact of contemporary history that points to a firmer foundation for this cultural doctrine. In a world riven with international fears, the pressure for national consensus grows stronger. Ethnic and racial fissures in the national polity cannot so lightly be endured. (Consider the concessions commonly given these groups in times of war.) This tendency is enhanced as Americans become sensitized to the balance of world population and recognize that firm alliances must be built with nonwhite peoples, ultimately, it is hoped, in a world alliance. From these pressures external to the nation, there develops an increasing movement toward translating the American creed from a less than fully effective ideology into a working code governing the actual behavior of men. Slight, yet not unimpressive, signs of this change are evident. In the realm of institutional organizations, there is growing pressure upon government, universities, trade unions, and churches to govern themselves by the words they profess. In the realm of interpersonal relations, one has a marked impression of increasing relations between members of diverse racial and ethnic groups. (This change in the pattern of private relations must remain conjectural, until social research searches out the needed facts. Periodic researches into the frequency of interracial and interethnic friendships would provide a barometer of interpersonal relations [necessarily invisible to the individual observer] that could be used to supplement current information on institutional changes and public decisions.)

These assumptions of the strategic significance of the three major fronts of social policy on race and ethnic relations and these impressions of secular trends now in progress on each front provide the basis for a consideration of social strategies for the reduction of discrimination.

Implications of the Typology
for Social Policy

This necessary detour into the assumptions underlying social policy leads us back to the main path laid down in the account of the four main types appearing in our typology of prejudice and discrimination. And again, however disconcerting the admission may be, it is essential to note that we must be wholly tentative in drawing out the implications of this typology for social policy, for the needed sociological theory and data are plainly inadequate to the practical demands of the situation. Yet if we cannot confidently establish the procedures that should be followed, we can perhaps exclude the procedures that are likely to be unproductive. The successive elimination of alternative procedures is some small gain.

In approaching problems of policy, two things are plain. First, these should be considered from the standpoint of the militant ethnic liberals, for they alone are sufficiently motivated to engage in positive action for the reduction of ethnic discrimination. And second, the fair-weather liberal, the fair-weather illiberal, and the all-weather illiberal represent types differing sufficiently to require diverse kinds of treatment.

Treatment of the Fair-Weather Liberal

The fair-weather liberals, it will be remembered, discriminate only when it appears expedient to do so, and experience some measure of guilt for deviating from their own belief in the American creed. They suffer from a conflict between conscience and conduct. Accordingly, they are relatively easy targets for the all-weather liberals. They constitute the strategic group promising the largest immediate returns for the least effort. Recognition of this type defines the first task for militant liberals who would enter into a collective effort to make the creed a viable and effective set of social norms rather than a ceremonial myth. And though the tactics that this definition of the problem suggests are numerous, I can here allude to only one of these, while emphasizing anew that much of the research data required for fuller confidence in this suggestion are not yet at hand. But passing by the discomforts of our ignorance for the moment, the following would seem to be roughly the case.

Since the fair-weather liberal discriminates only when it seems rewarding to do so, the crucial need is so to change social situations that there are few occasions in which discrimination proves rewarding and many in which it does not. This would suggest that ethnic liberals self-consciously and deliberately seek to draw into the social groups where they constitute a comfortable majority a number of the "expedient discriminators." This would serve to counteract the dangers of self-selection through which liberals come to associate primarily with like-minded individuals. It would, further, provide an interpersonal and social environment for fair-weather liberals in which they would find substantial social and psychological gains from abiding by their own beliefs, gains that would more than offset the rewards attendant upon occasional discrimination. It appears that people do not long persist in behavior that lacks social corroboration.

We have much to learn about the role of numbers and proportions in determining the behavior of members of a group. But it seems that individuals generally act differently when they are numbered among a minority rather than the majority. This is not to say that minorities uniformly abdicate their practices in the face of a contrary-acting majority, but only that the same people are subjected to different strains and pressures according to whether they are included in the majority or the minority. And the fair-weather liberal who finds himself associated with militant ethnic liberals may be expected to forgo his occasional deviations into discrimination; he may move from category II into category I; this at least is suggested by our current Columbia-Lavanburg researches on ethnic relations in the planned community.

This suggestion calls attention to the possible significance for policy of the composition of a local population with respect to the four types found in our typology, a consideration to which I shall presently return in some detail. But first it is necessary to consider briefly the problems attending policies for dealing with the illiberal.

Treatment of the Fair-Weather Illiberal

Because their *beliefs* correspond to those of the full-fledged liberal, the fair-weather liberals can rather readily be drawn into an interpersonal environment constituted by those of a comparable turn of mind. This would be more difficult for the fair-weather illiberals, whose beliefs are so fully at odds with those of ethnic liberals that they may, at first, only be alienated by association with them. If the initial tactic for the fair-weather liberal, therefore, is a change in interpersonal environment, the seemingly most appropriate tactic for the fair-weather illiberal is a change in the institutional and legal environment. It is, indeed, probably this type that liberals implicitly have in mind when they expect significant changes in behavior to result from the introduction of controls on ethnic discrimination into the legal machinery of our society.

For this type—and it is a major limitation for planning policies of control that we do not know their numbers or their distribution in the country—it would seem that the most effective tactic is the institution of legal controls administered with effectiveness. This would presumably reduce the amount of *discrimination* practiced by fair-weather illiberals, although it might *initially* enhance rather than reduce their *prejudices*.

Despite large libraries on the subject, we have little by way of rigorous knowledge indicating how this group of prejudiced but coercible conformists can be brought to abandon their prejudices. But something is known on a research basis of two methods that are *not* effective, information important for social policy since groups of ethnic liberals do commonly utilize these two apparently ineffectual methods. I refer, first, to mass propaganda for "tolerance" and second, the formation of interracial groups seeking to promote tolerance among their members.

Available evidence suggests rather uniformly that propaganda for ethnic equity disseminated through the channels of mass communication does not appreciably modify prejudice. Where prejudice is deep-seated, it serves too many psychological and social functions for the illiberal for it to be relinquished in response to propaganda, emanating from howsoever prestigeful a source. The propaganda is either evaded through misinterpretation or selectively assimilated into his prejudice system in such a fashion as to produce a "boomerang effect" of intensified prejudice.[5] Seemingly, propaganda for ethnic tolerance has a more important effect upon the propagandist, who comes to feel that he "is doing something" about diffusing the American creed, than upon the prejudiced people who are the ostensible objects of the propaganda. It is at least plausible that *the great dependence of ethnic liberals upon propaganda for tolerance persists because of the morale function the propaganda serves for the liberals who feel that something positive is being accomplished.*

A second prevalent tactic for modifying the prejudice of fair-weather illiberals is that of seeking to draw them into interethnic groups explicitly formed for the promotion of tolerance. This, too, seems largely ineffectual, since the deeply prejudiced individual will not enter into such groups of his own volition. As a consequence of this process of self-selection, these tolerance groups soon come to be comprised of the very ethnic liberals who initiated the enterprise.

This barrier of self-selection can be partially hurdled only if the ethnic illiberals are brought into continued association with militant liberals in groups devoted to significant common values, quite remote from objectives of ethnic equity as such. Thus, as our Columbia-Lavanburg researches have found, many fair-weather illiberals *will* live in interracial housing projects in order to enjoy the rewards of superior housing at a

5. There is a large literature bearing on this point. For recent discussions, see P. F. Lazarsfeld, "Some Remarks on the Role of Mass Media in So-called Tolerance Propaganda," *Journal of Social Issues* (Summer, 1947) ; P. F. Lazarsfeld and R. K. Merton, "Media of Mass Communication, Popular Taste, and Organized Social Action," in Bryson, ed., *Communication of Ideas*; M. Jahoda and E. Cooper, "Evasion of Propaganda: How Prejudiced People Respond to Anti-prejudice Propaganda," *Journal of Psychology*, 23 (1947), pp. 15–25. For an appraisal of the inadequate research to date on this problem, see R. M. Williams, Jr., *The Reduction of Intergroup Tensions* (New York, Social Science Research Council, 1947), p. 32 ff. The absence of adequate evidence attesting the *pragmatic* (not statistical) significance of tolerance propaganda suggests that propaganda programs now represent an act of faith on the part of propagandists.

given rental. And some of the illiberals thus brought into personal contact with various ethnic groups under the auspices of prestigeful militant liberals come to modify their prejudices. It is, apparently, only through interethnic collaboration, initially enforced by pressures of the situation, for immediate and significant objectives (other than tolerance) that the self-insulation of the fair-weather illiberal from rewarding interethnic contacts can be removed.

But however difficult it may presently be to affect the *prejudicial sentiments* of fair-weather liberals, their *discriminatory practices* can be lessened by the uniform, prompt, and prestigeful use of legal and institutional sanctions. The critical problem is to ascertain the proportions of fair-weather and all-weather illiberals in a given local population in order to have some clue to the probable effectiveness or ineffectiveness of anti-discrimination legislation.

Treatment of the All-Weather Illiberal

It is, of course, the hitherto confirmed illiberal, persistently translating prejudices into active discrimination, who represents the most difficult problem. But although he requires longer and more careful treatment, it is possible that he is not beyond change. In every instance, his social surroundings must be assiduously taken into account. It makes a peculiarly large difference whether he is in a cultural region of bigotry or in a predominantly "liberal" area, given over to verbal adherence to the American creed at the very least. As this cultural climate varies, so must the prescription for his cure and the prognosis for a relatively quick or long delayed recovery.

In an unfavorable cultural climate—and this does not necessarily exclude the benign regions of the Far South—the immediate resort will probably have to be that of working through legal and administrative federal controls over extreme discrimination, *with full recognition that, in all probability, these regulations will be systematically evaded for some time to come.* In such cultural regions, we may expect nullification of the law as the common practice, perhaps as common as was the case in the nation at large with respect to the Eighteenth Amendment, often with the connivance of local officers of the law. The large gap between the new law and local mores will not *at once* produce significant change of prevailing practices; token punishments of violations will probably be more common than effective control. At best, one may assume that significant change will be fitful, and excruciatingly slow. But secular changes in the economy may in due course lend support to the new legal framework of control over discrimination. As the economic shoe pinches because the illiberals do not fully mobilize the resources of industrial manpower nor extend their local markets through equitable wage payments, they may slowly abandon some discriminatory practices as they come to find that these do not always pay—even the discriminator. So far as discrimination is concerned, organized counteraction is possible, and some small results may be expected. But it would seem that wishes father thoughts, when one expects basic changes in the immediate future in these regions of institutionalized discrimination.

The situation is somewhat different with regard to the scattered, rather than aggregated, ethnic illiberals found here and there throughout the country. Here the mores and a social organization oriented toward the American creed still have some measure of prestige and the resources of a majority of liberals can be mobilized to isolate the illiberal. In these surroundings, it is possible to move the all-weather illiberal toward Type III—he can be brought to conform with institutional regulations, even though he does not surrender his prejudices. And once he has entered upon this role of the dissident but conforming individual, the remedial program designed for the fair-weather illiberal would be in order.

Ecological Bases of Social Policy

Where authenticated data are few and scattered and one must make *some* decision, whether it be the decision to act in a given fashion or not to take action at all, then one must resort to reasonable conjecture as the basis for policy. That is what I have done in assuming throughout that policies designed to curb ethnic discrimination must be oriented toward differences in the composition of a population with respect to the four types under discussion. It is safe to assume that communities and larger areas vary in the proportion of these several types. Some communities may have an overwhelming majority of militant liberals, in positions of authority and among the rank-and-file. Others may be short on ethnic liberals but long on fair-weather illiberals who respond promptly though reluctantly to the pressure of institutional controls. It would seem reasonable to suppose that different social policies of control over discrimination would be required as these ecological distributions of prejudice–discrimination types vary.

This assumption is concretized in the conjectural distributions of these types set forth in the following charts. Consider the same legislation aimed at curbing job discrimination against the Negro as this might operate in a community in the Far South and in New England. Since it runs counter to the strongly entrenched attitudes of the large majority in the one community and not in the other, we may suppose that the same law will produce different results in the two cases. This must be put in a reasonable time perspective. Conceivably, the short-term and the long-term effects may differ widely. But with respect to both the long and the short term, it matters greatly whether there is a sufficient local nucleus of ethnic liberals in positions of prestige and authority. The ecological and social distribution of the prejudice–discrimination types is of central importance in assessing the probable outcome. Whether a law providing for equitable access to jobs will in fact produce this result depends not only on the law itself as on the rest of the social structure. The law is a small, though important, part of the whole. Unless a strong economic and social base for its support exists in a community, the law will be nullified in practice.

Charts C and D set forth, again conjecturally, the distribution of the prejudice–discrimination types with respect to the Jew among middle-

HYPOTHETICAL CLASS AND REGIONAL PROFILES AND CULTURAL CLICHÉS
FOR THE PREJUDICE-DISCRIMINATION TYPOLOGY

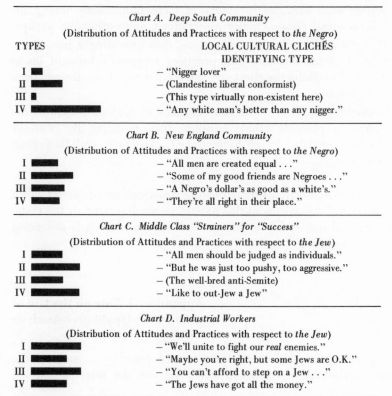

Chart A. *Deep South Community*

(Distribution of Attitudes and Practices with respect to *the Negro*)

TYPES	LOCAL CULTURAL CLICHÉS IDENTIFYING TYPE
I	— "Nigger lover"
II	— (Clandestine liberal conformist)
III	— (This type virtually non-existent here)
IV	— "Any white man's better than any nigger."

Chart B. *New England Community*

(Distribution of Attitudes and Practices with respect to *the Negro*)

I	— "All men are created equal . . ."
II	— "Some of my good friends are Negroes . . ."
III	— "A Negro's dollar's as good as a white's."
IV	— "They're all right in their place."

Chart C. *Middle Class "Strainers" for "Success"*

(Distribution of Attitudes and Practices with respect to *the Jew*)

I	— "All men should be judged as individuals."
II	— "But he was just too pushy, too aggressive."
III	— (The well-bred anti-Semite)
IV	— "Like to out-Jew a Jew"

Chart D. *Industrial Workers*

(Distribution of Attitudes and Practices with respect to *the Jew*)

I	— "We'll unite to fight our *real* enemies."
II	— "Maybe you're right, but some Jews are O.K."
III	— "You can't afford to step on a Jew . . ."
IV	— "The Jews have got all the money."

class "strainers" and industrial workers. Should research find that the industrial worker stratum indeed has a larger proportion of militant ethnic liberals than the middle classes, then initial support of an active anti-discrimination policy might most effectively be sought there. But whatever the actual facts might show, policy-makers attuned to the realities as well as the objectives of the problem would do well to take these into account in the design of programs.

If makers of policy are to escape utopianism on the one hand and pessimistic inaction on the other, they must utilize diverse procedures for modifying attitudes and behavior according to the distribution of these prejudice–discrimination types.

Finally, though action cannot, perhaps, wait upon continued research, it is suggested that the following kinds of information are needed as a basis for effective anti-discrimination policy:

1. An inventory to determine the relative proportions in various areas of the four prejudice–discrimination types;
2. Within each area, an inventory of these proportions among the several social classes, major associations, and nationality groups;
3. Periodic audits of these proportions, thus providing a barometric map of ethnic attitudes and practices repeatedly brought up to date and marking the short-run and secular trends in diverse areas and groups;
4. Continuing studies of the consequences of various programs designed to promote ethnic equities, thus reducing the wastage presently entailed by well-intentioned, expensive, and ineffectual programs.

This is a large research order. But the American creed, as set down in the basic moral documents of this nation, seems deserving of the systematic exercise of our social intelligence fully as much as it is deserving of our moral resolution.

Appendix: A Note on the Use of Paradigms in Qualitative Analysis

Something should be said of the purposes of paradigms, such as the prejudice–discrimination typology, which set out the interrelations of qualitative items. Otherwise, the paradigm will be mistaken for simply a notational device rather than taken for what it is, a logical design for analysis, implicitly present even when it is not explicitly set forth. I believe that paradigms such as this one and others which have been developed for functional analysis in sociology, for the sociology of knowledge, and for the analysis of deviant behavior,[6] have great propaedeutic value. They bring out into the open the array of assumptions, concepts, and basic propositions employed in a sociological investigation. They thus dampen the inadvertent tendency to hide the hard core of analysis behind a veil of logically unconnected though possibly illuminating observations. Although there are some preliminary efforts to assemble propositional inventories of sociological knowledge, the discipline still has few formulae— that is, highly abbreviated symbolic expressions of stable relationships between variables. Sociological interpretations tend to be discursive. The logic of procedure, the key concepts, and the relationships between them and observation often become lost to view. When this happens, the critical reader must laboriously fend for himself in trying to identify the tacit assumptions of the author. The paradigm serves to reduce this tendency for the theorist to employ tacit concepts and assumptions.

Paradigms for qualitative analysis have at least five closely related functions.

First, paradigms have a notational function. They provide a compact, parsimonious arrangement of the central concepts and their interrelations as these are utilized for description and analysis. Having one's concepts set out in sufficiently brief compass to permit their *simultaneous* inspection is an important aid to self-correction of one's successive interpretations, a result difficult to achieve when one's concepts are scattered and hidden in page after page of discursive exposition. (This, it appears, as may be seen from the work of Cajori on its history, is one of the major reasons for the importance of mathematical symbolism: it permits the simultaneous inspection of terms entering into the analysis.)

6. For these examples of what I understand by qualitative paradigms in sociology, see R. K. Merton, "Paradigm for Functional Analysis in Sociology," and "Paradigm for the Sociology of Knowledge," in *Social Theory and Social Structure* (New York: The Free Press, [1949] 1968), pp. 104–109, 514–15; and for delimited paradigms, "Social Structure and Anomie," *ibid.*, p. 195, and "Intermarriage and the Social Structure: Fact and Theory," *Psychiatry* 4 (1941), pp. 361–74 (reprinted as the following paper in this volume). For apposite logical analyses, see C. G. Hempel and P. Oppenheim, *Der Typusbegriff im Lichte der neuen Logik* (Leiden: A. W. Sijthoff, 1936), esp. pp. 44–101; P. F. Lazarsfeld, "Some Remarks on the Typological Procedure in Social Research," *Zeitschrift für Sozialforschung* 6 (1937), pp. 119–39.

Second, the explicit statement of analytic paradigms lessens the likelihood of inadvertently importing hidden assumptions and concepts, since each new assumption and each new concept must be either *derivable* from the previous terms of the paradigm or explicitly *incorporated* in it. The paradigm thus supplies a pragmatic and logical guide for the avoidance of *ad hoc* (i.e., logically irresponsible) hypotheses.

Third, paradigms advance a *cumulation* of theoretical interpretation. In this respect, we can regard the paradigm as the foundation upon which the house of interpretations is built. If a new story cannot be built directly upon the paradigmatic foundation, i.e., if it is not derivable from it, then it must be treated as a new wing of the total structure, and the foundations (of concepts and assumptions) must be extended to support the new wing. Moreover, each new story that *can* be built upon the original foundations strengthens our confidence in their substantial quality just as every new extension, precisely because it requires additional foundations, leads us to suspect the soundness of the original substructure. To pursue the figure further: a paradigm in which we can justifiably repose great confidence will in due course support an interpretative structure of skyscraper dimensions, with each successive story testifying to the substantial and well-laid quality of the original foundations, whereas a defective paradigm will support only a rambling one-story structure, in which each new set of observations requires a new foundation to be laid, since the original cannot bear the weight of additional stories.

Fourth, by their very arrangement, paradigms suggest modes of systematic cross-tabulation of putatively significant concepts and thus sensitize the investigator to empirical and theoretical problems that might otherwise be overlooked. Paradigms promote analysis rather than continued description of concrete details. They direct our attention, for example, to the components of social behavior, to possible strains and tensions between these components, and so to social sources of deviation from socially prescribed behavior.

Fifth, paradigms make for the codification of qualitative analysis in a way that approximates the logical if not the empirical rigor of quantitative analysis. The procedures for computing statistical measures, like their mathematical foundations, are codified as a matter of course; the procedures and assumptions are readily open to critical scrutiny. By contrast, the sociological analysis of qualitative data often resides in a private world of inquiry in which the often interesting results cannot be reproduced by others. Discursive interpretations not based upon paradigms are of course often perceptive and evocative. As the phrase has it, they are rich in "illuminating insights." But it is not always clear just which operations and analytical concepts were utilized in arriving at those insights. In some quarters, even the suggestion that these private experiences must be reshaped into publicly certifiable procedures is taken as a sign of impiety or downright ignorance. Yet the use of concepts and procedures for investigation by even the most qualitative-minded sociologists must be reproducible if they are to be given credence. Science, and this includes sociological science, is public, not private. It is not that we ordinary sociologists wish to cut all talents to our own small stature; it is only that the contributions by the great and small alike must be reproducible and codifiable if they are to advance sociological knowledge.

All virtues can easily become vices merely by being carried to excess and this applies to the sociological paradigm. It can become a temptation to mental indolence. Equipped with a paradigm, the sociologist may shut his eyes to strategic data not expressly called for by the paradigm. It can thus be transformed from a sociological field-glass into a sociological blinker. Misuse results from absolutizing the paradigm rather than from using it as a tentative point of departure. But if they are recognized as provisional and changing, destined to be modified in the immediate future as they have been in the recent past, these paradigms are preferable to sets of tacit assumptions.

Upon proposing this conception of paradigms in sociology back in the 1940s, I discovered that it was regarded as an unusual, not to say bizarre, usage. One candid friend went so far as to inform me that the notion of a "paradigm" was "really appropriate" only as an exemplar for declension or conjugation that exhibits all the inflectional forms of a class of words. In rebuking me, he of course managed to put aside Plato's idea of paradeigmata as well as centuries-long usage of the word in the extended sense of pattern or exemplar. Over the past quarter-century, the notion of paradigm in the indicated sense became thoroughly domesticated, not alone in sociology and psychology but in other social and behavioral disciplines as well.

With the appearance in 1962 of Thomas S. Kuhn's vastly consequential book, *The Structure of Scientific Revolutions*, the term "paradigm" has acquired a substantially different set of meanings and far wider usage. In a recent overview,[7] Raymond Firth instructively summarizes the dif-

7. Raymond Firth, "An Appraisal of Modern Social Anthropology," in *Annual Review of Anthropology* 4 (1975), pp. 1–25, at pp. 12–15. For other recent discussions of related kind, see Robert W. Friedrichs, "Dialectical Sociology: An Exemplar for the 1970s," *Social Forces* 50 (1973), pp. 447–55; Raymond Boudon, "Notes sur la Notion de Théorie dans les Sciences Sociales," *Archives Européennes de Sociologie* 11 (1970), pp. 201–51; S. B. Barnes, "Paradigms—

ferences and, to some degree, the conceptual relations between the two usages, in a passage which can be instructively quoted at length:

> Some might characterize the present situation in social anthropology as the paradigmatic phase. Paradigm has become the key word for a lot of interpretation. Paradigm, a word derived from classical sources, has been in use in English since at least the seventeenth century to mean a pattern to follow, an exemplar. It also has a hint of providing the basic components underlying any variation which a phenomenon might assume. In this sense the term was used by Robert Merton long ago when he was arguing for stricter methodology and greater awareness of the theoretical framework of sociological analysis. Merton used what he called the device of the analytical paradigm to present in a succinct way "codified materials" on concepts, procedures, and inferences over a range of problems from the requirements of functional analysis to social pressures leading to deviant behavior. Merton pointed out that any sound sociological analysis inevitably implies some theoretical paradigm, and he held that an explicit statement of such analytical model allows assumptions which would otherwise be hidden to be brought to the surface and laid open to scrutiny. He also argued that such analytical paradigms suggest systematic cross-tabulation of concepts, help to give more rigor in codifying qualitative data, and generally aid the symbolic expression of relationships between sociological variables. (The synoptic charts used by Malinowski for study of Trobriand agriculture or African culture change are examples of analogous paradigms primarily directed to research in the field.)
>
> Modern social anthropologists use the notion of paradigm rather differently, borrowing it not from Merton but from de Saussure and Thomas Kuhn. Moreover, one tendency is to attribute the paradigm not to the analytical observer but to the people whose behavior and ideas are being analyzed. In this setting a paradigm is a framework of ideas which the people have for envisaging and dealing with a specific set of circumstances and problems relating thereto—a kind of mental map of a sector of the natural and social world. Hence actors may

Scientific and Social," *Man* 4 (1969), pp. 94–102; James T. Duke, *Conflict and Power in Social Life* (Provo, Utah: Brigham Young University Press, 1976), pp. 305–13; Derek L. Phillips, "Paradigms and Incommensurability," *Theory and Society* 2 (1975), pp. 37–61; Don Martindale, "Sociological Theory and the Ideal Type," in Llewellyn Gross, ed., *Symposium on Sociological Theory* (Evanston: Row, Peterson, 1959), pp. 77–80. See also the pages in Chapter 7 of this volume on the multivalent meanings of "paradigm" and, in particular, the reference to Margaret Masterman, "The Nature of a Paradigm," in Imre Lakatos and Alan Musgrave, eds., *Criticism and the Growth of Knowledge* (Cambridge: University Press, 1970), pp. 59–90.

be spoken of as encoding those circumstances in terms of preexisting paradigms.* It is not easy to determine how far we are confronted here with a new mode of anthropological analysis or only with a new language. It is my impression that when the analysis can come down to actual cases, much of it is congruent with what has formerly appeared as treatment of social structure or social norms. More specifically, much of what I have described as "attitudes," that is, intellectual and emotional patterns, of the Tikopia about suicide, or of what Fortes has described as "ideological landmarks" of totemic and other ritual symbols that keep an individual Tallensi on his course, could be put easily into paradigm language. But much modern anthropological use of paradigm has an extra component, overtly stressed as of critical importance, namely, its basis in metaphor or analogy.

The history of the rise of analogy to the surface of anthropological analysis would be interesting to trace, including such diverse threads as McLennan's interest in legal symbolism and Evans-Pritchard's interest in the famous equation of Nuer twins with birds. Since analogy is the process of reasoning whereby recognition of similarity of attributes in different objects is presumed to indicate other similarities also, examination by anthropologists of the objects and attributes concerned can be very revealing about thought processes in various social contexts. This is particularly so when analysis of behavior is linked with the study of analogic thought process as exemplified in language—hence the many fruitful recent expositions of relations between symbol, ritual, and myth. Yet one should not forget *Kunapipi* and *Djanggawul* by R. M. Berndt, or *Chisungu* by Audrey Richards, rich contributions to the study of symbolic ideas and behavior in initiation and allied cults, which appeared 20 or so years ago. In the modern field the powerful analyses of Victor Turner have emerged in the concept of the "root paradigm." This is not only a set of rules from which many kinds of social actions can be generated, but also a consciously recognized cultural model of an allusive metaphorical kind, cognitively delineated, emotionally charged and with moral force, so impelling to action. Notions of such loaded images lift the anthropologist's interpretation from the mundane level of social relations on to a metaphorical, even metaphysical plane. So Turner sees "root paradigms," insofar as they are religious in type, as involving some element of sacrifice of self in favor of survival of the group.

Thus paradigms tend to be concerned with type rather than with instance, with thought rather than with action. Paradigmatic structures

* Terms such as code and encode are used metaphorically and loosely. They indicate the tendency of many modern social anthropologists to use primarily linguistic analogies, even to refer to nonlinguistic phenomena.

are essentially structures of ideas rather than structures of social relationships. As such, they can be conceived as having creative power for the actor. For the analyst, they can appear to have a higher power of comparison and prediction through their more abstract, analogic quality. But sharp-edged instruments need more care in handling. Sometimes the notion of paradigm is used in almost a mechanistic sense: one is given the impression of people being fitted out with portfolios of paradigms which encode their circumstances and experiences—pulling out the appropriate blueprint for use as occasions present themselves. And the notion of collectivity inherent in most definitions of paradigm carries with it the well-known difficulties of abstraction—in the last resort, whose paradigm is it, the actor's or the analyst's? Long ago, Merton pointed to some of these dangers of possible abuse of the sociological paradigm. He called it roundly a temptation to mental indolence, to shutting one's eyes to strategic data not expressly called for in the paradigm, to using it as a sociological blinker rather than a sociological fieldglass. "Misuse results from absolutizing the paradigm rather than using it tentatively, as a point of departure." Fortes & Dieterlen made a parallel point by implication when they indicated how in studies of ritual and symbolism French anthropologists who began with accounts of cosmological beliefs, doctrines, and myths were able to display conceptual systems with all-embracing interpretative powers, while British anthropologists who started with an analysis of the structure of social positions tended to find conflict and discrepancy as well as consistency and cooperation. But Fortes & Dieterlen continued to make the significant suggestion that this could reveal a basic difference between the symbolic and the pragmatic, the ritual and the secular spheres of life. So, granted the interpretative value as well as the intellectual excitement of analysis in terms of paradigm and allied concepts, there is also a good case for analysis in more direct behavioral and social terms. A focus on the world of ideas should complement, not replace, a focus on the world of action.[8]

8. Reprinted, with permission, from *Annual Review of Anthropology*, Volume 4. Copyright © 1975 by Annual Reviews Inc. All rights reserved.

12

Intermarriage
and the Social Structure

The paradox is now fully established that the utmost abstractions are the true weapon with which to control our thought of concrete fact.—A. N. Whitehead

INTERMARRIAGE IS A CONCRETE ACTION involving numerous facets, the more dramatic of which have been accorded considerable attention by students of interpersonal relations. The dramatic, however, is not always the theoretically significant; human interest and scientific relevance do not invariably coincide. Among the more prosy aspects of intermarriage is the role of the social structure. Rates and patterns of intermarriage are closely related to cultural orientations, standardized distributions of income and symbols of status. The conflicts and accommodations of mates from socially disparate groups are partly understandable in terms of this environing structure. A provisional theory of structural components in intermarriage, then, can contribute to the analysis of interpersonal relations although, as Sapir has noted, the sociological abstractions refer to consistencies in cultural definitions rather than to the actions of particular persons. The theory of social structure complements the theory of personal interaction; from a functional standpoint, regularities in the two spheres are mutually implicative.

No society lacks a system of marriage. In no society is the selection of a marriage partner unregulated and indiscriminate. The choice, whether by the contractants themselves or by other delegated persons or groups, is subject to regulation by diffuse cultural controls and sometimes by specific social agencies. These regulations vary in many respects: in the

Read at the annual meeting of the Southwestern Sociological Association 11 April 1941, Dallas, Texas. This article appeared in *Psychiatry: Journal of the Biology and Pathology of Interpersonal Relations* 4 (August 1941), pp. 361–74. Reprinted by special permission of The William Alanson White Psychiatric Foundation, Inc. Copyright 1941 by the Foundation; copyright renewed.

degree of control—permission, preference, prescription, proscription; in the social statuses that are thus categorized—for example, kinship, race, class, and religion; in the sanctions attached to the regulations; in the machinery for carrying the rules into effect; in the degree to which the rules are effective. All this can be said with some assurance but there still remains the problem of systematizing these types of variation into some comprehensible order. To assume that the variations are random is to provide a spurious solution of the problem by abandoning it. The apparent chaos must be shaped into a determinable order. The task of organizing these data has of course long since been taken up. Such concepts as endogamy, exogamy, preferential mating; as caste, class, and estate; and a host of related concepts reflect preliminary victories of an attack upon the problem. In this paper we seek to extend these conceptual formulations by suggesting some means for their further integration in the field of intermarriage.

Kinds of Intermarriage

Speaking literally, all marriage is intermarriage in the sense that the contractants derive from different social groups of one sort or another. This follows immediately from the universal incest taboo that forbids marriage at least between members of the same elementary family unit and derivatively restricts marriage to members of different family groups. Marriage contractants invariably[1] come from different elementary family groups; often from different locality, occupational, political, nationality groups; and at times from different religious and linguistic groups, races, and castes. Thus, if the term intermarriage is used to denote all marriage

1. "Invariably" on the basis of a study of 220 societies by George P. Murdock, *Sex Mores and Social Structure*, an unpublished paper presented at the annual meetings of the American Sociological Society, 29 December 1940. "All societies prohibit sexual intercourse and marriage between mother and son, father and daughter, and brother and sister. Our 220 cases reveal no genuine exception to any of these three universal incest taboos. To be sure, in two instances brother-sister marriages are customary in the royal family, and in one case a paramount chief may marry his own daughter, but in all three societies such incestuous unions are rigorously forbidden to the rest of the population and special factors explain their occurrence among the chosen few of highest status." Ralph Linton, *The Study of Man* (New York: Appleton-Century, 1936), p. 125, holds that "the prohibition of marriage between mother and son is the only one universally present." Whether occasional exceptions to this taboo are "genuine" or not, the approximation to universality is not questioned.

between persons of *any* different groups whatsoever, without any further specification of the groups involved, it becomes virtually synonymous with the term marriage and may well be eliminated. In other words, differences in group affiliation of the contractants may occur, but if these affiliations—for example, political, neighborhood, social clubs—are not defined as relevant to the selection of a spouse, then the case is one of marriage, not intermarriage. The fact is, however, that certain types of marriage are sufficiently distinctive with respect to the group affiliations of the contractants as to mark them off as a special category. Intermarriage, then, will be defined as *marriage of persons deriving from those different in-groups and out-groups other than the family that are culturally conceived as relevant to the choice of a spouse.* Thus, a given marriage may be, within one frame of reference—for example, the caste—inmarriage, and within another frame of reference—for example, social class—intermarriage. The distinction is analytical.

The standardized rules of intermarriage range from prescription, and social approval, to proscription, and social disapproval. These polar extremes give rise to two distinguishable types of intermarriage: the first, representing conformity to the rules, called *exogamy*; the second, involving prohibited deviations from the rules, may be called *cacogamy*. Prescribed marriage with*in* a specified group is, of course, *endogamy*. The combination of *rules* requiring or forbidding in-marriage and of *practices*, which may or may not conform to the rules, thus generates four type-cases of marriage. These are set forth in the following table.

This set of distinctions may help to eliminate that theoretical confusion in interpretations of intermarriage that stems from the failure to distinguish clearly between the two levels of rules and practices. Marriages that are superficially similar should not be classified as though they were significantly alike. Thus, marriages between persons with grandparents of different nationalities are often categorized as internationality-marriage even in those cases where there is no consciousness by the contractants or the community of such group "affiliation" and, more importantly, even where there are no norms in the law or mores prescribing, preferring, or proscribing such marriages. Cases such as these are not profitably classified as intermarriage since the ultimate group origins of the contractants are not culturally defined as relevant to the choice of a spouse. They are socially and culturally in-marriages, not intermarriages. The failure to discriminate between norms and practices also obscures the necessary distinction between those intermarriages that are approved and those disapproved by the community. Clearly, cacogamous intermarriages, which repudiate social norms, are not to be classified with

RULES GOVERNING CHOICE OF SPOUSE

		In-Group Marriage Prescribed = Out-Group Marriage Proscribed	In-Group Marriage Proscribed = Out-Group Marriage Prescribed
PRACTICES IN CHOICE OF SPOUSE	Conformity to Rule: Agathogamy[2]	Endogamy	Exogamy
	Deviation from Rule: Cacogamy[3]	Inter-group mesalliance	Intra-group mesalliance (incestuous marriage)[4]

(inmarriage ... intermarriage shown diagonally across the table)

exogamous marriages, which represent conformity to these norms. The confusion here lies in not discriminating between significantly different types of marriage just as in the previous instance it lies in discriminating between essentially similar types. Our fourfold table provides a ready guide for the avoidance of such errors.[5]

The distinctions between norms and practices of mate selection is further necessary because practices are influenced not only by the rules but also by certain *conditions* [structural constraints] that facilitate or hinder conformity to the rules. In other words, the actual practices are

2. *Agathogamy*: marriage which conforms to the norms governing selection of a spouse. From *agathos* = good, virtuous + *gamos* = marriage. At present there is no word to denote that class of marriages which conform to these norms. Agathogamy is intended to fill this gap.

3. *Cacogamy*: marriage which involves tabooed deviations from the norms governing selection of a spouse. From *kakos* = bad + *gamos* = marriage.

4. Incestuous marriages are often termed *intermarriage*. This would appear to be an instance of the rhetorical fallacy of catachresis, in which one term is wrongly put for another. Its source is possibly the following. In lay language, the term intermarriage commonly denotes those marriages which *deviate* from *endogamous* norms. This attribute of *non-conformity and group disapproval* has come to be the identifying characteristic of intermarriage. Hence, incestuous marriage—surely at the polar extreme from inter- (group) marriage—which is also commonly *condemned*, comes mistakenly to be assimilated to the category of intermarriage, which is interpreted as tabooed marriage. The usage is misleading for analytical purposes and should be dropped from the sociological if not the folk lexicon.

5. It will be noted, however, that this classification is not exhaustive for it does not distinguish between permissive, preferential and assortative mating. Uniform patterns of mate-selection and the standardized ratings of potential spouses constitute a familiar phenomenon in many societies. Both preferential mating, which occurs in accordance with definite rules setting forth the particular statuses from which the spouse is to be selected, and assortative mating, which involves selection on the basis of more diffuse cultural values, are contained within the foregoing categories. Rules of preferential marriage simply specify in more detail the status attributes of the potential spouse; assortative mating is also usually within the normative framework—that is, agathogamous. A more detailed analysis would follow through the special features of preferential marriage but this problem is beyond us here.

resultants of the norms *and* specifiable conditions of group life. Among the non-normative conditions affecting actual rates of in- and out-marriage are size of groups, sex composition, age composition, and degree of contact between members of different groups. These conditions, it will be noted, are not directly matters of standardized attitudes, sentiment, or cultural definitions although they are interdependent with normative factors. Norms may affect the degree and type of social contact; as embodied in immigration laws, for example, they may influence the size of nationality groups and indirectly even their sex and age composition. But the conditions may best be treated as largely independent factors in the selection of mates, quite apart from the cultural norms. As Romanzo Adams has indicated in this connection, "the larger the group the higher the percentage of in-marriage, irrespective of any sentiment relative thereto."[6] Likewise, a radical disproportion in the sex ratio, as in the case of Chinese and Filipinos in this country, exerts a pressure for outmarriage. These pressures may be more than counterbalanced by in-group sentiments but analytically it is necessary to recognize their significance. Comparisons between rates of intermarriage in different populations should take account of the relative numbers of potential in-group mates, as affected by size, sex and age composition, territorial distribution, and technologically determined opportunities for contact. Norms and actual frequencies of intermarriage, then, are not to be confused.

When, with a changing social structure, the functional significance of certain norms governing choice of a spouse diminishes, the antagonism toward violations and finally the norms themselves will tend to disappear. When the in- and out-groups are in fact progressing toward social and cultural assimilation; when pathways for group consolidation are established; when a considerable part of the population is alienated from traditional group distinctions; when social mobility is notably high; when physical and cultural marks of group distinction have largely disappeared and group "differences" persist merely as a matter of purely technical definition—as, for example, with the third generation of native-born white Americans—then a state of affairs is reached where the quadrisyllable, "intermarriage," is whittled down to a bisyllable, "marriage." The groups previously defined as severally endogamous become redefined as jointly endogamous; the circle of permissible mates is enlarged and the change in social organization is registered by newly modified norms concerning the selection of marriage partners.

6. Romanzo Adams, *Interracial Marriage in Hawaii* (New York: Macmillan, 1937), p. 191. Adams has an excellent discussion of the problem of distinguishing between practices and norms in the field of intermarriage.

Whether permitted or tabooed, intermarriage does not occur at random but according to more or less clearly describable patterns. Two of these patterns may be selected for special attention. The first may be called *hypergamy*, a term that we adapt from its usage in connection with the Hindu caste system to denote institutionalized or non-institutionalized patterns of intermarriage wherein the female marries into a higher social stratum, in a system of caste, class, or estates (*Stände*). We may introduce the term *hypogamy* to denote the pattern wherein the female marries into a lower social stratum. *Institutionalized* hypergamy and hypogamy denote those instances where the practice conforms to a norm contained in the law or mores; *non-institutionalized* hypergamy and hypogamy denote statistical uniformities of a hypergamous or hypogamous nature that are not, however, explicitly governed by a norm. Thus, Hindu hypergamy is an institutionalized pattern; American caste–hypogamy, a non-institutionalized pattern or a statistical uniformity but not a normatively prescribed arrangement.

We have now reviewed certain types of regulations and practices in the field of intermarriage. We have distinguished between endogamous and exogamous norms; between prescription, proscription, preference, and permission; between agathogamy, or conformity to marriage rules, and cacogamy, or nonconformity; between hypergamy and hypogamy; between institutionalized and non-institutionalized practices. It is suggested that these conceptual distinctions provide a framework for the observation and arrangement of relevant intermarriage data. In other words, one of the more general theses of this paper is that *an explicit conceptual outfit, a part of theory, is necessary even for fruitful discoveries of fact.* It is our second general thesis that much of the available statistical materials on intermarriage are of relatively little value because the fact-finders, so-called, have not assembled and classified *relevant* facts and that this inadequacy is tied up with their neglect of a coherent theoretical system in terms of which relevance of facts might be determined.[7] Studies of intermarriage concerned simply with "the facts" may be of use for the scientific study of the subject but only when they tacitly relate to a system of theory. A science without a matrix of logically interrelated propositions is a contradiction in terms. A canvass of empirical studies of intermarriage suggests that these views need to be labored for the "factual materials" are often discrete, scattered and arranged in what seems to be a wholly private and unusable fashion.

7. In this general connection, reference is made to Talcott Parsons, "The Role of Theory in Social Research," *American Sociological Review* 3 (1938), pp. 13–20.

Negro–White Intermarriage

A survey of the scanty statistical materials on Negro–white intermarriage in the United States will illustrate the basis for this judgment. The relations of "fact" and "theory" will be further instanced by setting forth a theoretically oriented taxonomy for the fruitful classification of such data. Accordingly, although our general categories apply to other types of intermarriage as well, the rest of our discussion will be devoted to the caste–class aspects of Negro–white intermarriage in this country. To refer to these cases merely as "interracial marriage" is an insufficiently analytic statement of a complex kind of event. It fails to bring out the fact that such intermarriage involves intercaste, and sometimes interclass, as well as interracial marriage. Furthermore, it does not direct attention to the racial, caste, and class origins of each of the marriage contractants. Yet there are significant sex differentials in the rate of Negro–white intermarriage. These interracial marriages, then, must be resolved into their elements, of which we shall attend to three: the caste, class, and sex of each contractant. A classification of these attributes suggests categories in which statistical data on Negro–white intermarriage might profitably be arranged and provides a benchmark for evaluating the available data. The *logically possible* combinations of the three attributes give rise to eight types of Negroes and whites who may enter into marriage.

These eight types of potential mates may be arranged into 16 logically possible marriage pairs, which are readily classifiable into four major

	Racial caste	Social class[8]	Sex
A.	Negro	lower class	female
B.	White	lower class	female
C.	Negro	upper class	female
D.	White	upper class	female
E.	Negro	lower class	male
F.	White	lower class	male
G.	Negro	upper class	male
H.	White	upper class	male

8. The evident simplification involved in dealing with only two social classes, loosely termed "upper" and "lower," is not of crucial importance at this point. Consideration of further class differentiation would serve only to multiply the possible types of mates without materially affecting the analysis. This twofold class distinction is advisedly a first approximation designed to indicate the general lines of the classification.

I
**Caste and
class
endogamy**

1. AE
2. BF
3. CG
4. DH

II
**Caste endogamy
Interclass marriage**

5. AG—class hypergamy
6. BH—class hypergamy
7. CE—class hypogamy
8. DF—class hypogamy

III
**Intercaste marriage
Class endogamy**

9. AF—caste hypergamy
10. BE—caste hypogamy
11. CH—caste hypergamy
12. DG—caste hypogamy

IV
**Intercaste marriage
Interclass marriage**

13. AH—caste and class hypergamy
14. BG—caste hypogamy; class hypergamy
15. CF—caste hypergamy; class hypogamy
16. DE—caste and class hypogamy

categories: those that conform to norms of both caste and class endogamy; those that involve caste endogamy and interclass marriage; those that involve class endogamy and intercaste marriage; those that deviate from norms of both caste and class endogamy.

Although these 16 pairings are logically possible, it is evident that they are not, in fact, equally probable. At this juncture the proper procedure would be, of course, to determine the relative frequency with which these possible combinations actually occur in order to test theoretically derived hypotheses concerning the selection of marriage partners.[9]

9. For the logic of this procedure, consult Paul F. Lazarsfeld, "Some Remarks on the Typological Procedure in Social Research," *Zeitschrift für Sozialforschung* 6 (1937), pp. 119–39; Carl G. Hempel and Paul Oppenheim, *Der Typusbegriff im Lichte der neuen Logik* (Leiden: A. W. Sijthoff, 1936), in particular, pp. 44–101. For other examples of this procedure, consider Robert K. Merton, "Social

Significantly, this cannot be done for the available statistical series do not include the necessary data, possibly because the empiricism of "fact-finders" included no canons of theoretical relevance. The statistical data will be briefly reported, and the rest of our discussion will be devoted to an interpretation that these data are not altogether adequate to sustain. It should be noted, however, that our hypotheses are such that they are clearly subject to confirmation or refutation when the relevant facts have been assembled.

In view of the fact that Negro–white intermarriage is forbidden by law in 30 states and condemned by the mores throughout the nation [as of 1941], it is scarcely surprising that such marriages seldom occur. Reuter's estimate of "perhaps less than one hundred per year"[10] since the Emancipation may be a slight understatement, but as the scattered statistics in the table below indicate, the figure is not appreciably higher. Moreover, there is no tendency for this negligible rate to increase.

NEGRO–WHITE INTERMARRIAGE

	Negro males–White females		White males–Negro females		Total	
	Per cent[11]	No.	Per cent[11]	No.	Per cent[11]	No.
New York City, 1908–12[12]	1.78		.44		1.08	
New York State, 1919–29[13] ...	2.92		1.00		1.95	
Rhode Island, 1881–93[14]		51		7		58
Michigan, 1874–93[14]		93		18		111
Connecticut, 1883–94[14]		..		..		75
Boston, 1855–90[14]		..		..		624
Boston, 1900–07[15]		203		19		222
Massachusetts, 1900[16]		43		10		53

Structure and Anomie," *American Sociological Review* 3 (1938), pp. 672–82; Karl Menger, "An Exact Theory of Social Groups and Relations," *American Journal of Sociology* 43 (1938), pp. 790–98; George A. Lundberg, *Foundations of Sociology* (New York: Macmillan, 1939), pp. 353 and 372–73.
10. Edward Byron Reuter, *The American Race Problem* (New York: Crowell, 1938), p. 143.
11. These are percentages of "all Negro marriages."
12. Julius Drachsler, *Intermarriage in New York City* (New York: Columbia University Press, 1921), p. 50.
13. J. V. De Porte, "Marriages in the State of New York with Special Reference to Nativity," *Human Biology* 3 (1931), pp. 376–96; in particular, p. 393. These figures are exclusive of New York City.
14. Frederick L. Hoffman, *Race Traits and Tendencies of the American Negro* (New York: Macmillan, 1896), pp. 198–200.
15. Gilbert T. Stephenson, *Race Distinctions in American Law* (New York and London: D. Appleton, 1910, p. 98. Alfred H. Stone, *Studies in the American*

This low rate of intermarriage is not particularly problematical; it simply reflects a high degree of conformity to strongly entrenched norms. In view of the vigorous taboos on intercaste marriage, we expect that most marriages in this country will be caste-endogamous—categories I and II. What is problematical, what does require generalized explanation, is the presence of these endogamous norms. Three related problems require consideration. First, what are the structural and functional bases[17] of the current norms governing Negro–white intermarriage? Second, what are the putative sources of deviations from these norms? Finally, how can we account for the prevalently caste–hypogamous pattern of these deviations?

Although the taboos on Negro–white intermarriage are primarily a matter of caste, as distinct from social class, the class affiliations of potential interracial spouses are not altogether irrelevant. In our open-class system, the preferred type of marriage, so far as *both* partners are concerned, is class endogamy. However, this norm is flexible and anything but rigorous for reasons that derive from the class structure itself and from other aspects of the culture. It is of course advantageous to marry a person of high class position. Interclass marriage has an acknowledged place as a means of consolidating class gains within a structure that contains mobility as a primary aspiration. Thus, despite preferential class endogamy, we should expect relatively frequent interclass unions. Paradoxically, this pattern is supported by the prevalent *romantic complex*, which emphasizes the dominant importance of "love" rather than utilitarian calculations in choosing a marriage partner. Romance is presumably blind to class differences. The marriages of the heiress and the chauffeur, the wealthy scion and the shop-girl, when love conquers all, are enshrined in our folklore, our folksongs and drama. The romantic complex is largely but not wholly integrated with preferential class endogamy. Unless closely restricted by the prior importance of class-endogamous preference, romanticism interferes with the smooth function-

---

Race Problem (New York: Doubleday Page, 1908), p. 62, reports that 13.6 per cent of all Negro marriages in Boston, 1900–04, were intermarriages with whites. Although Edward Byron Reuter, *The Mulatto in the United States* (Boston: Badger, 1918), p. 136, quotes this percentage, it appears to be implausibly high and Stone's original sources should be rechecked.

16. Reference footnote 15, *Studies in the American Race Problem*, p. 62. This refers to 37 Massachusetts towns and cities.

17. We are primarily concerned with the generalized, not the historical, basis of these norms. A full analysis would deal with the historical or diachronic as well as the structural-functional or synchronic elements involved. The two approaches are readily integrated in this case.

ing of the regulations regarding choice of a spouse; it makes for some instability and lack of consensus in appraising certain interclass marriages that may be disapproved in terms of the endogamous norms but praised in terms of romanticism. Such lack of consensus also derives in part from our *democratic creed*, which officially denies strict class lines and thus subverts the effectiveness of preferential class endogamy. These interdependent definitions—preferential class endogamy, on one hand, and romantic and democratic values, on the other—prevent class endogamy from being a stable, unchallenged norm in our society. It is a tendency, not a strict uniformity. We expect the majority of marriages to occur within a social class, if only for reasons of mutual accessibility and participation in common social groups by members of the same class, but the norm is sufficiently flexible to allow frequent interclass unions. Class endogamy is loosely preferential, not prescriptive.

Insofar as Negro–white intermarriage is a matter of social class, that is, insofar as we may temporarily abstract from other considerations affecting such intermarriage, a loose class endogamy with some interclass marriage is to be expected. Of course, it is abundantly clear that Negro–white marriage in our society is *not simply* a matter of the class affiliation of the contractants, but this is no reason for assuming that the class positions of the mates are wholly irrelevant to the probability of certain types of pairing. The class origins of spouses in interracial cacogamy are distinctly relevant to patterns of such intermarriage.[18] However, considerations of social class are supplemented by the norms of caste that prescribe, not merely prefer, endogamy.

In our racial-caste system,[19] the taboos on intermarriage are not

18. In fact, Miller goes so far as to say that the objection to Negro–white intermarriage is "merely a class objection and strong as it is, it is no stronger than has prevailed between clearly defined classes within the same race." H. A. Miller, "Race and Class Parallelism," *The Annals* 140 (1923), pp. 3–4. This view attaches too much weight to class whereas others have completely ignored this element in interracial cacogamy.

19. Kingsley Davis has distinguished between racial castes, non-racial castes and non-caste systems of race relations. He indicates that the differences lead to different types of regulation of intermarriage. "Intermarriage in Caste Societies," *American Anthropologist* 43 (1941), pp. 376–95. The nature of my extensive debt to Davis's analysis will be evident to those who consult his excellent paper. Despite some differences in terminology, our substantial agreement on certain independently conceived classifications and interpretation may be held to enhance the cogency of both papers. The convergence of independent researches toward common conclusions is, after all, a significant test of reliability. This applies particularly to the following items: conformity to and deviations from norms of mate-selection (agathogamy and cacogamy); ascription to endogamy of the function

materially counteracted by the influences of romanticism and the democratic creed. The romantic complex operates largely within the confines
of a caste and, when it fails to do so, it is more than outweighed by caste
controls. Moreover, in a racial-caste structure, the criteria of pulchritude
are commonly derived from the physical traits characteristic of the dominant caste, so that even in these terms, lower caste members will usually
be deemed "unattractive." These derived aesthetic criteria thus reduce
one possible source of deviation from the endogamous norm. Another
such potential source, the democratic creed, has been largely accommodated to the caste structure so that its "subversive" influence with respect
to the non-democratic caste system is negligible.[20] In other words, although the caste structure is not integrated with the democratic and
romantic values, it persists by being largely insulated from the application
of criteria contained in these value systems. Conflict arising from this
lack of integration is minimized by segmentation of attitudes and rationalization: democratic and romantic criteria are largely restricted to intra-
caste evaluations, and elaborate explanations account for the necessity,
justice, and desirability of doing so. Intercaste marriage is not granted
even qualified approval as subserving the function of social mobility for
mobility is ruled out by the very nature of caste structure. Finally, the
contacts between members of different racial-castes are regulated by
codes of racial etiquette so that there are few opportunities for relationships not involving considerable social distance. This in turn largely
reduces the type of contact that might result in marriage.

Thus, various characteristics of the social and cultural structure support the prevalent code of racial-caste endogamy in the United States.
But all this does not account for the existence of such endogamy. What,
then, are the structural and functional bases of racial-caste endogamy?

Endogamy is a device that serves to maintain social prerogatives and
immunities within a social group.[21] It helps prevent the diffusion of
power, authority, and preferred status to persons who are not affiliated
with a dominant group. It serves further to accentuate and symbolize the
"reality" of the group by setting it off against other discriminable social

---

of making for cultural compatibility of spouses; ascription to the taboo on
cacogamy of the function of precluding disruption of the matrix of kinship and
other interpersonal relations in which the spouses are embedded; the concept
of compensatory intermarriage.

20. Robert K. Merton, "Fact and Factitiousness in Ethnic Opinionnaires." *American Sociological Review* 5 (1940), pp. 13–28; in particular, pp. 23–28 [reprinted as
the following paper in this volume].

21. Linton, *op.cit.*, p. 204.

units. Endogamy serves as an isolation[22] and exclusion device, with the function of increasing group solidarity and supporting the social structure by helping to fix social distances that obtain between groups. All this is not meant to imply that endogamy was deliberately instituted for these purposes; this is a description in functional, not necessarily purposive, terms.

Facts that apparently controvert this functional account seem, upon analysis, to lend it further support. Thus, in American society where the class structure involves preferential rather than prescriptive endogamy, interclass marriage acts as a means of social mobility. When groups are relatively permeable, when new class status may be attained through socially recognized achievements, the endogamous norms are sufficiently relaxed to be integrated with mobility. Contrariwise, in a caste system with gaps between strata where individual mobility is the exception, the endogamous norms are rigid. This interpretation is consistent with historical changes in endogamous norms. It appears that notable increases in group consciousness and solidarity involve a tightening of endogamous prescriptions. The Nazi taboo on interracial and interreligious marriage is a case in point.

The structural basis for endogamous rules may be seen by examining their bearing upon the conjugal family units themselves. Endogamy ensures to a certain extent that the marriage contractants will have a rough similarity of cultural background inasmuch as they have been socialized in groups with similar culture.[23] A universe of discourse common to the contractants lessens the likelihood of that intrafamilial conflict which derives from different sets of values of the spouses. Moreover, by precluding diverse group loyalties of the mates, the conjugal unit is integrated with the larger social structure. Both class and caste endogamy prevent that familial instability that occurs when children identify themselves with the upper-status parent and condemn the lower-status parent in terms of the cultural values that they have assimilated. This potential split of loyalties becomes especially disruptive within a racial-caste system where the child's animosity may be directed against himself as well as the lower-

---

22. E. T. Hiller has introduced the useful term *isolation device* to denote arrangements and symbols which mark off in-groups from out-groups. His usage may be profitably modified to this extent: *isolation devices* are those employed by subordinate groups for this function; *exclusion devices*, those employed by dominant groups. E. T. Hiller, *Principles of Sociology* (New York: Harper, 1933), pp. 24 and 325.
23. Kingsley Davis—Reference footnote 19—properly stresses the importance of this fact.

caste parent who bears the invidious racial marks. This interpretation in terms of the functions of endogamy for the conjugal family unit may account in part for the widespread tendency to conceive of the conjugal unit as involving equality of status in the framework of stratification.[24]

A further structural basis for the taboo on intercaste marriage is found in the effect of such marriage upon the network of social relationships in which the contractants are implicated. Marriage introduces the mates into a new set of kinship relations. Kinship relatives, with exceptions such as mother-in-law avoidances which are not relevant here, are culturally defined as standing in a relation involving ready social accessibility.[25] Cacogamous intercaste marriage introduces an abrupt breach into this network of social relations for with it comes a conflict between the super-ordinate–subordinate relations deriving from status differences of the new-made kin and the mutual accessibility in terms of equality deriving from the kinship structure. Nor does the conflict cease at this point. Each of the persons in the new kinship group is normally embedded in a matrix of friendships and cliques. Usually, such friendship groupings are, apart from age and sex differences, potentially accessible to one another.[26] Intermarriage between persons of radically different social status thus conflicts with the existing organization of cliques and friendship groups involving the spouses and their kin. Rules of avoidance or social distance and rules of accessibility are brought into open conflict. The taboo on such intermarriage may be construed as a socially evolved defensive arrangement for restricting the incidence of such conflicts. A cross-caste mésalliance would entail a considerable readjustment of established systems of social relationships which, since they are affectively significant, are most resistant to abrupt and profound alterations. Intercaste marriage is thus seen to involve not only an internally contradictory relationship

24. Kingsley Davis, "The Forms of Illegitimacy," *Social Forces* 18 (1939), pp. 85–87; Talcott Parsons, "An Analytical Approach to the Theory of Social Stratification" *American Journal of Sociology* 45 (1940), pp. 841–62; in particular, p. 850. These two papers may be profitably read in conjunction with the present study since they all involve the same general theoretical system.
25. Reference footnote 24; Davis, p. 86.
26. To be sure, friendship groupings are often confined to a single sex and a single generation, but this limits rather than eliminates the potential accessibility of friends and kin of members of the group. [The implications of this observation have been extensively investigated in a community context: R. K. Merton, Patricia S. West, and Marie Jahoda, *Patterns of Social Life* (New York: Columbia University Bureau of Applied Social Research, 1951), and the findings have been summarized in Jean Maisonneuve, *Psycho-Sociologie des Affinités* (Paris: Presses Universitaires de France, 1966), pp. 270–87.]

between the spouses but to influence directly an elaborate network of social relations ramifying through the immediate families, the extended kinship group, and their friends. Viewed in such a context, the profound emotional resistance to racial-caste intermarriage becomes largely comprehensible. These outbursts of moral indignation are defensive devices that stabilize the existing organization of interpersonal relations and groups.

In a society where certain types of intermarriage are forbidden, several alternative adjustments by cacogamous pairs are possible. The relative frequency of these attempted adjustments depends at least in part on the larger social organization. In any case, the "adjustment" will involve the rupture of some social systems involving the offending pair. In a society such as our own, with its pattern of virtual independence of conjugal groups and with high rates of geographic mobility, ostracism of the offending couple involves a minimum of social readjustment, particularly should the pair leave the immediate community. Such ostracism, when the marriage provoking it is not widely known, *approximates*—though it is not affectively identical with—a recognized cultural pattern in which new conjugal pairs maintain relatively few active relations with their families of orientation and their native community. If the cacogamous pair leaves the local community, the families of orientation are *publicly* little more depleted than if the departure were in response to economic opportunities elsewhere. A highly mobile, segmented society, then, to this extent minimizes the disturbing influences of cacogamy upon the local community and affords somewhat more loopholes for such normatively irregular unions.

In the case of intercaste mésalliances, however, the problem is not solved by such makeshift "escapes" to another community, for here the problem of establishing new social relationships is encountered. This problem becomes acute in cases of racial-caste intermarriage where physical badges of affiliation with different castes bar the way to a reintegration of the conjugal pair with new social groups. Similarly, when status differences are correlated with marked cultural differences leading to high visibility of another kind, flight from the native community fails to solve the problem. Under these conditions, new relationships can no more easily be established than the old relationships could be maintained. In cases of intermarriage where both physical and cultural visibility are absent, the temporarily atomized pair may gear into a satisfactory set of new social relationships as a conventional family group. But all such adjustments by the deviant pair that, in the optimum case, may attain some measure of personal success are still at the expense of the social relationships that have been sloughed off by ostracism and mobility. Successful evasions indicate loopholes in the structure of community control, not modifications of the marriage structure. Hence, although a segmented, mobile society may reduce the animus directed toward certain types of cacogamy, it is functionally necessary to maintain such effective antagonism if the going arrangement of social relationships is not to be endangered.[27] Metaphorically, intercaste marriage may be viewed as a catalyst that activates and intensifies group consciousness. It symbolizes the repudiation of standardized cultural values that have been defined as sacrosanct and inviolable. A cultural axiom is being challenged. Cultural orientations are, by virtue of this challenge, presumably no longer secure. The response is immediate and familiar. The violation is intensely condemned; the nonconformists are stigmatized; the cultural norms are reaffirmed. All this has little of design, of the predetermined plan. It resembles rather the automatic, the prompt trigger-like response ensured by socialization and rooted in sentiment. The pattern is an integrated arrangement of action, sentiment, and reaction serving to order social relationships. It may suggest a premeditated structure but it is more nearly reminiscent of the ordered integration of reflexive behavior. The crisis arouses self-consciousness; in this instance, consciousness of self as a member of the in-group.

The Pattern of Caste Hypogamy

Structural and functional elements, then, would appear to account for [not justify] the prohibition of racial-caste intermarriage in our society. The taboo appears to be largely supported by the standardized sentiments of both Negroes and whites and, consequently, the rate of intermarriage continues to be low. But what of the intermarriages that do occur, in spite of the taboo? The most striking uniformity in the statistics of Negro–white intermarriage is the non-institutional pattern of caste hypogamy, i.e., marriage between white females and Negro males. In our samples, such pairings are from three to ten times as frequent as the Negro female–white male combination. This uniformity has often been remarked by students of the subject. Even the collection of mixed marriages assembled from cases "personally known" to a group of students consists of 18 caste-

27. This functional statement does *not* imply a value-judgment favoring or rejecting the current social arrangements. Only a perversion of functional analysis systematically results in rationalizations of the *status quo* in various areas of social life.

hypogamous unions to seven hypergamous unions.[28] What is the basis of this uniformity?

The hypogamous pattern is clearly not attributable to non-normative conditions affecting intermarriage. There is no significantly unbalanced sex ratio among either the Negro or white populations that can be taken to account for this pattern.[29] Similarly, neither the etiquette of race relations nor sheer propinquity would make for more frequent contacts between white females and Negro males than between Negro females and white males.[30] We may entertain the hypothesis that hypogamy is understandable in terms of the social structure; a view that is not invariably shared by other students of the subject. Thus, Baber raises the question in these non-structural, individualistic terms: "Surely there is no more stigma attached to the white man who marries a Negro woman than to the white woman who marries a Negro. Is color difference in the mate less repulsive to the white woman than to the white man?"[31] This way of posing the problem illustrates the necessity of systematic theory if empirical data are to be made intelligible. An *ad hoc* common-sense hypothesis such as Baber's contains no reference to social structure and ignores the fact that most illicit miscegenation involves Negro women and white men. "Repulsiveness" is not a datum; it is a cultural artifact requiring sociological analysis.

28. Ray E. Baber, "A Study of 325 Mixed Marriages," *American Sociological Review* 2 (1937), pp. 705–16. Reference is also made to Ray E. Baber, *Marriage and the Family* (New York: McGraw-Hill, 1939), pp. 163–73.
29. Consult, for example, relevant data presented by Oliver C. Cox, "Sex Ratio and Marital Status Among Negroes." *American Sociological Review* 5 (1940), pp. 937–47.
30. If at all involved, the contrary is more probable since Negro females and white males are more likely to have sustained contacts than are the complementary pairs, in view of the fact that the ratio of Negro women to Negro men engaged in domestic and personal service is about 4 to 1. [It should be added, however, that this disproportion did not obtain prior to 1910, the period to which all but one of our statistics of Negro–white intermarriage refer. Consult Abram L. Harris and Sterling D. Spero, "Negro Problem," *Encyclopedia of the Social Sciences* 11 (New York: Macmillan, 1937), p. 342; Elizabeth R. Haynes, "Negroes in Domestic Service in the United States," *Journal of Negro History* 8 (1923), pp. 384–442, in particular, pp. 386–93.] In any event, such contacts scarcely serve to account for the caste-hypogamous pattern, in view of the social distance deriving from both caste and class differences.
31. Reference footnote 28: "A Study of 325 Mixed Marriages," p. 706. [Note that Baber does not raise the symmetrical rhetorical question: "Is color difference in the mate less repulsive to the Negro man than to the Negro woman?" And note, too, that in those ancient times of a third of a century ago, I did not call attention to Baber's highly selective formulation.]

Dealing with this same general question, Park asserts that hypergamy is "one principle which seems to have been everywhere operative in determining the amount of miscegenation." It appears to be true that inter-caste sex relations largely involve upper-caste males and lower-caste females, but clearly "hypergamy," which denotes a form of *marriage*, is far from universal. Park further holds that hypergamy "seems to be a principle in human nature . . . which operates spontaneously."[32] A third hypothesis holds that "the disposition of men to go abroad for wives and of women to welcome these roving strangers is probably part of original nature. Human beings are naturally exogamous." Here again, certain abstract characteristics are attributed to human nature as such and, in contrast to Park's usual analytical insight, with no regard for the role of social organization. How would one test the hypothesis that exogamy is fixed in original nature? What theoretical or factual basis exists for this hypothesis? In any case, these gratuitous assumptions do not clarify the prevalently hypogamous pattern of Negro–white intermarriage.

Donald Young[33] and Kingsley Davis[19] have severally advanced hypotheses that can be elaborated to account for the relative frequencies of the logically possible pairings of Negroes and whites. Inasmuch as the statistics show a marked predominance of caste hypogamy, we know that most of the actual intercaste pairings are contained among the following types: Numbers 10 BE; 12 DG; 14 BG; 16 DE. It is suggested that the frequencies of these pairings may be interpreted within the context of the generalized scheme shown on pages 223–24.

Limitations of space and the absence of sufficient concrete data prevent a detailed analysis of the multiple structural factors involved in patterns of interstratum marriage. The general lines of analysis may be briefly illustrated. In our twofold racial-caste and open-class structure, all Negro–white marriages are cacogamous, that is, they deviate from endogamous norms and are attended by the sanctions of ostracism and the ascription of lower-caste status to offspring. Within such a context, it is likely that pairing Number 10 will be found among the pariahs of the society, among those persons who have become, as it where, "cultural aliens" denying the legitimacy of much of the social structure in which

32. Robert E. Park, "Race Relations and Certain Frontiers" in E. B. Reuter, ed., *Race and Culture Contacts* (New York: McGraw-Hill, 1934), in particular, pp. 80–81. Park's essay contains an excellent summary of comparative materials on interracial marriage.
33. Donald Young, *American Minority Peoples* (New York: Harper, 1932), p. 409.

they occupy disadvantaged positions.[34] Interracial cacogamy is, in this instance, simply a special case of the larger repudiation of cultural means and goals. There is little in the way of mutual socio-economic compensa-

VARIABLES IN THE ANALYSIS OF INTERMARRIAGE BETWEEN PERSONS
FROM DIFFERENT SOCIAL STRATA

I. *The System of Stratification*
  A. Open-class ⎫ these may be combined in concrete
  B. Estates or *Stände* ⎪ social systems: racial caste-and-class
  C. Caste ⎬ in United States; estate-and-class in
    1. Racial ⎪ England, Prussia—especially 18th &
    2. Non-racial ⎭ 19th centuries

II. *Bases of Ascribed or Achieved Status in the System of Stratification*[35]
  A. Membership in a kinship unit   D. Possessions
  B. Personal qualities—including race E. Authority
  C. Achievements   F. Power

III. *Types of Intermarriage*
  A. Exogamy—agathogamous   B. Intergroup mésalliance—
    intermarriage   cacogamous intermarriage
    1. Compensatory[36]   1. Compensatory
      a. hypergamy ⎫ institutionalized   a. hypergamy
      b. hypogamy   or non-   b. hypogamy
    2. Non-compensatory institutionalized 2. Non-compensatory
      a. hypergamy   a. hypergamy
      b. hypogamy ⎭   b. hypogamy

IV. *Status of Children of Cross-Stratum Marriage*
  A. Matrilineal
  B. Patrilineal
  C. Positional (that is, status of either upper-stratum or of lower-stratum parent)

V. *Status of Conjugal Pair*
  A. Same as prior status of husband
  B. Same as prior status of wife
  C. Same as prior status of upper-stratum spouse
  D. Same as prior status of lower-stratum spouse
  E. Status of pariahs, outcaste, déclassé

34. For an account of the structural sources of the cultural alien, see Robert K. Merton, "Social Structure and Anomie" *American Sociological Review* 3 (1938) 3, pp. 672–82.
35. For a discussion of these bases of differential valuation, consider Parsons, reference footnote 24.
36. Ernst Kohn-Bramstedt, *Aristocracy and the Middle-Classes in Germany* (London: P. S. King, 1937), p. 244, properly stresses the importance of social or economic compensation in cacogamous intermarriage.

tion between the cross-caste mates. This particular pairing, however, would not be expected to occur any more frequently than its complementary hypergamous type, Number 9, involving a lower-class Negro female and a lower-class white male. Concubinage, rather than marriage, would be the probable type of durable sex relationship in these cases.

Type Number 12, when it occurs, will also not involve mutual compensation with respect to socio-economic position, since here the class positions of the upper-class mates are roughly equal. The relation is asymmetrical inasmuch as the Negro male does not compensate for the upper-caste status of his wife. Such marriages would be expected to occur among "emancipated" persons, so-called radicals, who repudiate legitimacy of caste distinctions. The sole formal difference between types Numbers 10 and 12, then, is that in the former the contractants are disadvantaged persons who relinquish social norms because of the ineffectiveness of their efforts to gear into the social structure and achieve a "respectable" status, whereas in the latter type, the contractants enjoy eminently satisfactory status as judged by conventional standards but have become alienated from the values, institutional ideologies, and organization of the caste system.[37]

We should expect pairing Number 14—lower-class white woman and upper-class Negro man—to occur most frequently for it involves a reciprocal compensatory situation in which the Negro male "exchanges" his higher economic position for the white female's higher caste status.[38] This does not at all imply that the "exchange" is necessarily the result of an explicit utilitarian calculus in which the contractants deliberately weigh the economic and social returns to be gained from the marriage. The event may be experienced by them as simply an affectional relationship, but this psychic reaction is manifestly structured by the social organization. A comparable reciprocity pattern often emerges even more clearly in hypergamous unions in caste or estate systems of stratification.

37. One of the cases reported by Baber appears to fall more or less in this category. The white woman "was very well educated, a member of Phi Beta Kappa, and from a highly respected family." The Negro male, evidently highly mobile within the class system, was a law student who came of a poor family. "They were both radicals. . . ." Reference footnote 28: Baber, p. 708. The distinction between the personality types in pairings Numbers 10 and 12 corresponds to those established by Merton as "retreatism" and "rebellion." Reference footnote 34: p. 676.
38. This is the special case of hypogamy with which Kingsley Davis was primarily concerned: when the dual caste-class structure "makes it economically profitable for some white women to marry some Negro males." Reference footnote 19. [As the text plainly indicates, the theoretical model of "social exchange" is not at all alien to this mode of structural and functional analysis.]

In the Hindu caste system, for example, the bride's family "have to pay for marrying her to a man above her in rank, whilst they also desire to make a show of wealth as a set-off to the bridegroom's social advantages."[39] In an estate system where titles descend patrilineally, the hypergamous exchange of wealth for noble status is often quite explicit, as in the patterns involving American heiresses and foreign nobles since the middle of the last century. Thus, the marriage settlement between Conseuelo Vanderbilt and His Grace the ninth Duke of Marlborough was set forth in an official document in which the Duke was guaranteed for life the income from $2,500,000 of Beech Creek Railway stock.

Among the hypogamous pairings, type Number 16 would, on our hypothesis, occur least frequently. Here *both* the class and caste positions of the white female are superior to that of the Negro male, and there is no element of social or economic compensation involved. Such a marriage abjures all prevailing social and cultural considerations, and for this compound deviation from class and caste standards it would be most difficult to find culturally acceptable motivation.

This brief canvass of types of caste hypogamy is avowedly hypothetical, but it involves theoretically derived hypotheses that lend themselves to empirical confirmation or refutation. Furthermore, it sets forth the particular attributes that must be included in future statistical and case materials in order to test this interpretation. Baber has apparently made a step in this direction. However, the available data are too unsystematic and fragmentary to provide an adequate test although, so far as they go, they are consistent with our analysis. Thus, Reuter observes that uniformly in intercaste marriages, the Negro "groom is of some importance and the white bride a woman of the lower class."[40]

We have yet to examine the structural bases for the greater frequency of caste-hypogamy as compared to caste-hypergamy in our society. Two

39. E. A. H. Blunt, *The Caste System of Northern India* (London: Oxford University Press, 1931), p. 70.

40. Reference footnote 15: Reuter, p. 138. Reuter cites Hoffman's study of 57 mixed unions which were predominantly between members of the lower classes of both castes—pairing No. 10—and included a generous proportion of criminals and prostitutes. This again concurs with our analysis but since Hoffman does not indicate the basis on which he selected his cases, his study cannot be accorded much weight. Only 23 of Hoffman's cases were actual marriages. Although Reuter refers to Hoffman's canvass as a "careful investigtion," it should be noted that Hoffman gives only the following indication of the source of his information and the basis of selection of cases: "I have been able during a number of years to collect information of a fairly reliable character in regard to 37 mixed relations. . . ." Reference footnote 14: p. 204. In view of Hoffman's bias and naiveté in other respects, there is no reason to assume that this sample was representative.

aspects of the roles ascribed to males and females appear to be primarily relevant. The latitude permitted women to seek an occupational career has increased greatly but it does not approximate that accorded men. Moreover, even in the most "emancipated" circles the status of a conjugal unit is primarily that of the male head of the family. The standardized case is one in which the social rank of the female is largely derivative from that of her husband or, prior to social adulthood, her father. In a society where this is the case, intrafamilial conflict often occurs when the wife has outdistanced her husband in the occupational sphere since feminine careers are hedged about by conceptions of the impropriety of competition between husband and wife. Occupational achievement is still considered the usual if not the exclusive prerogative of the male, despite the larger participation of women in economic and public life. The male is "the provider," the chief source of economic status. The second difference in sex roles is contained in the prevalent code of sex morality wherein, despite some slight modifications, the female of the species is more circumscribed in the range of allowable activity. Moreover, it is commonly considered more appropriate that sex relations be initiated by the male; that the male will propose and the female dispose; and that the male will seek out the female, for examples. These social definitions are not unchallenged but they exercise a discernible control.

Given these differences in role definitions, then, an upper-caste male, by virtue of his sex role, may more properly make advances than an upper-caste female and, secondly, he may more readily flout the caste taboos, by virtue of his upper-caste status than a lower-caste male may dare. In short, the sex morality supports sex advances by the male; the caste morality more easily enables the dominant upper-caste member to initiate cross-caste sexual overtures. Thus, the individuals who incorporate the "male attribute" and the "upper-caste attribute," that is, white males, may more readily initiate cross-caste sexual relations than either the white female, who lacks the male prerogative, or the Negro male, who lacks the upper-caste prerogative. This enables us to see structural sources of the fact that most intercaste *sex relations*—not marriages—are between white men and Negro women.

It remains to be seen, then, why the durable relationships between white men and Negro women are usually extramarital. Once again, sex roles and the caste and class structure would appear to account for the facts. Given the dominance of the white male with his relative immunity from active retaliation by the lower-caste male, there is no pressure to legitimatize his liaison by marriage. Concubinage and transient sex relations are less burdensome and less damaging to his status, since these may be more easily kept secret and, even if discovered, are less subject to violent condemnation by fellow caste members, since they do not imply equality of the sex partners. Furthermore, as Davis has suggested, the marriage of a lower-class white male with a wealthy Negro woman is less likely than the complementary hypogamous pairing in view of the standarized role of the male as "economic provider."

We may tentatively conclude that most cross-caste sex relations will be clandestine and illicit. Within a racial-caste structure, the non-institutionalized statistical pattern of the few intermarriages that do occur will be largely hypogamous. In a non-racial caste structure, as in India, the institutionalized pattern of hypergamy may be interpreted as a system manifesting the prerogatives of upper-caste males who thus have *legitimate* access to women of their own caste *and* to women of the immediately inferior subcaste. In a racial-caste structure, the institution of hypergamy is not probable because the ambiguous position of cross-caste offspring would introduce an instability in the caste system by eventually eliminating the identification of race and caste.[41]

The classification and interpretation presented in this paper are highly provisional and rudimentary: the one needing to be further tested for convenience, the other requiring a larger body of systematically collated data than is yet at hand. The random collection of facts will not lead to further understanding of the phenomenon of intermarriage; the collection of facts in terms of our conceptual framework may do so. Confirmed by whatever relevant facts are available, our interpretation enjoys a measure of plausibility; consistent with a wider body of theory that in turn is supported by systematic empirical inquiry, it may lay claim to a further degree of validity; stated in such terms as to be testable by freshly accumulated facts, it is, at the very least, open to further confirmation or disconfirmation.

Postscript: Private History of a Published Paper

Like most scholarly or scientific articles, the preceding one on intermarriage has a private history that cannot be reconstructed from its public version. The historically evolving conventions and format of the scientific paper do not allow it to be otherwise, calling as they do for an impersonal account of the procedures of investigations, the findings, and the interpretations, all this put forward in a form that gives next to no idea of how the work actually proceeded. The tidy public record gives no hint of the typically untidy private realities. It tells little or nothing of the intuitive

41. Consult the article by Davis for a comparative analysis. Reference footnote 19.

leaps come to nothing, the misperceptions and false starts, the downright errors of inference, the loose ends, and the opportunistic adaptations to this array of troubles. Nor does the paper in its public form ordinarily convey the occasional happy accident or, most significantly and frequently, the many cognitive interactions that enabled the work to proceed as it did.[42]

The preceding paper does provide a few markers or traces of such cognitive interactions in the half-dozen or so discursive footnotes and citations referring to Kingsley Davis. Particularly in footnote 19, there is reference to "my extensive debt to Davis' analysis [which] will be evident to those who consult his excellent paper." Even so, these brief allusions to the public record cannot begin to convey the character of the give-and-take between Kingsley Davis and myself that took place during the time that his paper and my own were being developed.

The gap between the public and private record of scientific work is occasionally, but with growing frequency, being narrowed. The long-delayed but now rapidly growing interest in the sociology of science with its concern in discovering how scientific inquiry is actually carried out brings with it an interest in assembling materials full of pertinent particulars, amongst them particulars bearing on cognitive and social influences on specific inquiries. Having long shared those interests and having long urged colleagues to convert some of the private record of actual inquiry into a public record, I want now to take that sage advice myself. I therefore append the correspondence with Kingsley Davis having to do with the writing of our two related papers on intermarriage. It is of some small interest to note that, after all these years, some ideas appearing in that exchange of letters that might still hold relevance today failed to find their way into his paper and mine.

From RKM to KD
[Cambridge, Mass.]
August 8, 1939

Dear Kingsley,

Your intermarriage paper has just arrived. Since we have begun our preparations for the long jaunt to our new home, I fear I shan't have as

42. For more on the contrast between the private and public records of science, and on continuities and discontinuities in sociology specifically, see Chapter 1 in R. K. Merton, *Social Theory and Social Structure* (New York: The Free Press, 1968, 3rd, enlarged edition).

much time to examine it as carefully as I should like. My "first impressions," after reading it thru just once, may be briefly summarized. After I get my immediate reactions down on paper, I shall attempt to find the time to study your analysis in more detail and to restate my opinion of it more fully. In general, I believe that you are on the right track, but it also seems to me that (1) there is some evidence of "over-simplification"; (2) that some of the concrete cases don't fall too readily into line with your present analysis; (3) that other empirical cases—especially in the direction of intermarriage in an open-class system—will serve to clarify the problem; (4) that the treatment of what might be called sex differentials in intermarriage is in some respects inadequate; (5) that possibly you did not have too clearly in mind the "typical" (more accurately, perhaps, the "ideal-typical") features of different types of class systems (i.e. systems of status stratification). Now, mind you, these are my first impressions; upon reexamination, I may have ample reason to retract or modify some or all of these criticisms. Perhaps, I can clarify the general bases of my remarks by transcribing a brief outline of the "minimum variables" which I have considered necessary in an analysis of intermarriage.

Variables in the Analysis of Intermarriage Between Social Strata

I. The system of stratification
    a. open-class
    b. Stände or estate
    c. Caste
        1. racial
        2. non-racial

    these may be interwoven in concrete social systems; e.g. caste-class in U.S.; *Stände* and class in England, Prussia (esp. 18th–19th centuries)

II. Factors determining or validating position of person in system of stratification
    a. race   d. personal qualities   g. power
    b. kinship   e. achievements
    c. possessions   f. authority

III. Types of more or less permanent cohabitation
    A. Intermarriage
        1. compensatory connubium
            a. hypergamy
            b. hypogamy
        2. non-compensatory connubium
            a. hypergamy
            b. hypogamy

    institutionalized or simply statistical uniformities (e.g. India in contrast to Negroes–Whites in U.S.)

    B. Concubinage
       1. compensatory concubinage
          a. lower stratum ♀ —upper stratum ♂
          b. lower stratum ♂ —upper stratum ♀
       2. non-compensatory concubinage
          a. lower stratum ♀ —upper stratum ♂
          b. lower stratum ♂ —upper stratum ♀

IV. System of reckoning initial "class" position of children of cross-strata relationships
    A. Legitimate offspring
       1. matrilineal
       2. patrilineal
       3. positional
    B. Illegitimate offspring
       1. matrilineal
       2. patrilineal
       3. positional—neither mat. nor pat.
          i.e. either status of upper or lower status parent, or intermediate

V. Position in system of stratification of conjual pair after connubium
    A. same as prior position of ♂
    B. same as prior position of ♀
    C. same as prior position of spouse from higher stratum
    D. same as prior position of spouse from lower stratum
    E. ostracised, outcaste, déclassé

A may concretely coincide with C or D; B may concretely coincide with C or D

Now let me make myself clear before I turn to your paper. I don't believe that the foregoing items are all of crucial importance in the analysis of any case, nor do I delude myself into believing that they constitute all the features which are important. All I mean to imply is that "a theory of intermarriage between social strata" would do well to consider their interrelations. Note that I say "social strata," rather than caste or class, because I think that even a tentative theory of intermarriage in caste societies will be more satisfactory if it is drawn up in the light of the wider problem of connubium in various systems of stratification. I have the impression that the reason why *some* (and not necessarily the most important part) of your interpretation does not click at a first reading is this: you don't introduce some of the elements I have listed above which seem to be necessary to an understanding of the structure of intermarriage in various instances.

But all this is much too abstract AND vague. Let me clarify it a bit before turning to your paper. These various items (the 5 major "categories") are closely interrelated. For example, one can't determine whether one concrete pattern of connubium is compensatory or non-compensatory without knowing the changes in stratum-position of the spouses after intermarriage (category V), without knowing the scale of values embodied in a concrete system of social stratification (category II—you were leading up to this more general point, it seems to me, in your distinction between racial and non-racial "castes"), without knowing the general pattern of establishing the stratum-position of offspring of such intermarriages (whether mésalliances or institutionalized—category IV), and without a *very clear idea* of what type or types of social stratification characterizes the society (category I). Thus, one may have compensatory hypergamy in an exclusively caste society if the female shares the caste-status of her husband, or, even if *she* doesn't, if their children do, or if it redounds to the prestige-or-economic-advantage of *her* parents, *providing* that the upper-caste male is compensated by his wife contributing some social value (e.g. wealth, beauty, achievement-prestige, i.e., the artiste). Moreover, unless one has the data to decide the degree and types of compensation involved, the pattern becomes difficult to interpret, altho it can be *partly* analyzed in functional terms. Likewise, in attempting to explain the fact that in one society one finds, instead of hypergamy, a widespread system of lower-stratum females being the concubines of upper-stratum males (type-III, B, 1, a), data of the same type are necessary. I have the impression that the reason why your interpretations seem more successful in some cases than in others is due to the dual fact that in some instances you have both more detailed data and have introduced more variables than in other cases. I hope that the general tenor of my remarks is clear, altho I haven't the time right now to elaborate upon them in the detail which is obviously necessary if their full implications are to become apparent. In general, I think that you will find empirically every type of "system of cohabitation"; that, moreover, certain types will be found to occur more frequently than others, simply because a certain combination of these "variables" occurs more frequently than other combinations; and that hypergamy is, at least apriori, no more probable than hypogamy. The reason why hypergamy seems to be in fact (i.e. concretely) more common in caste or *Stände* systems is that stratum-position of the conjugal pair is *ordinarily* that of the male spouse (hence, this readily leads to compensatory hypergamy).

Well, it is now 1:30 A.M. and I'm beginning to get bleary-eyed, so I shall revise my original intention and get this initial statement off to you before discussing your paper in greater detail. If you think you would like me to send you my not fully articulated statement, I shall try to do so very soon after getting to New Orleans. Let me know if you want me to return your MS before we leave for the South; a letter designed to reach me at 1839 Trapelo Rd, Waltham, by Monday of next week will do the trick. We intend to leave Tuesday or Wednesday of next week, making the trip by easy stages. . . .

From KD to RKM
August 25, 1938

Now, having got some current preoccupations off my chest, I want to express my belated appreciation of your reading the intermarriage paper and taking the time to transmit some of your own ideas on the topic. I had a feeling that the paper is inadequate, but I couldn't diagnose what was wrong. Your comments make it much clearer to me, and I won't publish it without another revision. I sent a copy of it to Linton, mainly to get his reaction to that type of article; I seriously doubt that he will consider publishing it. What exasperates me is that I have loads of concrete material which I was unable to use in the paper because there is no room for it (or so it seems to me). I simply haven't learned, as you apparently have, to condense a great deal of empirical evidence into small space. As a result, the instances of caste systems that I do give seem sketchy, and I do not seem to give enough instances anyway. Your outline of the variables in the analysis of intermarriage is excellent; it is similar, though better than my own formulation of the important variables. Only one thing prevented me from understanding it completely; that was the precise meaning you attach to "compensatory" under Types of Durable Cohabitation. I realize that to discuss caste intermarriage adequately it is necessary to do so against a background of an entire scheme such as you have suggested. This is what I do in the book—or attempt to do. But do you think I can get enough of the general scheme into an article to make the attempt worthwhile? My present inclination is to do the whole thing over again, continuing however to limit the scope to caste systems. (This business of taking a hunk out of a book and trying to make an article out of it is not so satisfactory.)

I hate to publish on something that you have devoted so much attention to. Since this subject is one where our special interests come together and our ideas are fairly compatible, I should like to renew my invitation to have you join me in writing it up. It might constitute our first exercise in preparation for the more important functionalism collaboration. If you wish to do this, I shall avoid the burden of writing the next draft. If you don't, I will continue to tinker with it for awhile.

From RKM to KD
August 31, 1939

And now for something which is more like business. Unfortunately, your Intermarriage MS and my own notes are coming down in the van and will not be here for another week, so I shan't be able to do anything with the paper until then. As for the possibility of a joint article, I think I should like to do it, but certainly not because I have, in any sense, a "claim" on the subject. After all, if you were to forego working on any of the problems with which I have dabbled, you would be considerably restricted in your choice. How would it be if we left the matter stand this way? The moment our things arrive, I'll sit down to the paper and see just what I can add or modify. When this is done, I'll send the revised MS to you and then we can consider whether it is to be a joint paper or no. In any case, don't—for God's sake (and mine)—hesitate to publish it as soon as you wish simply because I've happened to poke my inquisitive nose into the field of the family (via the back entrance). (What a lovely metaphorical jumble.)

From KD to RKM
October 18, 1939

The main purpose of this letter is not such idle palaver but to tell you that much to my surprise I received a long letter from Linton yesterday accepting the Intermarriage article. This bowled me over. As George remarked some time ago, the section on Nazi Germany, if nothing more, would exclude it from the *Anthropologist*, and I think any editor previous to Linton would have returned it virtually unread. Now what do you think I should do? On the assumption that you have not got to work on a revision, and realizing that having finished my paper for the Christmas meeting I have some "free" time for the next three weeks, I am inclined to think that the best for me to do is to put it through a revision, acknowledge your aid in the paper, and, as you express it, "put a fence around" this topic for our general approach and point of view. Then later, if we can possibly find the time, we might be tempted to tackle the problem on a broader basis—say, Reproductive Institutions and Social Stratification, which literally makes my mouth water. If this is agreeable to you, let me know. If not, I am ready to go through with our collaboration on it and tell Linton so. My only feeling is that having definitely secured a publication commitment, and knowing that I am at least on fairly firm ground (as judged by George's and Linton's comments), it might be better to go through with it and one more revision than to risk further delay and uncertainty. But let me know what you think.

From RKM to KD
February 1, 1941

I'm now quite certain that I haven't made clear the grounds for my estimate of the Dollard, and especially the Murdock paper. I said that I considered them "important" and I still do, but not, God knows, because of the *theory* which they embody. Dollard's "theory" is simply a slightly-modified version of conditioned-response conceptions; moreover, his paper is solely concerned with an interpretative account of psychological mechanisms in "matched-dependent learning." Likewise, Murdock's "theory" is confused because it operates on two levels—the psychological and sociological—without M. showing any appreciation of this fact. He evidently accepts a functional interpretation of incest-tabus *within* the family and then shifts to the "psychological" level in accounting for extensions in terms of generalization-discrimination. I recognize all this and still think that the papers have considerable merit, but merit of methodology rather than sociological theory. Let me take the M. paper as a case in point. He states the problem: to order the apparently chaotic incidence of statuses to which incest tabus are applied in different societies. He begins with the theorem of the functional significance of the tabu within the immediate family. He introduces a hypothesis: that the *mechanisms* thru which the tabu was extended are those of generalization and discrimination. The more specific and testable formulation of this hypothesis would read: the tabu is extended to those statuses outside the immediate family which *most resemble* the statuses of parent, cross-sexed sibling or child. It is then explicitly assumed that the culture and social organization *define* and fix the degree of recognized similarities or dissimilarities between those in various statuses. The next step is to "hit upon" (intuit, derive, deduce, guess, or otherwise ascertain) the ways in which social organization emphasize or minimize similarities between persons occupying different kinship statuses. M. explicitly tests the hypothesis that rules of residence and descent may be sufficient to define these similarities. (Note: he does not assume a "psychological" interpretation here at all.) Then, BEFORE LOOKING AT HIS STATISTICALLY ORDERED DATA, he *predicts* that the term "sister," e.g. for mother's brother's daughter evidences in general a culturally defined similarity between m's-b's-d and cross-sexed sibling and that the tabu would be extended to such a status in a bilateral descent system. This is the crucial step: the *prediction* is made prior to the compilation of the data; it is a prediction and not a post-hoc interpretation. I questioned Murdock closely on this and he insisted that he had set up the "indexes of culturally defined similarity and dissimilarity" BEFORE examining the "correlation-table"; that he was NOT merely reading off the tabulated results and THEN fitting his interpretation to them. The latter type of procedure is the typical one in the social sciences and it is for that reason that so much of our work is unconvincing. There is a multitude of PLAUSIBLE explanations of data which are before us; the important step is so to set up our research that we *predict* the observations before they are actually made. This is the crucial difference between ad hoc and post-hoc "explanations" on the one hand and confirmed hypotheses on the other. Murdock was not simply interpreting the tabulated data *after* he had examined them, but, he says (and I shan't challenge his honesty), he set up the indexes of similarity before examining the facts. Now, mind you, I not only freely grant, but insist, that he has not carried his work far enough; that he should return to the sociological level by seeing the functional significance of incest tabus outside the immediate family. But, so far as he has gone, he seems to me to have succeeded in satisfying the fundamental rule of valid scientific procedure: of deducing definite consequences from a theorem which can be and are checked by *future* observations. Explanations *after* the facts to be explained are in is inevitably questionable if only because a host of plausible interpretations are equally available. M.'s research has many minor methodological flaws and even more theoretical limitations—for example, he has done nothing with his "most important" cases, i.e. the negative cases which do not support his hypothesis—but in the main, it seems to me to represent a basic methodological contribution to social science.

KD to RKM
P.O. Box 15
Lares, Puerto Rico
July 28, 1941

Dear Bob:

Bowed is my head, tortured my conscience, and raw my skin, I am a sinner twice over, truly repentant but so blind as not to fathom the cause of my arrant ways. As time went on and my sin grew, my consternation and my shame grew apace. Now, without excuse or reason, I can only pray that the fountains of forgiveness are as bountiful as they are eternal.

Tomorrow your paper on intermarriage will be in the mails, and if a wandering submarine doesn't sink the boat, it will arrive in due time. Needless to say I greatly enjoyed reading it, not only because of the excellent reasoning it contains but also because it is the first time we have treated the same subject. I judge from the autobiographical note that the publication of the paper has been assured. Any remarks I may now make, therefore, will possibly seem like the post-partum arrival of the obstetrician.

In some ways I think this is the neatest paper you have ever done. The conceptual clarification and systematization you have employed are marvels of lucidity and simplicity, important because they involve the very core of the problem. In short, this is sociological taxonomy in the highest form, such as we seldom if ever see in the literature. If any muddlehead attempts to do research in this field without relying on your paper, he will be a candidate for a branding ceremony at one of the annual meetings. I propose to use at least half of it in my "chapter" on the subject.

I have taken the liberty, since the copy was a carbon one, of scratching things in the margins. In addition, I will note here one or two items which seem worth mentioning. In general I agree so well with your argument that there is not much to talk about.

(1) I feel that your definition of *intermarriage* is a bit too inclusive

in one sense and too narrow in another for the things you really wish to include. There are perhaps things culturally conceived as relevant to the choice of a spouse which are not definable as groups and yet are of interest in intermarriage. E.g. standards of beauty, education and wealth. In other words, I feel that "in-groups" and "out-groups" in the definition may suggest something a little too concrete. In addition, I feel that being relevant to the choice of a spouse may include a class of cultural conceptions greater than what one would think of as intermarriage. For instance, membership in a social club is apt to be highly relevant to the choice of a mate, indeed to intermarriage as such; yet marriage to another person belonging to a different unit of the same social club, a different social club, or no social club at all, will not necessarily be intermarriage. These points of course are piddling, but it is a matter over which I have sweated at length and I am not quite satisfied with either your definition or mine.

(2) There is quite a difference, I think, between an endogamous rule proscribing marriage in an out-group, so-called, and one prescribing marriage in an in-group—for the reason that it is sometimes difficult to make the out-group non-specific. Thus, a rule that I cannot marry within specific outside communities is not tantamount to a rule that I must marry only within my own community. The caste rule in some cases is not really that I should marry always within my caste, but that I should never marry anyone below me in caste; and the same for class. Again, I realize that this is not very important.

(3) For purposes of exposition, I think you need to make clear, about p. 10, that the rest of the paper will deal with an application of your method to class and caste. The general part, as you well know, is built to take care of all forms of intermarriage, but you treat only caste and class. It would not hurt, in the conclusion, again to make reference to this characteristic of the paper. You introduce the discussion of class and caste by reference to a methodological issue, which further obscures the transition in intrinsic subject matter.

(4) This is not so much a criticism as a comment, and it may not be a clear one at that. Do you notice that when you begin to deal with intercaste marriage in the U.S., you are forced to bring in not only the caste but all the other factors as well? Naturally this is because, as you point out on the first page, every marriage is a concrete act. What both of us aimed at but didn't accomplish, then, is a systematic treatment of theoretical relations between the various bases of group differentiation and hence of marital selection. We each got off onto the class and caste

angle and, except for supplementary purposes, let the rest of it slide. Sometime before long I would like to discuss with you a further extension of the *general system*.

(5) Perhaps you were a little tired, thinking about that coming Southwest meeting and the tribulations of a father. Anyway, it seems to me you slowed down just a bit in the last part of the paper and didn't make the effort of a conclusion that would "round things off."

Now, I have mentioned every possible thing I could find wrong with the paper. Everything else I agree with 100%. With slightly more polishing I think it would be your best paper to date. Actually, I am a poor critic, because we agree too well on this subject for me to find any fault. Anyway I am glad you are finally awake to the supreme importance of my "field." I guess it all began when you gave that lecture on "Sex and the Future of the Orgasm" in New Orleans. Are you collaborating with Himes on any books?

13

Fact and Factitiousness
in Ethnic Opinionnaires

"FOR A DESPERATE DISEASE, A DESPERATE CURE"; therefore, if opinionnaires are to be used they must be discussed. This is a report on one phase of a study of opinions on ethnic groups. The major objectives are (1) to suggest certain lines of internal and external criticism of opinionnaire "results" and (2) to present certain materials pertaining to group differences in the endorsement of a range of judgments about Negroes.[1]

It has been largely agreed for the last decade that the various "attitude scales" introduced by L. L. Thurstone represent the most exact means of assaying group attitudes toward various social values. It is argued here that some of the procedures used in the scoring and interpretation of Thurstonian "scales" involve methodological contradictions and sociological inadequacies. Although it is believed that this is true of the various Thurstonian opinionnaires (on War, Prohibition, Communism, "the" Church, "the" Negro, etc.), the present discussion is restricted to ethnic opinionnaires.

Reprinted with permission from *American Sociological Review* 5 (February, 1940), pp. 13–28. Read at the annual meeting of the American Sociological Society, Dec. 28, 1938. The writer is indebted to the Tulane University Council on Research for financial aid.

1. Limitations of space preclude the extended discussion merited by each of the several points in question. Hence, the full evidence for various conclusions and inferences can be only imperfectly reported. The fault is not necessarily lessened by its admission.—Throughout the paper, certain terms have been consistently set off by quotation marks ("thus"). Terms thus qualified are to be read: so-called. This device lessens the likelihood of equivocation, of using the same term to denote two or more significantly different concepts. [The criticism of "attitude scales" evidently led to use of the more modest term "opinionnaires." What I still do not know, 35 years later, is whether this term was coined for the occasion or adopted from prior use. This is mildly embarrassing. For, as the "outside consultant" in sociology for Webster's Unabridged Dictionary, Third edition, where the word "opinionnaire" (or "opinionaire") is securely recorded, I should presumably know.]

"Attitudes" of Religious Groups
toward "the" Negro

The following tabulation is presented as an introductory basis for this discussion. The table summarizes results obtained through a printed opinionnaire concerning "the" Negro which was administered to 679 college students registered in sociology courses at Harvard University, Radcliffe College, Pennsylvania State College, Tulane University, and Louisiana State University, at various times between October 1938 and October 1939.[2] The opinionnaire consists of thirty statements about the Negro. It was adapted from a "scale" constructed by I. D. MacCrone according to the Thurstone-Chave-Droba method of equal-appearing intervals.[3]

The following computations exhibit uniformities that appear to be statistically significant, despite the paucity of cases in some of the subgroupings. In all eight samples, the Catholics rank first in the endorsement of judgments "unfavorable" to "the" Negro. With almost equal regularity, the Protestants rank second; the Jews are usually third, and those with no religious affiliation rank fourth (or "least unfavorable"). Conventional indexes of statistical significance suggest that these are "real" differences, particularly between the "Northern" religious aggregates. (However, as the critical ratios indicate, the differences between the Jews and the "non-religious" groups are anything but significant.) The consistency of these results is so pronounced that, despite occasion-

2. The opinionnaire (appended to this paper) is part of a larger test battery not treated here. I am indebted to the following for aid in administering these opinionnaires: at Harvard and Radcliffe, E. Y. Hartshorne, Logan Wilson, Edward Devereux and Dudley Kirk; at Pennsylvania State, Kingsley Davis and Gordon T. Bowden; at Louisiana State University, Edgar E. Schuler, T. Lynn Smith and M. B. Smith. The Harvard-Radcliffe sample was obtained between October 1–11, 1938 (except for retests not reported here); the Pennsylvania State sample, between February 18 and March 5, 1939; the Tulane-Newcomb sample on Sept. 30, 1939; the Louisiana State sample between Oct. 13–19, 1939.

3. See I. D. MacCrone, *Race Attitudes in South Africa* (New York, 1937), Chap. IX. The original opinionnaire referred to the South African 'native' and the scale-values were based upon the judgments of 200 persons of European descent and 100 Bantu. Only those statements which were ordered similarly by both groups were included in the inventory. It will be noted that substitution of the term 'Negro' for the term 'the native' leads to a series of judgments which are substantially similar to those in the Hinckley-Thurstone 'attitude-toward-the-Negro scale.' The same assumptions underlie our adaptation of MacCrone's inventory and the use of 'generalized scales,' except that our adaptation involves the generalizing process to a lesser extent. See H. H. Remmers and E. B. Silance, "Generalized Attitude Scales," *Journal of Social Psychology* 5 (1934), pp. 298–312.

"MEAN SCORES" ON OPINIONNAIRES CONCERNING "THE" NEGRO, ACCORDING
TO SEX, COLLEGE AND RELIGIOUS AFFILIATION OF SUBJECTS

Colleges	MALES																
	Catholics			Protestants			Jews			None			Unknown			Total	
	N	MS	R[a]	N	MS	R	N	MS	R	N	MS	R	N	MS	N	MS
Harvard	25	4.3	1	82	3.9	2	51	3.1	3	22	2.6	4	35	3.8	215	3.6
Penn State	15	5.0	1	27	3.9	2	16	3.0	4	5	3.4	3	13	4.0	76	3.9
Tulane	18	6.3	1	12	5.2	2	4	4.3	3	1	4.0	4	—	—	35	5.5
L.S.U.	25	6.1	1	56	6.0	2	2	3.4	4	8	5.4	3	1	5.4	92	5.9
Total	83	—	—	177	—	—	73	—	—	36	—	—	49	—	418	—

Colleges	FEMALES																
Radcliffe	21	4.4	1	40	3.4	2½	18	3.4	2½	5	2.7	4	5	3.9	89	3.6
Penn State	6	4.8	1	24	3.5	2	3	3.1	3	1	3.0	4	3	4.1	37	3.7
Newcomb	5	7.1	1	14	5.6	2	1	3.5	3	—	—	—	—	—	20	6.1
L.S.U.	40	6.1	1	66	5.5	2	5	4.1	3	4	2.3	4	—	—	115	5.6
Total	72	—	—	144	—	—	27	—	—	10	—	—	8	—	261	—

CRITICAL RATIOS $\left(\dfrac{\text{diff.}}{\delta \text{ diff.}} \right)$

Classes of Subjects Compared	"Northern" Subjects[b] (males and females)[c]	"Southern" Subjects[b] (males and females)[c]
Protestants versus Catholics	3.4	2.2
Protestants versus Jews	3.6	3.1
Protestants versus No Religious Affiliation	4.4	2.1
Catholics versus Jews	5.6	3.9
Catholics versus No Religious Affiliation	6.2	2.9
Jews versus No Religious Affiliation	1.8	0.7

[a] R is the rank order of religious groups according to an interpretation that will be presently criticized; MS is the "mean score."
[b] "Northern" subjects are: Harvard, Radcliffe, and Pennsylvania State subjects; "Southern" subjects are: Tulane, Newcomb and Louisiana State subjects.
[c] Inasmuch as the differences in means between males and females of the same geographical region and the same religious affiliation are insignificant, these groups have been combined in the computation of critical ratios.

ally insignificant differences between averages, there would appear some justification for proclaiming that "Catholics are least favorable toward the Negro whereas the nonreligious and Jews are most favorable, with the Protestants consistently between these extremes." In point of fact, conclusions of this general sort based upon the same kind of evidence are current in the literature on ethnic and racial attitudes.[4] When so based, such conclusions may be at once impugned.

4. *E.g.*, for sex differences in "mean attitude scores," see V. F. Sims and J. R. Patrick, "Attitude toward the Negro of Northern and Southern College Students," *Journal of Social Psychology* 7 (1936), pp. 196–97.

Methodological Fallacies of
Thurstone Attitude Scales

The basic objections to such a conclusion questions the meaning of summed or averaged scores of group responses to "scales" using the Thurstone technique of construction. What do these "averaged scores" denote? The usual answer is that they constitute an "index" of the degree of "favorableness" or "unfavorableness" toward "the" Negro. This answer is based on the conviction that the judgments that make up the inventory represent a "linear continuum" and that the scale-values of endorsed judgments may be algebraically summed and averaged.[5] This assertion can be and has been challenged but, to my knowledge, the various criticisms have not been satisfactorily met.[6] The objections to the assumption of a linear continuum (involving additivity and determination of central tendencies) are of at least three interrelated kinds.

1. It can be shown that Thurstone's scale-values are not additive, inasmuch as his collections of statements do not have the "group-property," i.e., do not constitute closed systems.[7] To put this more concretely, let us

5. See the explicit statement of L. L. Thurstone and E. J. Chave on this point. "It is legitimate to determine a central tendency for the frequency distribution of attitudes in a group. Several groups of individuals may then be compared as regards the means of their respective frequency distributions of attitudes. The differences between the means of several such distributions may be directly compared because of the fact that a rational base line has been established." *The Measurement of Attitudes* (Chicago, 1929), p. 82.

6. For basic methodological criticism of the Thurstonian assumption of a linear continuum, see the incisive papers by H. M. Johnson, "Pseudo-Mathematics in the Mental and Social Sciences," *American Journal of Psychology* 48 (1936), pp. 342–51, and by Clifford Kirkpatrick, "Assumptions and Methods in Attitude Measurements," *American Sociological Review* 1 (1936), pp. 75–88. See also Kirkpatrick's further papers on this subject cited therein, and the general methodological discussions of measurement by N. R. Campbell, *An Account of the Principles of Measurement and Calculation* (New York, 1928), and by Morris R. Cohen and Ernest Nagel, *An Introduction to Logic and Scientific Method* (New York, 1934), Chap. xv. For a paper which purports to demonstrate the logical validity of such techniques of 'measurement' as those of Thurstone, see George A. Lundberg, "The Thoughtways of Contemporary Sociology," *American Sociological Review* 1 (1936), pp. 703–23. Relevant to this discussion is the unpublished critique of Lundberg's paper read by R. K. Merton at the Eastern Sociological Conference, New Haven, April 18, 1936.

7. For a demonstration of this inadequacy, see Johnson, *op. cit.*, 349–350. For a brief discussion of the group-property, see Cassius J. Keyser, *Mathematical Philosophy* (New York, 1922), Chap. XII.

examine Thurstone's assertion that "we may assign the scale-value to each of the statements that a subject has indorsed and then calculate their arithmetic mean."[8] Suppose (1) that a person, *A*, who is extremely unfavorable toward "the" Negro, endorses Statement 6 ("I consider that the Negro is more like an animal than a human being") with a scale-value of 10.6. Suppose (2) that individual *B* is even more intensely unfavorable to "the" Negro, and that he likewise endorses Statement 6 and also several other statements disparaging to Negroes (e.g., Statements 1, 2, 8 and 30, with scale-values of 10.3, 10.2, 9.7, and 8.8 respectively). *B's* "score" (arithmetical mean) thus becomes 9.9, less "unfavorable" than *A's* score of 10.6, which contradicts the hypothesis. The inevitable result of multiple endorsements of statements lying at either extreme of the "scale" is a score that is less extreme than that obtained by endorsing *only* the limiting statements in the series. Given a finite number of statements, the "score" of endorsed statements may thus become an inaccurate index of subjects' convictions concerning the values in question.[9]

2. That Thurstone's inventories do not constitute a linear "scale" may be seen in another connection. Were the inventory a linear scale, endorsement of a statement with a given scale-value would involve "acceptance of all positions less extreme and in the same direction from the neutral position."[10] In other words, were the Thurstone inventory actually a "scale," in the strict sense, persons endorsing items graded as "very unfavorable" might be assumed to endorse all statements involving slightly less deprecation of the social value in question. Likewise, endorsements of statements with scale-values of 8 and 10.3, let us say, would logically entail endorsement of all statements with scale-values falling between 8

8. Thurstone and Chave, *op. cit.*, p. 64. In the Hinckley-Thurstone "attitude-toward-the-Negro scale," "scores" are constituted by the median scale value. This is a difference which makes no difference to our argument. Likewise, the use of MacCrone's statements and scale-values, rather than Hinckley's, does not affect the *logical* basis of our discussion.
9. For Thurstonian inventories which contain statements of the "A" and "E" types ("All," "No") this difficulty becomes readily apparent. The "A" proposition includes all the "I" propositions, yet the subject who endorses both the "A" statement and any or all of the "I" propositions will obtain a lower score than the subject who simply endorses the "A" statement. As Johnson suggests, "Perhaps the procedure should be worked over." *Op. cit.*, p. 350.
10. G. Murphy, L. B. Murphy and T. M. Newcomb, *Experimental Social Psychology* (New York, 1937), p. 906. The fact that Thurstone has chosen not to indicate a "neutral" position on his "scale" is irrelevant for, as he indicates, "The origin is arbitrarily assigned. We could have placed the origin in the middle of the scale, but that would necessitate dealing with negative class-intervals and nothing is statistically gained thereby." Thurstone and Chave, *op. cit.*, p. 63.

and 10.3. This is a most elementary consideration. "No one could use a ruler on which he could not tell whether the point marked 7 would fall between 6 and 8 or whether it would have a capricious preference for some other point on the instrument."[11] In actual practice, however, as those who have used Thurstone's inventories can testify, there is no assurance that subjects will check all the statements with scale-values intermediate between the extremes of those actually endorsed. If this be a linear "scale," it is one belonging to a newly created species of scales.

3. Not unrelated to these considerations is the question of *interchangeability of units* in a measurable collection. The Thurstone units are not interchangeable, as can be illustrated by the following case. Individual *A* endorses Statement 6 ("I consider that the Negro is more like an animal than a human being") with a scale-value of 10.6 and also endorses Statement 25 ("I consider that the white man is neglecting to do his duty by not doing more to improve the lot of the Negro") with a scale-value of 2.8. By the Thurstone method of scoring, his score is 6.7. Individual *B* endorses Statement 24 ("I think that all the Negro needs to make him happy is the satisfaction of his material needs") with a scale-value of 6.7. In both cases, then, the score is 6.7. In what sense can we conclude that these two persons are equally "favorable" (or equally "unfavorable") to "the" Negro? *Interviews with various subjects who have identical "scores" indicate that they will not readily substitute endorsement of one set of endorsed statements for another set of statements, even though the two sets result in identical or insignificantly different "average scores."* If so, what is the denotation of "equally favorable" scores? Can we conclude with such proponents of unalloyed operationalism as Lundberg that in this way "the *attitude* would . . . have a very much narrower but a more definite meaning than at present?"[12] Narrower, perhaps, but hardly more definite, Thurstone *assumes* an interchangeability of judgments with identical scale-values that does not in fact exist. Statistical fiat does not make empirical fact.

In this connection, various investigators have maintained that these "scales" are not designed to represent "attitudes" pictorially. They assert that Thurstone's "scales," like scientific measuring instruments in general, do not measure *all* aspects of events. These instruments respond selectively to one aspect or property, e.g., "favorableness," just as the balance responds only to one property, weight. Hence, it is argued, criticisms that hold that Thurstone's "scales" force complex attitudes into one dimension

11. Murphy, Murphy and Newcombe, *op. cit.*, p. 897.
12. Lundberg, *op. cit.*, p. 711.

are wholly beside the point, since no scientific construct "attempts to cover all enumerable details of a class of phenomena."[13] To my mind, the analogy seems to be slightly misplaced. The fault of Thurstone's constructs is not their abstractness but their failure to constitute a continuum involving assignable magnitudes. Despite the complicated operations involved in the construction of these "scales," there is no introduction of *cardinal* numbers at any point. Thurstone's inventories are usable if they are treated for what they are: ordered series of statements concerning social values. In terms of certain criteria, they rank, but they do not "measure," opinions.

Sociological Inadequacies of Thurstone Attitude Scale

When we shift our attention from the inventory as a whole to its component statements, several sociological assumptions come into view. In an effort to eliminate "undifferentiating elements" from his "scale," Thurstone introduced such criteria as "ambiguity" (Q-value) and "irrelevance." To be sure, these criteria are necessary if the sole objective is to develop an instrument that will "measure" a given property, but this very emphasis on linearity may obscure the sociological utility of including in an inventory some statements that, on the basis of these criteria, are not "differentiating," i.e., statements endorsed with equal frequency by persons with differentiated responses to other statements. In other words, if we abandon or modify the notion that these inventories "measure" a single "attitude," opinions involving the coalescence of several cultural values may be included in the inventory, although conventional tests of reliability may lead us to designate these opinions as "undifferentiating." Otherwise, we rule out access to *those opinions that are shared* by most of our sample, irrespective of their differences about other opinions.

In the case of such opinions, we are no longer dealing with "pure," highly distilled opinions concerning "the" Negro (as a "pure" abstraction) but rather with complex opinions concerning Negroes within certain cultural contexts. Thus, using Thurstone's criteria, such statements as "I think that the Negro ought to be given every opportunity of education and development—just like the white man" would be discarded because they are endorsed by a large proportion of subjects with "scores" lying near both extremes of the "scale." This statement would be suspect, for

13. L. L. Thurstone, *The Vectors of Mind* (Chicago, 1935), pp. 44–48; see also Lundberg, *op. cit.*, p. 714.

although our "Northern" samples consistently endorsed it more frequently than did our "Southern" samples, yet 45 percent of the latter also endorsed it. Apparently, then, this statement does not exclusively reflect "attitudes" toward "the" Negro, as such, but involves also the "halo effect" induced by the prestige of "universal education" as a cultural value in our society. Endorsement may thus be a resultant of opinions concerning "the" Negro and of opinions concerning the cultural premise that "every American citizen has a right to an education." Thus, even though statements of this type are irrelevant by Thurstonian standards, frequency of endorsement can be adopted as a crude index of current opinions concerning Negroes and education as a value complex. Combining separate tests of "attitudes toward education" and "attitudes toward the Negro" would no more provide an index of this opinion configuration than combining encyclopedia articles on "France" and on "disease" would provide discussion of "the French disease." Otherwise stated, the effort to attain a linear scale should not be permitted to divert all attention from the sociologically and psychologically relevant question of opinion configurations.[14] Group differentials in the endorsement or rejection of complex opinions constitute valuable descriptive data.[15]

If opinionnaires are to serve as indexes of current opinion concerning social values, their component statements should be analyzed with reference to values besides those to which the inventory as a whole is devoted. This assertion has implications for determining "internal consistency" of an inventory by means of the association between each statement in the inventory and the total score. An item is said to be discriminating according to the extent to which it leads to differential responses by persons with markedly different total scores. It is further believed that nondis-

14. Clifford Kirkpatrick and Sarah Stone have evolved a "belief pattern method" of appraising configurations of opinions. However, they also assert the "unsatisfactory" nature of inventory-statements which are "ambiguous since either factual, evaluational or logical considerations may have motivated the acceptance or rejection of the statements." It may be suggested, however, that statements which are "ambiguous" in terms of imputable motivation may nevertheless prove useful in ascertaining group differences in maintaining complex opinions. See Kirkpatrick and Stone, "Attitude Measurement and the Comparison of Generations," *Journal of Applied Psychology* 19 (1935), p. 575.

15. G. Murphy and R. Likert note "the importance of considering the qualitative significance of each item as well as the significance of the whole scales." *Public Opinion and the Individual* (New York, 1938), pp. 50–51. See also Keith Sward's observation that "mean scores" in rating scales are inadequate "except as the very roughest of devices." He finds that item-analysis contains an assortment of traits that are significant numerically and qualitatively." See his "Patterns of Jewish Temperament," *Journal of Applied Psychology* 19 (1935), pp. 410–25.

criminating items should be discarded. Although this procedure is statistically impeccable,[16] it obscures fallacious assumptions by assuming a disputable "logic of relations" between judgments involving social evaluations. Let us turn to cases.

The investigator who shelves his psychology and sociology while he deals with mathematical formulas will doubtless conclude that if a considerable proportion of subjects endorse both of the following statements, the "internal consistency" is to this extent lessened.

> To my mind the Negro is so childish and irresponsible that he cannot be expected to know what is in his best interests (scale-value = 8.4, i.e., "unfavorable").

> I think that the Negro ought to be given every opportunity of education and development—just like the white man (scale-value = 1.1, i.e., "very favorable").

Endorsement by the same subjects of both these statements, rated as "unfavorable" and "favorable" respectively, will presumably cast suspicion on their reliability and validity.[17] A reconstruction of the implicit reasoning may be hazarded. If a person believes Negroes to be childish and irresponsible, he will scarcely favor their being given every opportunity of education. Hence, if the same subjects endorse both these judgments, they are not giving their "real" opinions but are checking statements facetiously or at random. Or, it is inferred, the statements do not adequately reflect "attitudes" toward the same entity, "the" Negro. Both of these inferences contain a suppressed premise which, I suggest, is fallacious. This premise holds that subjects do not "really" subscribe to "logically" contradictory judgments. In making this assumption, the investigator is playing the role of logician rather than psychologist or

16. However, R. F. Sletto has demonstrated that "measurement of a single common variable cannot be safely inferred from the fact that items satisfy the criterion of internal consistency, as usually applied." See his "Critical Study of the Criterion of Internal Consistency in Personality Scale Construction," *American Sociological Review* 1 (1936), pp. 61–68; and the valuable discussion of this paper by R. V. Bowers, *ibid.*, pp. 69–74.

17. The explicit relevant statement reads: "If we find considerable inconsistency [in endorsements], we might attribute it to the carelessness of the subjects in making their check marks more or less at random, or we might attribute it to defects in the statements themselves. ... But the inconsistencies vary with the statement that is chosen as a basis of comparison with all the rest, and such differences are due primarily no doubt to defects in the statements themselves. We have so regarded them. ..." Thurstone and Chave, *op. cit.*, 46–47.

sociologist. He is, in effect, tacitly assuming that these presumably incompatible assertions *should not* be endorsed by the same persons. Such a prejudgment minimizes the possibility of securing an adequate representation of the inconsistencies of social judgments that in many instances actually obtain. This "test of internal consistency" is based on a dubious rationalist assumption. In making this assumption, the investigator is using *norms* of logic, not facts of sociology.

Once we shift from the level of logical norms to the level of psychosocial fact, we observe that incompatible judgments are often made by the same person.[18] Thus, in the previous illustrations, persons who subscribe to both the national democratic ideology—including the belief in education as a "moral right"—and to the regional ideology that insists on the childishness and irresponsibility of the Negro, will readily and honestly endorse both statements. To assume, as Thurstone does, that persons hold rigorously consistent social opinions is to fly in the face of a store of clinical observations by psychologists, sociologists, anthropologists, and John Doe himself. It is not pertinent to our present problem to discuss the level on which these coexisting judgments are "not consistent." It is sufficient to indicate that Thurstone's criterion of "irrelevancy" is loaded with assumptions that are contrary to fact; that here again mathematical technique has supplanted and obscured sociological considerations.[19]

On Opinion and Overt Behavior

A further mooted point in connection with opinionnaires is the relation of opinion to overt behavior. The current vogue of semanticism and Paretoism leads some to draw questionable inferences from these systems of thought and to urge that verbal responses are "really of minor importance." The metaphysical assumption is tacitly introduced that in one sense or another overt behavior is "more real" than verbal behavior. This assumption is both unwarranted and scientifically meaningless. In some

18. A paraphrase of an observation by Jean Piaget is pertinent. "For it is not by taking the ready-made schema of adult reasoning (and of explicit scientific . . . reasoning at that) and by submitting this schema to, say syllogistic tests so as to see whether the [subject] conforms to our practical and scholastic habits of thought, that we shall succeed in finding the true nature of [social opinions]." *Judgment and Reasoning in the Child* (New York, 1928), p. 135.

19. A close reading of the method of constructing the criterion of "irrelevance" shows that these invalid assumptions underlie the "index of similarity." See Thurstone and Chave, *op. cit.*, 46–56.

situations, it may be discovered that overt behavior is a more reliable basis for drawing inferences about future behavior (overt or verbal). In other situations, it may be found that verbal responses are a tolerably accurate guide to future behavior (overt or verbal). It should not be forgotten that *overt actions may deceive; that they, just as "derivations" or "speech reactions" may be deliberately designed to disguise or to conceal private attitudes.* The question of the relative "significance" of verbal and overt responses must as yet be solved anew for each class of problems. The a priori assumption that verbal responses are simply epiphenomenal is to be accorded no greater weight than the assumption that words do not deceive nor actions lie. It is unnecessary to repeat additional considerations in this connection except to state, in company with Thurstone, Murphy, Likert and others, that the expression of opinion is itself a recurrent phase of social activity. Hence, reliable and valid opinionnaires may be useful even if unrelated to overt behavior.

Another issue in this controversy has not received adequate attention. It is not simply a question of whether or not overt behavior "coincides" with expressed or endorsed opinions. This way of formulating the problem obscures one of its basic aspects, namely, *may we assume the amount and direction of spread between opinion and action to be relatively constant for members of different groups?* To my knowledge, no systematic research on this problem has been carried out.[20] It may be tentatively (and speculatively) suggested that the spread between opinion and action is not the same for different groups but that the "differences in direction of spread" are relatively constant. Thus, the hypothesis may be advanced that "the Northern index of *verbalized* tolerance" of Negroes is consistently *higher* than their "index of *behavioral* tolerance" of Negroes. And, contrariwise, that "the Southern index of *verbalized* tolerance" is consistently *lower* than their "index of behavioral tolerance." Put in more idiomatic and possibly more intelligible terms, it is possible that Northerners treat Negroes less "favorably" than they talk about them and that Southerners talk about Negroes less "favorably" than they treat them.[21] Or possibly the difference is one of degree rather than direction. In any event, setting the problem in these terms shifts the discussion from the question of correlation between opinion and action *in general* to comparisons of degree and direction of correlation in various groups. To be sure, these notions about possibly consistent group differences in spread between

20. Cf. Richard T. LaPiere, *Collective Behavior* (New York, 1938), pp. 49–50.
21. The terms "favorable" and "unfavorable" are suspiciously inexact and at times misleading. They should be interpreted within the context of considerations introduced in the next note.

opinion and action are largely speculative at the present juncture.[22] But the very hypothesis emphasizes the need for caution in the use of "attitude scores" derived from opinionnaires as indexes of predispositions to act in a determinate fashion toward a given value. Identical scores may well be associated with sharply diverging forms of overt behavior.

Regional Differences in Opinions
Concerning "the" Negro

With these strictures in mind, we may now consider a preliminary report of regional differences in endorsement of statements about "the" Negro. Some studies have assumed that student subjects hold opinions that represent the mores of the region where they attend school. This assumption may or may not square with the facts; in any event, it should not be assumed without further ado that subjects represent the particular geographical region in which they are tested. Using the sixfold division into

22. "Largely speculative," because the theory of social stereotypes suggests that such difference in spread may occur through the varying roles played by stereotypes in propositions and in overt behavior. Thus, "Southerners," when asked to respond to propositions about "the" Negro may show an unequivocally "unfavorable" and "intolerant attitude," although their relations with specific Negroes may involve a larger component of "intimacy," "favorableness" and "tolerance" than would be the case with "Northerners" interaction with specific Negroes. In the proposition, there may be a response to a verbal stereotype, "the Negro"; in behavior, there may be response to a concrete personality standing in a complex set of relations to the white, e.g. Herman-the-colored-handyman-who-has-been-with-the-family-for-years-and-knows-more-about-my-dahlias-than-I-do, etc. (John Dollard's speculations concerning the relative frequency and intensity of stereotypes of Negroes among Northern and Southern whites partly agree and partly disagree with these suggestions. See his *Caste and Class in a Southern Town* (New Haven, Conn., 1937), pp. 73, 84, 390. These suggestions indicate the vacuity of such one-dimensional terms as "favorableness," "tolerance," "appreciation," "depreciation," and the like. It would seem expedient to reassess the denotations of such crude abstractions, especially when one investigator can conclude that "Northerners" have greater "*good-will*" toward "the" Negro than "Southerners"; while others conclude that "on the whole, a greater '*aversion*' was shown toward 'the' Negro by Northern than by Southern students"; and a third study informs us that Northern students are "more favorable" to "the" Negro than are Southern students. Item-analyses of actual frequencies of endorsements of specific statements would do much to eliminate or to minimize such indulgence in verbalism. See C. W. Hunter, *A Comparative Study of the Relationship Existing Between the White Race and the Negro Race in the State of North Carolina and in the City of New York* (unpublished Columbia University M.A. thesis) summarized by G. and L. B. Murphy, *Experimental Social Psychology* (New York, 1931), pp. 639–45; D. Katz

"regions" developed by Odum,[23] we find considerable variations between our samples with regard to the percentages of subjects who have lived for the past decade in the same region as that in which their school is located. Thus, in the Harvard–Radcliffe sample, 68, or 21.6 percent had their residence outside the Northeastern region; of the Pennsylvania State sample, only 4, or 3.5 percent, derived from outside this region; of the Tulane–Newcomb sample, 5, or 9 percent, and of the Louisiana State University sample, 28, or 13.5 percent, had their homes outside the Southeastern region.[24] Thus, with respect to these samples, the assumption that the subjects' endorsements were those of persons living in the cultural region wherein their schools are located would lead to a significant error. The original data were reclassified according to the subjects' place of residence for 10 years prior to 1938–39. This shifts the frequency distributions of endorsements to some extent and decreases the standard deviations.[25]

The following item-analyses, then, pertain to 346 subjects recruited from the Northeastern region and 233 from the Southeastern region. A synopsis of the percentages of these two samples who endorsed each of the 30 statements in the opinionnaire is presented in the following chart. An arbitrary definition leads to the inclusion of all statements endorsed by 50 percent or more of either sample in an "inventory of assent." It was likewise decided that statements endorsed by 10 percent or less of a sample would be taken to comprise the "inventory of dissent" for that group.[26] Thus, we obtain four classes of statements described as the "Northern credo," "the Southern credo," "Northern dissent" and "Southern dissent."[27]

---

and F. H. Allport, *Students' Attitudes* (Syracuse, 1931), p. 102; Sims and Patrick, *op. cit.*, pp. 194–195.

23. For an itemization of the states included in each of the six regions—Southeast, Southwest, Northeast, Middle States, Northwest, Far West—and a discussion of the criteria adopted in this classification, see Howard W. Odum, *Southern Regions of the United States* (Chapel Hill, N.C., 1936), pp. 1–205.

24. Fourteen cases in the Harvard–Radcliffe sample and four cases in the Pennsylvania State sample did not state their place of residence.

25. Of course, when the research is designed with "practical objectives of college administration" in mind, breakdowns by residence are not necessary. See, e.g., Katz and Allport, *op cit.*

26. These labels do not imply that these opinion-aggregates are typical of "the North" or "the South." The results (frequencies of endorsements) should not be extrapolated beyond the groups actually involved nor can we simply assume that these opinions are stable.

27. The arbitrariness of these definitions should be apparent. Differing magnitudes of critical ratios could instead be adopted as the criterion of the various credos.

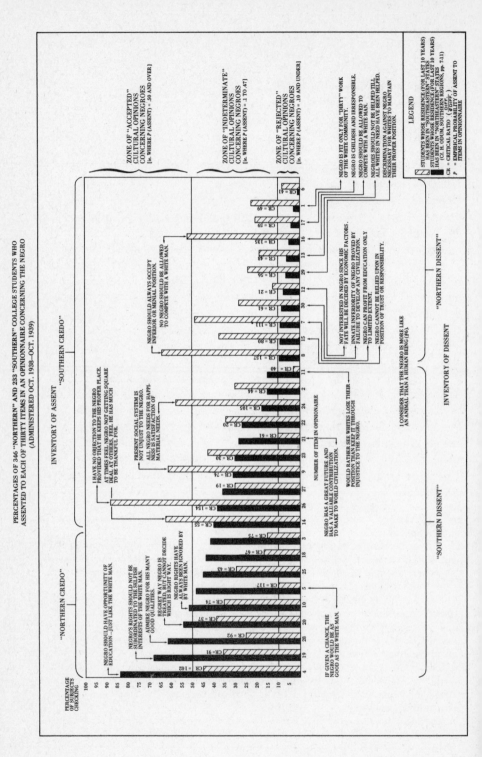

PERCENTAGES OF 346 "NORTHERN" AND 233 "SOUTHERN" COLLEGE STUDENTS WHO ASSENTED TO EACH OF THIRTY ITEMS IN AN OPINIONNAIRE CONCERNING THE NEGRO (ADMINISTERED OCT. 1938–OCT. 1939)

INVENTORY OF ASSENT

"NORTHERN CREDO"

"SOUTHERN CREDO"

NEGRO SHOULD HAVE OPPORTUNITY OF EDUCATION—JUST LIKE THE WHITE MAN.

NEGRO RIGHTS SHOULD NOT BE SUBORDINATED TO THE SELFISH INTERESTS OF THE WHITE MAN.

ADMIRE NEGRO FOR HIS MANY GOOD QUALITIES.

REGRET WAY NEGRO IS TREATED, BUT CANNOT DECIDE WHICH IS RIGHT WAY.

NEGRO RIGHTS HAVE ALWAYS BEEN IGNORED BY WHITE MAN.

IF GIVEN A CHANCE, THE NEGRO WOULD BE AS GOOD AS THE WHITE MAN.

I HAVE NO OBJECTION TO THE NEGRO PROVIDED THAT HE KEEPS HIS PROPER PLACE.

AT TIMES FEEL NEGRO NOT GETTING SQUARE DEAL AT OTHERS, FEEL HE HAS MUCH TO BE THANKFUL FOR.

PRESENT SOCIAL SYSTEM IS NOT UNJUST TO THE NEGRO.

ALL NEGRO NEEDS FOR HAPPINESS IS SATISFACTION OF MATERIAL NEEDS.

NEGRO SHOULD ALWAYS OCCUPY INFERIOR OR MENIAL POSITION.

NO NEGRO SHOULD BE ALLOWED TO COMPETE WITH A WHITE MAN.

NEGRO HAS A GREAT FUTURE AND HAS A VALUABLE CONTRIBUTION TO MAKE TO WORLD CIVILIZATION.

NUMBER OF ITEM IN OPINIONNAIRE

WOULD RATHER SEE WHITES LOSE THEIR POSITION THAN KEEP IT THROUGH INJUSTICE TO THE NEGRO.

"SOUTHERN DISSENT"

I CONSIDER THAT THE NEGRO IS MORE LIKE AN ANIMAL THAN A HUMAN BEING (#6).

INVENTORY OF DISSENT

"NORTHERN DISSENT"

ZONE OF "ACCEPTED" CULTURAL OPINIONS CONCERNING NEGROES [i.e. WHERE P (ASSENT) .50 AND OVER]

ZONE OF "INDETERMINATE" CULTURAL OPINIONS CONCERNING NEGROES [i.e. WHERE P (ASSENT) .1 TO .47]

ZONE OF "REJECTED" CULTURAL OPINIONS CONCERNING NEGROES [i.e. WHERE P (ASSENT) .10 AND UNDER]

NEGRO IS FIT ONLY FOR "DIRTY" WORK OF THE WHITE COMMUNITY.

NEGRO IS CHILDISH AND IRRESPONSIBLE.

NEGRO SHOULD BE ALLOWED TO COMPETE WITH A WHITE MAN.

NEGRO CAN PROFIT FROM EDUCATION ONLY TO LIMITED EXTENT.

NEGROS SHOULD NOT BE HELPED TILL ALL WHITES IN NEED HAVE BEEN HELPED.

DISCRIMINATION AGAINST NEGRO NECESSARY FOR WHITES TO MAINTAIN THEIR PROPER POSITION.

NEGRO CANNOT BE RELIED UPON IN POSITION OF TRUST OR RESPONSIBILITY.

NOT INTERESTED IN NEGRO SINCE HIS FATE WILL BE DECIDED BY ECONOMIC FACTORS.

INNATE INFERIORITY OF NEGRO PROVED BY FAILURE TO PERCENT WITH ANY CIVILIZATION.

LEGEND

STUDENTS WHOSE RESIDENCE (FOR LAST 10 YEARS) HAS BEEN IN SOUTHEASTERN" STATES

STUDENTS WHOSE RESIDENCE (FOR LAST 10 YEARS) HAS BEEN IN "WHITE" NON-SOUTHERN STATES (C. H. ODUM, SOUTHERN REGIONS, pp. 7-11)

CR = CRITICAL RATIO (DIFF./σDIFF.)

P = EMPIRICAL PROBABILITY OF ASSENT TO ITEMS IN OPINIONNAIRE

PERCENTAGE OF SUBJECTS CHECKING

An empirical classification of the Northern and Southern inventories follows.[28]

<table>
<tr><td colspan="2">NORTHERN CREDO</td><td colspan="2">SOUTHERN CREDO</td></tr>
</table>

A. *Expressions of Democratic Mores*

  4. Negro should have every opportunity of education and development—just like the white man. (83.2%)

  10. Negroes' rights have nearly always been ignored by the white man. (51.2%)

  19. Negroes' rights should not be subordinated to selfish interests of the white man. (68.5%)

A. *Expressions of Caste Mores*

  8. Negro should always occupy an inferior position in the community. (64.4%)

  9. Present social system is fundamentally not unjust to the Negro. (60.9%)

  16. No Negro should be allowed to compete with a white man. (52.8%)

  26. I have no objection to the Negro provided he keeps his proper place. (88.8%)

B. *Qualities Imputed to the Negro*

  28. I admire the Negro for his many good qualities. (61.6%)

B. *Qualities Imputed to the Negro*

  24. All the Negro needs to make him happy is the satisfaction of his material needs. (57.1%)

C. *Ambivalence toward Caste System, with Dominant Negative Valence*

  20. I am not very happy about the way the Negro is treated, but I find it difficult to decide which is the right way. (54.6%)

C. *Ambivalence toward Caste System, with Dominant Positive Valence*

  14. Sometimes I feel the Negro is not getting a square deal, but at other times I feel he has a lot to be thankful for. (62.7%)

NORTHERN DISSENT

SOUTHERN DISSENT

A. *Nonendorsement of Antidemocratic Mores*

  8. (See under Southern Credo, A.) (9.5%)

  13. Negro ought not to be helped until all the white people in need have been helped. (5.5%)

  16. (See under Southern Credo, A.) (5.5%)

A. *Nonendorsement of Anticaste Mores*

  11. I would rather see the white people lose their position in this country than keep it at the expense of injustice to the Negro. (3.4%)

Note also that "inventory of dissent" is a somewhat misleading phrase; it would be more accurate to say "inventory of nonassent," inasmuch as subjects were asked to check only those statements which they endorsed. Thus, failure to check a statement is ambiguous; it may signify anything from sharp disagreement to incomplete agreement with the opinion.

28. Numbers refer to statements in the *Opinionnaire* appended to this article.

Northern Dissent

29. I feel very strongly that the white man cannot maintain his proper position unless he discriminates against the Negro. (6.1%)

B. *Nonendorsement of Imputation of Qualities to the Negro*

  1. Negro is fit to do only the "dirty" work of the white community. (3.2%)
  7. Negro can profit by education only to a very limited extent. (9.0%)
  15. The Negro cannot be relied upon in a position of trust or responsibility. (9.2%)
  17. The Negro is childish and irresponsible. (4.0%)
  30. The Negro's failure to develop a civilization before he arrived in this country is proof of his innate inferiority. (8.1%)

Southern Dissent

B. *Nonendorsement of Imputation of Qualities to the Negro*

  5. If Negro were given the chance he would be just as good as the white man. (9.9%)
  21. Negro has a great future and a valuable contribution to make to world civilization. (9.9%)

Seldom Endorsed by Either

  6. I consider that the Negro is more like an animal than a human being. (Northern sample = .9%; Southern sample = 8.6%)

On the whole, 50 percent or more of our "Northern" subjects subscribe to the "democratic mores" expressing the right to equal opportunity for individual development, irrespective of race. These convictions are supported by a series of beliefs that deny the intrinsic inferiority of "the" Negro. Contrariwise, Southern subjects largely assent to statements that endorse the current caste structure and justify their convictions by imputing inferiority to "the" Negro. It should be noted, however, that the extreme statement that asserts that the Negro is more like an animal than a human is seldom endorsed by either Northerners or Southerners. It is the one item on which there is substantial agreement by both regional groups, representing, as it were, an asymptotic nadir in the Southerners' imputation of inferiorities to the Negro.[29]

29. In this connection should be noted Dollard's observation that some residents of "Southerntown" were quite prepared to assert that "the Negro is a mere animal." Some 9 percent of our Southern sample assented to this notion. This case incidentally illustrates the utility of opinionnaires; they help to establish, however crudely, the *relative frequency* of folk beliefs and thus serve as a check on observations of scattered cases. Opinionnaires do not supplant direct observations of opinions advanced in "life-situations," but they are a useful supplement as Hortense Powdermaker has shown in her study of "Southerntown." See her *After Freedom* (New York, 1939), pp. 381–91; also Dollard, *op. cit.*, pp. 368–69. On page

Two statements (14, 20) in the opinionnaire may be interpreted as expressions of *ambivalence* toward the caste system. The Northern sample more often endorses one of these, and the Southern sample, the other; yet, even in the choice of ambivalent statements, there is a consistent difference. The Northern sample more often endorsed that ambivalent statement which implicitly weights more heavily a negative opinion concerning the caste system; the Southern group more often assented to that ambivalent statement which weights more heavily a positive opinion concerning the caste system. However, this difference should not be permitted to obscure the similarity: *both groups are apparently subject to the conflict between coexisting democratic and caste ideologies.* In all this, it should be remembered, we are dealing with opinions and not with overt behavior.

It should not be inferred from the foregoing discussion that the "Northern" and the "Southern" samples are wholly homogeneous in their respective opinions concerning the Negro. It can be shown that there are more or less consistent differences of opinion between subjects coming from different localities within the same general "region." Thus, in the "Northeastern region," on eight items[30] the frequency of endorsement by Pennsylvania subjects is intermediate between the frequencies of Massachusetts and Louisiana subjects. Although only one of these differences between Massachusetts and Pennsylvania subjects is conventionally "significant"—26, with a C.R. of 3.7—the fact that the Pennsylvanians are *consistently* intermediate between the Massachusetts and Louisiana subjects suggests that the Pennsylvanians are, in a sense, "marginal" with respect to "Northeastern" and "Southeastern" opinion inventories. As far as these results are concerned, then, we are not justified in treating Odum's "Northeastern region" as reasonably homogeneous in opinions about the Negro. Pennsylvania subjects, although largely sharing the opinions of the Massachusetts sample, tend toward the "Southeastern" configuration of opinions, in some respects. However, differences in frequency of endorsement by Pennsylvania and Louisiana subjects even with regard to these eight statements are conventionally significant (except for statement 14, with a C.R. of 2.4). For Statement 14, which is taken to express

---

387, Dollard remarks that not all Southern whites hold all of the "defensive beliefs" which he itemizes, and adds that "it would be desirable, but it is impossible, to give a statistical delineation of the degree to which various attitudes are held." 30. The eight statements are numbers 5, 9, 13, 14, 16, 19, 24, 26, with critical ratios (Massachusetts subjects vs. Pennsylvania subjects) respectively, of 1.1, 2.2, 2.0, 1.8, 1.4, 1.7, 1.8 and 3.7. Note that all of these statements are included in the regional inventories.

ambivalence toward the caste system (with a dominant positive valence), the Pennsylvanians' frequency of endorsement more nearly approximates that of the Louisiana subjects. These data suggest that the populations of areas as extensive as Odum's regions may not have relatively similar distributions of opinions concerning the Negro (and, possibly, a range of other social values).

This report is to be taken primarily as an indication of one way in which opinionnaire results may be legitimately employed without recourse to dubiously applicable mathematical operations.

OPINIONNAIRE USED IN THIS RESEARCH[31]

CHECK (√) ONLY THOSE STATEMENTS WHICH MOST NEARLY EXPRESS YOUR
SENTIMENT TOWARDS THE NEGRO

Scale-
Values

10.3 1. I consider that the Negro is only fit to do the "dirty" work of the white community.

10.2 2. The idea of contact with the black or dark skin of the Negro excites horror and disgust in me.

3.1 3. It seems to me that the white man, by placing restrictions, such as the "Color Line," upon the Negro is really trying to exploit him economically.

1.1 4. I think that the Negro ought to be given every opportunity of education and development—just like the white man.

1.3 5. I think that the Negro, if he were given the chance, would prove to be just as good as the white man.

10.6 6. I consider that the Negro is more like an animal than a human being.

7.8 7. I do not think that the Negro is capable of profiting by education except to a very limited extent.

9.7 8. I think that the Negro should always occupy an inferior or menial position in the community.

6.5 9. I do not consider that the present social system is fundamentally unjust to the Negro.

2.6 10. It seems clear to me that the rights of the Negro in this country have nearly always been ignored by the white man.

.8 11. I would rather see the white people lose their position in this country than keep it at the expense of injustice to the Negro.

5.6 12. I am not interested in the Negro or in his relations to the white man because I think that in the end economic factors will decide his fate.

7.5 13. I do not think that we ought to help the Negro until all the white people who are in need have been helped.

5.4 14. Sometimes I feel that the Negro is not getting a square deal, but at other times I feel he has a lot to be thankful for.

8.6 15. I do not think that the Negro can be relied upon in a position of trust or of responsibility.

31. Adapted from MacCrone, *op. cit.*

9.4 16. I think that no Negro should ever be allowed to enter into competition with a white man.

8.4 17. To my mind the Negro is so childish and irresponsible that he cannot be expected to know what is in his best interests.

1.4 18. I consider that the Negro has been unjustly deprived of his rights by the white man.

1.7 19. I do not think that the rights of the Negro should be subordinated to the selfish interests of the white man.

4.8 20. I am not very happy about the way in which the Negro is treated in this country, but I find it very difficult to decide which is the right way.

1.2 21. I believe that the Negro has a great future ahead of him and that he has a valuable contribution to make to the world's civilization.

3.8 22. I consider that the white community in this country owes a real debt of gratitude to the churches for the way in which they have tried to uplift the Negro.

4.4 23. I would like to see the Negro advance in the scale of civilization, but only very slowly and step by step.

6.7 24. I think that all the Negro needs to make him happy is the satisfaction of his material needs.

2.8 25. I consider that the white man is neglecting to do his duty by not doing more to improve the lot of the Negro.

6.2 26. I have no objection to the Negro provided that he keeps his proper place.

5.1 27. Until the Negro has been given more time and opportunity of showing what he is capable of doing, I think that it is foolish to try to judge him.

2.2 28. I admire the Negro for his many good qualities and would like to see him being given an opportunity of developing them.

8.2 29. I feel very strongly that the white man cannot maintain his proper position in the United States unless he discriminates against the Negro.

8.8 30. The fact that the Negro had developed no civilization of his own before he arrived in this country is to my mind more than sufficient proof of his innate inferiority.

Indexes

Index of Names

Index of Subjects

Accountability, 82, 93
Accumulation
  of advantage, 124
  of ambivalence, 24–25
  selective, of scientific knowledge, 137
Accumulative imbalances, 139n
Ad hoc explanations, 247
Ad hoc hypotheses, 112
Advantage, accumulation of, 124
Advantages, differential, 201
Affective neutrality, 17, 18, 31
Affectivity, 18
Agathogamy, 220n, 222
Aggrandizement effect, 77
Alternatives
  functional, 179
  socially structured, 124
Altruism, institutionalized, 62
Ambiguity, 23
Ambivalence
  accumulation of, 24–25
  apprentice-, 4–5
  emotional (affective) type, 3
  intellectual (cognitive) type, 3
  of organizational leaders: see Organizational leaders, ambivalence of
  of physicians: see Physicians, ambivalence of
  psychological, 4–7, 19, 31
  of scientists: see Scientists, ambivalence of
  situational contexts of professional care and, 21–23
  social diffusion of, 30–31
  sociological: see Sociological ambivalence
  sources of, toward professions, 19–30

  structural sources of, 23–30
  voluntary (conative) type, 3
American Sociological Association, 179
Anomie, 11, 122, 127, 128
Anti-sociologists, 180–85
Anti-Whig perspective, 137
Anxiety, 22, 23, 28
Apprentice love, 4–5
Asceticism, 154
Assent, audits of, 95
Assortative mating, 220n
Attitudes, 215, 256–58
  norms and behavior, 191–93, 220–22, 260–61
Authenticity, 174
Authoritarianism, 80
Authority, 25–27, 80, 97, 124, 228

Behavior vs. norms in science, 40–46
Berkeleyanism, 175
Blue books, 160, 161, 165
Boomerang effect, 206
Bureaucracy, 7
Bureaucratic man, 184

Cacogamy, 219, 222, 230–32, 234, 235
Canons of anti-sociology, 180–85
Capitalism, 154
Caste, 218, 222, 223, 226–29, 235, 237, 241, 242, 244, 249
Caste hypogamy, 232–39
Causal imputation, 146, 148
Chance, 57, 59, 148n, 151
Change
  innovative and adaptive, 78
  social, 86, 125, 202, 207

This book is set in 11/12 Bodoni Book Linotype. This most popular of all present-day Bodoni types was adapted from one of Giambattista Bodoni's original designs, first shown about 1788. He is credited with the invention of the letter we now call "modern." Strictly speaking, this is not true because the mechanical trend and perfection of finish that are characteristic of the modern faces were noted many years before Bodoni designed and popularized his letters.

Composition, presswork, and binding by The Book Press.
The editorial supervisor was Robert Harrington, and the production supervisors were Robert Garfield and Joe Lynn.

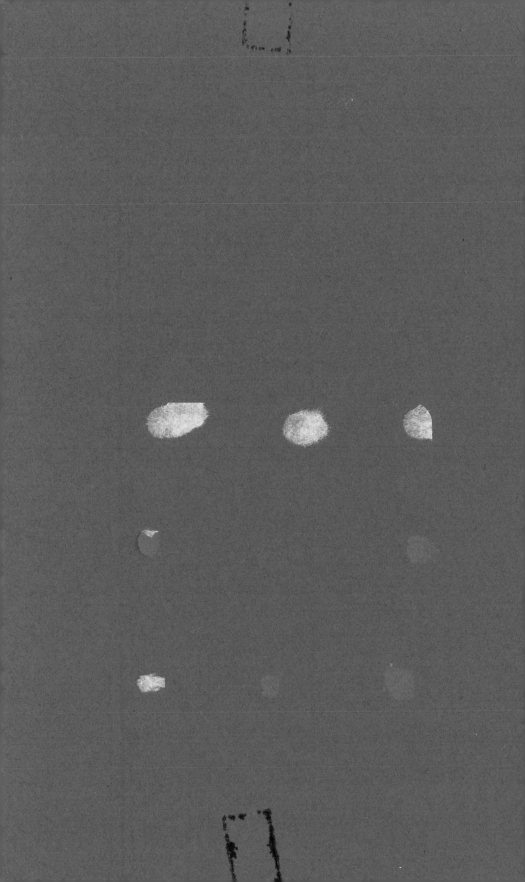